FRANCIS NORBERT BLANCHET
AND
THE FOUNDING OF THE OREGON MISSIONS
(1838-1848)

This dissertation was conducted under the direction of the Right Rev. Msgr. Peter Guilday as Major Professor, and was approved by Dr. Richard J. Purcell and Rev. Dr. John T. Ellis, as readers.

THE CATHOLIC UNIVERSITY OF AMERICA
STUDIES IN AMERICAN CHURCH HISTORY
UNDER THE DIRECTION OF RT. REV. MSGR. PETER GUILDAY
VOL. XXX

FRANCIS NORBERT BLANCHET

AND

THE FOUNDING OF THE OREGON MISSIONS
(1838-1848)

A Dissertation

SUBMITTED TO THE FACULTY OF THE GRADUATE SCHOOL OF ARTS AND
SCIENCES OF THE CATHOLIC UNIVERSITY OF AMERICA IN PARTIAL
FULFILLMENT OF THE REQUIREMENTS FOR THE DEGREE OF
DOCTOR OF PHILOSOPHY

BY

SISTER LETITIA MARY LYONS, M. A.
Sisters of the Holy Names
Marylhurst, Oregon

WIPF & STOCK · Eugene, Oregon

Wipf and Stock Publishers
199 W 8th Ave, Suite 3
Eugene, OR 97401

Francis Norbert Blanchet
and the Founding of the Oregon Missions
(1838-1848)
By Lyons, Letitia Mary
ISBN 13: 978-1-5326-4269-2
Publication date 10/31/2017
Previously published by
The Catholic University of America Press, 1940

PREFACE

The purpose of this dissertation is to present the story of the Catholic Church in the Oregon territory from the foundation of the first missions in 1838 until the formal organization of the country into the ecclesiastical province of Oregon City, which was completed ten years later when the first provincial council was held at St. Paul, Oregon, in February, 1848.

The pioneer priests, Francis Norbert Blanchet and Modeste Demers, had been but a few months in the Pacific Northwest when they realized the advantages that might result to their work from the presence of a bishop in Oregon. They sent, in 1839, the first of a series of petitions to the bishop of Quebec, asking that steps be taken thus to assist them but it was not until 1842, when Father De Smet, the Jesuit missionary, added his pleadings to theirs, that the project was given serious consideration. The following year, after recommendations from Quebec and Baltimore, the Holy See established the vicariate apostolic of Oregon and appointed Father Blanchet, first vicar apostolic. Three years later, in 1846, due to representations which Blanchet made at Rome, the province of Oregon City was erected. The Holy See elevated Blanchet to the metropolitan see and named as his suffragans, his brother, Augustine Magloire Blanchet, Bishop of Walla Walla, and Modeste Demers, Bishop of Vancouver Island. Archbishop Blanchet returned to Oregon in 1847 and several months later convened the first provincial council, which studied and legislated for the needs of the new province. It is this period of early foundations and development which is discussed in these pages.

Forty years after he established the first Catholic mission in the Pacific Northwest, Archbishop Blanchet published his *Historical Sketches of the Catholic Church in Oregon during the past Forty Years*, in which he recounts the story of the Church in that region from 1838 to about 1850. This appeared first as a series of articles in the *Catholic Sentinel*, Portland, continuing from February 7 to September 12, 1878, and in the same year was printed as a small volume. In 1911 the Most Reverend Edwin V. O'Hara, now Bishop of Kansas City, Mo., in the *Pioneer Catholic History of Oregon*, gave an account of the early period of missionary activity; and in 1938 the Reverend Gilbert J. Garraghan, S. J., devoted some pages to the Oregon missions in the second volume of his *Jesuits of the Middle United States*. Aside from these works and some periodical literature, largely based on Blanchet's *Sketches*, little else has been written and the complete story of these formative years has not yet been told. An attempt has been made here to reconstruct that story and to present it in the light of archival material, principally that in the archiepiscopal archives of Quebec and of Portland, Oregon.

I wish to thank all those who have assisted in the preparation of this work. To the Most Reverend Edward D. Howard, Archbishop of Portland-in-Oregon, with whose permission and good wishes this study was begun, I offer my sincere gratitude. To the Right Reverend Monsignor Peter Guilday, who directed the dissertation, I am deeply indebted. Especially am I grateful for the use of transcripts of many of the documents from the Quebec archives without which this work would have been impossible. To Professor Richard J. Purcell, Ph. D., head of the Department of History, and to Reverend John T. Ellis, Ph. D., Instructor in History, who read the manuscript, I wish to express my appreciation. To the many others who generously gave assistance, I am sincerely grateful: to the Right Reverend Monsignor B. P. Canon Garneau, archivist at the archiepiscopal archives in Quebec, for his kindly courtesy and many helpful suggestions; to the Right Reverend Monsignor Amadée Gosselein, formerly archivist at Laval University, and to his successor, Reverend Arthur Maneux, who gave me many details of Blanchet's early career; to the Right Reverend Monsignor N. Remilliard, who showed me interesting relics at Blanchet's old parish, The Cedars; to Reverend Zoel Landry of Richibucto and Reverend Elie J. Auclair; to Dr. James F. Kenny of the Public Archives of Canada, Ottawa, who collected and sent information regarding Blanchet; to Dr. W. Kaye Lamb of the Provincial Library and Archives, Victoria, B. C.; to Dr. Walter N. Sage of the University of British Columbia; to Dr. Erna Gunther of the Anthropology Department of the University of Washington; to Dr. Ronald Todd of the University of Washington library; to Miss Nellie B. Pipes, librarian of the Oregon Historical Society; to Mr. John O'Hara, who generously loaned me documents. Finally, to my community, the Congregation of the Sisters of the Holy Names of Jesus and Mary, the superiors of which have made possible my graduate studies at The Catholic University of America, it is a pleasant duty to express my appreciation.

CONTENTS

	PAGE
INTRODUCTION	xi

CHAPTER

I.	From Montreal to Fort Vancouver	1
II.	The First Missions	18
III.	Pioneer Priests and Missionaries	45
IV.	Dissensions and Problems	68
V.	The Apostolate of the Indians	97
VI.	The Vicariate Apostolic of Oregon	129
VII.	The Province of Oregon City	149
VIII.	The First Provincial Council	170
	ESSAY ON THE SOURCES	189
	INDEX	197

INTRODUCTION

Interest in the Oregon country, " an indeterminate stretch of coast north of San Francisco bay," was of long standing, but it first attained importance in the eighteenth century as the nations, one after another, recognized the value of this new field for trade. During the eighteenth and early nineteenth centuries, the ships of Spain, Russia, Great Britain and the United States [1] appeared off the north Pacific coast, to carry out instructions from the mother countries to explore and lay claim to the territory, which extended from the boundary of California to the Russian possessions in the far north, thus to secure the right to a share in the riches, principally furs, over which the native owners kept careful watch.

Spain, long established in Mexico and in California, had laid claim to the northwest, basing her sovereignty on a number of exploratory voyages, the first in the sixteenth century, which had led her ships north past the mouth of the great River of the West (1775), later to be called the Columbia, and on up the coast to Alaska (1779).[2] England, however, alert for an opportunity to check her traditional rival, challenged Spain's pretensions to exclusive control over the region and by the Nootka Sound Convention [3] (1790) forced her to recognize the right of Great Britain to

[1] France had been ambitious to extend her influence to the Pacific coast of North America and had sent out exploring parties about the middle of the century but was forced, shortly after, to withdraw her ships and to concentrate all her efforts on the protection of her interests in Europe.

[2] Spain's first claim to the Northwest was based on the bulls, *Inter Caetera* (May 3, 1493), *Eximiae Devotionis* (May 3, 1493) and *Inter Caetera* (May 4, 1493) of Pope Alexander VI and on the treaty between Spain and Portugal concluded at Tordesillas, June 7, 1494, by which recent discoveries were divided between Spain and Portugal. Copies of these documents may be found in Frances G. Davenport, *European Treaties bearing on the History of the United States and its Dependencies to 1648* (Washington, 1917).

[3] Spain had seized and dismantled a trading post on Vancouver Island, established by John Meares, a British subject. Great Britain protested vigorously and since Spain's ally, France, was at the time, unable to give

xi

trade and settle on the western coast of North America. Spain thus relinquished her attempt to maintain an exclusive monopoly but did not give up her whole claim to the country north of California until 1819, when by treaty,[4] she surrendered to the United States all her rights north of 42°.

Russian interest and influence were felt, also, during the eighteenth century as that country expanded eastward across and beyond Siberia. Following the initial voyage of the Danish explorer, Vitus Bering, to Alaska (1741), adventurous Russians carried on the fur trade between Siberia and the Alaska islands. In 1799 the Russian-American Fur Company began operations and during the next two decades extended its activities as far south as California, where in 1820 was established Fort Ross on what is now San Francisco bay.[5] But four years later (1824), the United States and Russia signed a treaty by which Russia agreed not to allow any establishment by its subjects south of 54° 40′ and the United States guaranteed that it would not permit its citizens to settle north of that latitude. The next year, Great Britain made a similar pact with Russia, setting at approximately 54° 40′, the boundary between their possessions on the Pacific coast.[6] By these two treaties Russia withdrew from any contest of territory south of 54° 40′ and abandoned her pretensions to exclusive sovereignty over any of the high seas on the Pacific

assistance, Spain was forced to agree to England's demands. William R. Manning, " The Nootka Sound Controversy," Annual *Report* of American Historical Association (1904), 281-477, discusses the significance of this incident.

[4] In February, 1819, a treaty was concluded between the United States and Spain, by which Spain ceded all her lands east of the Mississippi, together with her rights to the Oregon country to the United States in return for $5,000,000. A copy of the treaty is in *Treaties and Conventions concluded between the United States of America and other Powers since July 4, 1776* (Washington, 1889). See also Thomas M. Marshall, *A History of the Western Boundary of the Louisiana Purchase, 1819-1841* (Berkeley, 1914).

[5] Robert E. Riegel, *America Moves West* (New York, 1930), 302.

[6] Samuel F. Bemis, *A Diplomatic History of the United States* (New York, 1936), 274; Cardinal Goodwin, *The Trans-Mississippi West, 1803-1853* (New York, 1922), 200 ff. summarizes Russian claims and the negotiations which led to their adjustment. A translation of the convention from the original French is in *Treaties and Conventions*.

Introduction

Ocean off that shore. Spain having relinquished all her claims to the United States in 1819, the number of rivals for ownership of the territory between 42° and 54° 40′ was narrowed to two, the United States and Great Britain.

The claims of Great Britain were based on the voyage of Sir Francis Drake who skirted the coast on his journey around the world (1578). No further interest was taken in the region for two centuries and no Englishman set foot on the territory until Captain James Cook on an official journey of discovery and exploration, sailed as far north as Nootka Sound on the outer shore of Vancouver Island (1778). Cook took possession of the northwest coast for Great Britain. Some years later (1792), Captain George Vancouver led another expedition to the Pacific. His object was to execute the terms of the Nootka Sound Convention, as well as to explore the country. Vancouver's men discovered and named Puget Sound and sailed up the Columbia River for a hundred miles from its mouth. They owed their knowledge of its existence to Captain Robert Gray, an American, who had happened on to the river and named it after his ship a few weeks before the arrival of Vancouver (1792).[7]

The first American ships to appear in the waters of the north Pacific were the *Columbia*, Captain Robert Kendrick, and the *Lady Washington*, Captain Robert Gray, vessels from Boston, which opened up trading enterprise in the far Pacific in 1788. Three years later, encouraged by the success of the first venture, Boston merchants dispatched another expedition under the command of Gray, this time sailing the *Columbia*. He made extensive explorations and sailed (May 11, 1792) into the river which has since borne the name of his ship.[8] After 1792 ships from England,

[7] Cf. George Vancouver, *A Voyage of Discovery to the North Pacific Ocean, and Round the World*, etc. (London, 1798).

[8] Edmond S. Meany edited the account of John Boit, " Log of the Columbia, 1790-1792," in *Washington Historical Quarterly* (January, 1921), 1-50.

The first Americans to appear on the Pacific coast were two members of Captain Cook's crew. One of them, John Ledyard, spread the news of the profits to be made from the fur trade between the coast and China. It was he who first inspired the interest of Jefferson. His story was told by Jared Sparks, *The Life of John Ledyard, American Traveler; Comprising Sections from his Journals and Correspondence* (Cambridge, 1828).

Spain, the United States, even from some other nations frequented the northwest coast from the Columbia River to Alaska, and the trade begun by Captains Kendrick and Gray expanded with the passing years.

Overland expeditions followed closely the explorations of the northwest coast. The members of the North West Company [9] arrived in 1793 under the leadership of Alexander Mackenzie; some years later (1806-1808), Simon Fraser explored the river which now bears his name; and still later, David Thompson (1807-1810) penetrated the country to the mouth of the Columbia. Thompson had orders to follow the plans of Mackenzie and Fraser and to erect a chain of trading forts connecting the waters of the Columbia with the upper waters of the great rivers of Canada. The official voyages of Cook and Vancouver and the exploring and trading expeditions of the North West Company's representatives rapidly extended British trade into the region north of the Columbia, as well as along the western slope of the Rockies to some distance east and south of the river.

President Jefferson was responsible for the first official expedition of the United States to the Oregon territory when he sent Captains Lewis and Clark to make their perilous journey from St. Louis to the mouth of the Columbia. They spent the winter of 1805-1806 at a fort on the Pacific coast, formally taking possession of the region which Vancouver had also claimed twelve years previously for the British crown. Six years later (1811), John Jacob Astor of New York organized the American Fur Company, which made the first American settlement at Astoria, near the site of Lewis and Clark's old fort. However, the time for American occupation had not yet come and except for the intrusion of a few enterprising traders the Oregon country was left for the next thirty years to the exploitation of the powerful British concern, the Hudson's Bay Company.

The extension of the activity of the "Honourable Company" to

---

[9] The North West Company was a group of Canadian fur traders who vigorously opposed the attempts of the Hudson's Bay Company to maintain an absolute monopoly over the fur trade. The two companies were amalgamated in 1821. For an account of its policy and activities, see Gordon C. Davidson, *The Northwest Company* (Berkeley, 1916).

Introduction

the Pacific coast was a result of its amalgamation with the North West Company in 1821. The traditional warfare between the rivals had finally been recognized as injurious to both; indeed, as a probable cause of swiftly approaching annihilation. As a remedy, a merger was suggested and accomplished. The old royal charter of 1670 was the foundation on which the new concern was built. The fur trade was to be carried on under a clear cut monopoly, provided for, not only in the first charter, but endorsed as well by a statute of the British parliament in 1821, which granted an exclusive license for trade for twenty-one years in the British territory east of the Rockies and the sole right of trade west of those mountains. In effect, it made possible the control of nearly half a continent.[10]

The London committee chose George Simpson[11] as governor-in chief of its American holdings and assigned to John McLoughlin,[12] a former North West man, the work of reorganizing the Columbia territory. This was far from an easy task, due to the extravagant methods of his predecessors. Under his efficient control, however, the fur trade prospered and expanded. From Fort Vancouver, which replaced Astoria as the company headquarters in 1824,[13]

[10] Douglas MacKay, *The Honourable Company* (New York, 1936), 158; George W. Fuller, *A History of the Pacific Northwest* (New York, 1931), 110, says "Not only the 'whole trade,' but the possession, succession, government and defense of this region of unknown extent was turned over to the Company."

[11] George Simpson was born in Scotland in 1787. In 1809, as a clerk in a London firm he attracted the attention of Andrew Colville, member of the Hudson's Bay Company, who sent Simpson to America in the service of the Company. His advance was rapid; in 1820 he was placed in charge of a district and shortly after the coalition of the rivals in the fur trade, he became governor-in-chief of all the Hudson's Bay Company territory in America, a position he held until 1860. He was eminently successful in his administration and soon restored order and made the fur trade a prosperous business.

[12] John McLoughlin was born in Canada in 1784 of Scotch and Irish parentage. Educated as a physician, he began his career in Montreal and then at Fort William, post of the North West Company. He became intensely interested in the fur trade and eventually one of the wintering partners. After the union of the two companies in 1821 McLoughlin was placed in charge of the Columbia department, where he ruled until 1846.

[13] Bemis, *op. cit.*, 272, says that the change from Astoria to Fort Vancouver was made at the suggestion of Canning; Richard G. Montgomery in

brigades of trappers and traders journeyed each year—east, south and north—collecting the skins destined for eastern markets. Old posts were improved and strengthened; new ones erected as the need arose, until they numbered twenty-eight, scattered at strategic points in the Oregon country. Of these, Fort Vancouver was undoubtedly the center and under McLoughlin's able direction developed into a permanent settlement from which the ever-increasing business of the Hudson's Bay Company was managed. The first interest of the company was the fur trade but as the country developed furs became less easy to find and McLoughlin was persuaded of the necessity of enlarging the company's activities. Accordingly, agricultural pursuits were encouraged; trade was fostered with the Russian settlements in the north, with the Spanish possessions to the south and with the Hawaiian Islands, until the Columbia River region became a real source of wealth to the London-controlled corporation.

For more than ten years, McLoughlin had no serious competition. An occasional ship would come to the mouth of the Columbia and depart. At times American fur traders appeared east of the Blue Mountains. Such were Benjamin de Bonneville, William L. Sublette, Jedediah Smith and others, but none was more than partially successful. And so, McLoughlin ruled over the handful of white inhabitants in the valley and kept peace with the Indians while he carried out his instructions so to govern as neither to encourage citizens of the United States to settle nor to do anything to exclude them. Toward the middle of the 1830's there began the immigration of American settlers, which foreboded the end of the company régime. The missionary parties came first (1834), and after that, scarcely a year passed that did not add a few Americans to the population around Fort Vancouver; after 1842, the westward-bound groups grew steadily larger, finally forcing the once-powerful monopoly to the north.[14] The time had arrived for the settlement of the "Oregon question."

The White-Headed Eagle (New York, 1934), 68-76, discusses the considerations that influenced the selection of the site.

[14] The rulers of the Hudson's Bay Company had little, if any, hope of being able to hold all the Oregon territory for the British crown. They recognized the probability that settlers from the eastern United States

The far western boundary between the United States and Canada was a matter of concern to British and American statesmen for many years. The convention of 1818 between the two countries fixed the dividing line at the forty-ninth parallel from the Lake of the Woods to the Rocky Mountains, but left the Oregon country 'free and open' to citizens of both powers although it did not, strictly speaking, writes Bemis, provide a "joint occupation." The difficulty of arriving at a compromise and making a final settlement was due partly to a lack of knowledge regarding the boundaries of the Louisiana purchase, partly to the overlapping claims of Great Britain and the United States.

During the next ten years American citizens, following the example of the British fur-trading company, might have established themselves in the Oregon territory at any time but the interest of most Americans was still east of the Rocky Mountains.[15] However, as travelers' tales of the fertility of the soil and the magnificence of forests and streams were spread and as fur traders' stories of glorious adventure reached the eastern states, the desire of the people was aroused and the conviction grew that the United States

would take possession of the country south of the Columbia. But they did hope to keep possession of everything north of the river.

[15] From 1820 on there were periodic attempts to interest congress in plans to extend the jurisdiction of the United States over Oregon territory but with the exception of a few far-sighted members, the majority was opposed. In December, 1820, a committee was appointed to "inquire into the junction of settlements" in the Pacific northwest and into the "expediency of occupying the Columbia River." Its report was made in January, 1821, by the committee chairman, John Floyd of Virginia. It has since been recognized as a most important document but at the time it seemed ridiculous to most members of congress. In December, 1828, a bill was reported in congress to aid bands of prospective settlers from Massachusetts, Ohio, etc., who proposed to settle in Oregon. The bill provided for the organization of territorial government in the whole region, north to 54° 40′, the establishment of military protection, the erection of forts, a port of entry and donations of land to settlers. But the bill was checked by the opposition before it had proceeded far and congress heard much eloquence about the small importance of the country west of the Rockies, the impossibility of its ever becoming a state and the likelihood that the extension of the laws of the United States over it would be a violation of the convention of 1827.

was entitled to and should share in the offerings of that far western land.[16]

Meanwhile, it seemed impossible for statesmen to reach a satisfactory agreement. Negotiations, begun in 1824, were carried on until 1826 without any settlement being made. In 1827, representatives of the two powers, having failed to decide on a boundary, signed a new convention which continued indefinitely the terms of the treaty of 1818, providing, however, that it might be abrogated by either party after one year's advance notice. The Oregon problem was evidently no nearer a solution than before. No serious attempt was made to solve it until the meetings of the American Secretary of State, Daniel Webster, and the British statesman, Lord Ashburton, in 1842. Ashburton was sent to Washington as a special plenipotentiary with instructions to adjust the outstanding differences between Great Britain and the United States, one of which was the Oregon dispute. But the discussion of the northeast boundary preempted first place in the conversations of 1842 and the statesmen agreed to postpone the settlement of the "Oregon question" until some later time.

In the meantime, popular interest in the country west of the Rockies continued to grow and public sentiment to favor the demand for as much of Oregon as possible. The heavy immigration to the

---

[16] It was due to the interest and writings of Hall J. Kelley, a Boston schoolmaster, that a knowledge of the Oregon territory was first presented to the American public. His agitation began as early as 1815 and according to Bancroft, *History of the Northwest Coast* (San Francisco, 1886), II, 544, he did not "cease writing and raving until at the ripe age of eighty-five he was transferred from his New England hermitage, where . . . he had retired to brood in poverty over the wrongs inflicted by a soulless corporation and an ungrateful republic." An enthusiastic planner, Kelley drew up numerous plans for the colonization and government of Oregon which he insisted was the "finest on which the sun shines, and possesses natural advantages for agriculture and commerce, unsurpassed in any other part of the earth." In 1830 he was responsible for the establishment of the American Society for Encouraging a Settlement of the Oregon Territory and he wrote *A General Circular to All Persons of Good Character Who Wish to Emigrate to the Oregon Territory*, etc. (Charlestown, 1831). He also published *A Geographical Sketch of that Part of North America Called Oregon, Containing an Account of the Indian Title*, etc. (Boston, 1830), besides numerous letters, pamphlets, brochures.

Pacific coast in 1843-1844 [17] seemed to prove that the territory would eventually be an American possession and to justify immediate action by Congress to extend its jurisdiction westward. It began to talk of giving the necessary twelve months' notice for the abrogation of the treaty of 1827, and for the organization of an American Territory of Oregon with northern boundary at 54° 40'. The Oregon question now entered the political arena and the Democratic party fought and won the presidential election of 1844, at least partly, on account of its vigorous expansionist policy, which pledged it to "54° 40' or fight!" When Congress met in December, 1845 the annual message of President Polk came out vigorously for "54° 40'" and asked power for the executive to terminate the agreement of 1827. This was granted on April 23, 1846 and Polk immediately gave the necessary notice.

England was finally convinced of the necessity of settlement. In 1843, the British minister, Richard Pakenham, had brought to the United States several offers, the most favorable being that of a boundary at the forty-ninth parallel with free ports south of that line. American statesmen would at one time have been willing to accept that suggestion; indeed, it had several times been offered by Americans: John Quincy Adams had made it in 1818 to the British Secretary for Foreign Affairs, Lord Castlereagh; again in 1824 and in 1826 to George Canning, the British Foreign Minister; and Daniel Webster, until 1842, had thought it a fair division. But in that year, the report of Lieutenant Charles Wilkes, U. S. N. had convinced him that it would be to the advantage of the United States to increase its demands. John Calhoun held to the same opinion. After the election of 1844, Secretary of State James

[17] In addition to the speeches and writings of Kelley, various other publications spread interest in Oregon and encouraged immigration. After 1834 the missionary publications, the *Christian Advocate*, those of the American Tract Society, the annual report of the American Board of Commissioners for Foreign Missions gave accounts of the west. Of a number of official reports, those of John C. Fremont, Charles Wilkes, U. S. N., and William Slacum were important. The last inspired the bill which Senator Lewis Linn of Missouri presented to congress in 1837. It provided for the grant of a section of land to every male immigrant over eighteen years, settling in Oregon. The bill was defeated in the House but many immigrants believed that it had become law and made their way across the plains.

Buchanan continued the discussion of the question with Pakenham and suggested the boundary of the forty-ninth parallel with absolute American authority south of this line. The British minister had no authority to make such an agreement and refused to assent, making, however, an offer of arbitration, which Buchanan rejected. Meanwhile, came the action of Congress and the presidential notice to the British representative.

By this time, Lord Aberdeen, the British Secretary of State for Foreign Affairs, had become alarmed and took matters into his own hands, sending a proposal that the United States accept the forty-ninth parallel as the boundary with the exception that Vancouver Island should remain British. The proposal was sent to the Senate and that body advocated acceptance. A treaty embodying these terms was drawn up and signed on June 15. It was ratified by the Senate three days later, June, 18, 1846.

In this same month and year, June, 1846, in Rome, the Holy See sanctioned the erection of the province of Oregon City, thus definitely bringing to an end all doubt as to ecclesiastical jurisdiction over the region. The first attempt to establish the Catholic Church in the northwest had been made eight years before, when in November, 1838, the missionaries, Fathers Francis Norbert Blanchet and Modeste Demers, arrived at Fort Vancouver from Montreal. From some points of view, it seems to have been unfortunate that they should have come at this time, for they faced almost immediately a period of change—in ideals and ideas, in allegiances and loyalties. Sharing in the difficulties and the uncertainties of these years, they found their first ambitions altered; their advance halted; the very existence of their work seriously threatened. And yet, in spite of the disappointments and discouragements that accompanied their early attempts, progress continued and from the scattered mission stations of the pioneer years, there was formed in 1843 the vicariate apostolic of Oregon and three years later, in 1846, the province of Oregon City, the second in the present territory of the United States.

CHAPTER I

FROM MONTREAL TO FORT VANCOUVER

It was in 1834, at the suggestion of John McLoughlin, chief factor of the Hudson's Bay Company in the Columbia department, that the Catholic settlers in the Willamette Valley petitioned the nearest Canadian bishop, Joseph Norbert Provencher at Red River,[1] for a priest who would come to live among them and bring to them the joys and consolations of religion, of which they had been for so long a time deprived. There was no response to this first appeal; hence the following year a second was forwarded, which told of the dire need of the people of the far west and begged again for assistance.[2] These petitions seem to have had the approval of the officers of the Hudson's Bay Company at Fort Vancouver who urged that Canadian priests be sent immediately and offered free transportation under Company protection, either overland or by sea, as well as provision for their necessities until they could be permanently established.[3] Bishop Provencher had no priest to send but he was not unmindful of these far-away children of the Church and he wrote to them and to McLoughlin to assure them of his interest; to inform them of his plans; and to encourage them to hope that in the near future their desires might be fulfilled.[4] He brought the matter to the notice of Joseph Signay, the bishop of Quebec, and

---

[1] Provencher was sent as vicar general of Bishop Plessis of Quebec to Red River as its first missionary (1818). He was named Bishop of Juliopolis *in partibus* (1820), suffragan and auxiliary of the bishop of Quebec and vicar apostolic for the district of the Northwest. Cf. Sister M. Aquinas Norton, *Catholic Missionary Activities in the Northwest, 1818-1864* (Washington, D. C., 1930) for Provencher's mission at Red River.

[2] The first appeal was dated July 3, 1834, the second, February 23, 1835.

[3] Edmund Mallet, *Memoirs of Archbishop F. N. Blanchet, MS.* (unpub.) in library of l'Union St. Jean-Baptiste d'Amerique, Woonsocket, R. I.

[4] These letters are given in Francis N. Blanchet, *Historical Sketches of the Catholic Church in Oregon and the Northwest* (Ferndale, Wash., 1910), 6-7.

with the latter began the long process that was necessary before the ambitions of the Canadian habitants could be realized.

The only available means of transportation from Montreal to the Oregon country in 1835 was in the canoes of the Hudson's Bay Company and in order to make use of these, express permission from the governor and London committee of the Company was required. The officers in control of the great fur trading monopoly were not overly enthusiastic about the proposed missionary project. The "Oregon question" had not yet become a topic of general interest but the Company officials seem to have believed that any settlement south of the Columbia would lie in territory that would eventually pass under the control of the government of the United States. Hence, we find them at first refusing to give the matter any consideration and then, as a condition for the permission to establish a mission, requiring that it be located, not among the Willamette settlers who had sent the petition, but at some point north of the Columbia to be determined by the Company. It was only in March, 1838 that Bishop Signay received letters from Governor George Simpson, in charge of the Company's vast holdings in North America, and from James Keith, the agent at Lachine, telling him that final arrangements had been made and that the London authorities had given their consent.[5]

Months before this, the bishop of Quebec had selected the priest, at that time pastor at The Cedars in the district of Montreal, to whom he was to delegate power as his vicar general to establish and rule over the Church on the Pacific coast.[6] He chose Francis Norbert Blanchet, the son of Pierre and Rosalie Blanchet, both members of families which had furnished distinguished leaders to church and state in Canada. Blanchet was born in 1795 at St. Pierre, Rivière du Sud, Lower Canada, and was baptized September 4 of that year at the neighboring village of St. François. He and his younger brother, Augustine Magloire, who was later to share his work in the northwest, were sent to the parish school in the village of St. Pierre, where in 1808 Francis received his First

---

[5] *Ibid.*, 7; Keith to Signay, March 28, 1838. Quebec Archdiocesan Archives, henceforth cited as QAA.

[6] Blanchet was suggested for the post by Provencher who praised his zeal and good will. Provencher to Signay, January, 1837. QAA.

Communion and where he was confirmed the following year. In 1810 he and his brother enrolled at the minor seminary of Quebec and in 1816 Francis went to the superior seminary. Here, after a distinguished theological course, he was ordained to the priesthood, July 19, 1819, and celebrated his first Mass the next day. The ordination ceremony was performed by Bishop Bernard Panet, coadjutor to Joseph Plessis, the bishop of Quebec, during the absence of the latter in Europe.

After his ordination Father Blanchet was stationed for several months at the Cathedral of Quebec. But in 1820 he began his missionary career when, in answer to an appeal for a French-speaking priest, he went to New Brunswick to care for the Acadians of that region. The vast territory under his charge was a wilderness, in which the young priest experienced some of the difficulties that he was later to find on the other side of a vast continent. Edmund Mallet gives this description of missionary life:

> The Abbé Blanchet's mission, which was visited regularly at least twice a year, involved the travel of about 225 miles to reach the several stations, situated on rivers, bays and capes. In summer this was done in birch canoes along the rivers; in log canoes called pirogues, when crossing the arms of the sea; on horseback across the country, and in winter, on skates or snow-shoes or in dog trains, and this in a region where the thermometer marks thirty degrees below zero and where for some months the earth and ice are covered with several feet of snow. The oldest inhabitants still tell of his heroism in storms and dangers of every kind; how he encouraged his good Acadian or Indian guides, and shared with them their arduous labors and perils. His zeal never flagged, and after one of these long journeys to his distant stations, or after attending a sick call at a distance of a hundred or two hundred miles, he would return to his humble dwelling in the village as cheerful and joyous as did the Acadian farmer from his day's labor in his fields. Thus was the missionary being schooled for the duties of his apostolate in the wilds of distant Oregon.[7]

But, although conditions of living were hard, the priest had many a consolation among the Acadians who reverenced their missionary and acknowledged him their father, teacher and advocate.

---

[7] Mallet, *op. cit.*, 15.

The Indians, too, responded to his teaching and gave evidence of his devoted service to their interests. Each year in July there took place the pilgrimage in honor of St. Anne, one phase of missionary life which particularly appealed to Father Blanchet. The Indians of the whole surrounding country assembled on the northern shore of the Miramichi Bay to celebrate the feast of the saint on July 26. After weeks of preparation, the neighboring tribes gathered at the Bay. The Micmacs, dressed in their best, formed a flotilla in their brightly decorated pirogues and amid the firing of guns, started on their journey to the north with their missionary at their head. The coming of the group from Richibucto occasioned friendly demonstrations among the tribesmen. Then followed a week of religious exercises and instructions conducted by Rev. Thomas Cook, afterwards bishop of Three Rivers, Canada, which ended with the general reception of Holy Communion on the feast of St. Anne.[8]

In the spring of 1827, Father Blanchet accompanied an old friend, Joseph Lavignon, to Quebec. He expected to be absent only a short time from his mission but his appointment to the parish of The Cedars, or St. Joseph de Soulanges, in the district of Montreal, temporarily put an end to his missionary work. The little village of The Cedars was a rendezvous for boats passing up and down the river, a meeting place for travelers and voyageurs. Here the missionary met for the first time the fur trader and the adventurer who had braved the dangers of the journey to the west and had come back with tales of the fortune to be won from dealings with the Indians. There is no evidence that the priest was especially interested in these frontiersmen; no indication that he might have been ambitious to resume a missionary career. In fact, the letter of Bishop Signay, suggesting Blanchet as his delegate to the Columbia country, was, if we may judge from his reply to it, evidently a surprise:

> My Lord,
> It is only after several weeks of reflection and of prayer and a novena to the miracle worker of this century that I dare at last to answer your letter of October 28.

[8] *Ibid.*, 16; Edwin V. O'Hara, *Pioneer Catholic History of Oregon* (Paterson, N. J., 1939), 13-19.

It amazed me that you could consider me for the Columbia when you have in the dioceses of Quebec and Montreal so many holy priests, much more capable than I am of corresponding with the views of your Lordship. Alas! I have not the knowledge, the virtue or the piety necessary for a missionary on the Columbia. After seven years at the mission on the Gulf and nine years at The Cedars, of which six have been at the head of 2000 communicants, look at me and see if I am the man you seek.

I am not indifferent to the glory of God, nor to the salvation of souls redeemed by the blood of our Savior; but when I consider the isolation in which the missionaries of the Columbia will find themselves; the dangers and difficulties by which their mission will be surrounded; it seems to me that they will need a *divine vocation* with all the graces which accompany it; and even then, they will still have to fear that after having preached to others, they may be lost themselves.

I cannot then decide for myself; the consequences might be too terrible. It would be folly to seek this mission or even to accept it imprudently. Jesus Christ called His apostles, *sequere me*; He commanded them to go, *hos duodecim misit Jesus, praecipiens eis*; the vocation of St. Matthiam; *Domine quid me vis facere.*

This holy vocation must be manifested by the voice of superiors; God be blessed, my destiny is in His hands and in theirs; let his Lordship of Montreal examine and pronounce; my duty will be to obey; that will be to do the will of heaven, to walk in the ways of Providence.... When one obeys he has consolation in his sufferings; he has the confidence and the hope of being aided and sustained by heaven in the midst of dangers. These are my sentiments and my dispositions.[9]

The Bishop of Montreal considered the matter and sent his verdict to Bishop Provencher, February 9, 1837. He was willing to allow the Abbé Blanchet to go to Oregon on condition that the bishop of Quebec replace him by a man of equal capacity: a man of good conduct, of good health, one who could speak English. Blanchet was a priest, "très utile," and his Lordship could not easily replace him.[10] Superiors had spoken and the priest was ready to obey. He wrote to Bishop Signay signifying his willingness to

---

[9] Blanchet to Signay, November 19, 1836. QAA.
[10] Lartigue to Provencher, February 9, 1837. QAA.

accept the new appointment and asked information regarding the proposed site of the mission and the means of getting there.[11]

The first plans did not materialize. The Hudson's Bay Company could find no place in its canoes and so the Abbé Blanchet stayed on at The Cedars and the habitants of the Columbia were forced to wait. But the enterprise was not abandoned and Blanchet's interest in the far distant country did not lag. In the spring of 1838, Signay wrote to assure himself that the dispositions of the priest were the same. He also revealed a change made in regard to the situation of the mission; it was now planned to establish it, "not precisely in the spot where there was first question of placing it, but at a location, not far away, where there will be more opportunity of doing good." Word had not yet come from Governor Simpson as to whether or not he would grant the request that had been made but it was expected momentarily; meanwhile, Blanchet should be ready to leave at any time.[12] Blanchet's reply indicates his interest in the new country:

> It was with the liveliest concern that I read your letter. I rejoiced sincerely when I learned that the plan for the Catholic mission of the Columbia seems destined to succeed. The reasons which Governor Simpson gives for changing the place of the mission are excellent: the Catholic mission will not only be on British territory but separated from the trade, which is carried on at Vancouver where the vessels arrive, and at Willamette a little lower down and more exposed than Cowlitz. Another reason for rejoicing is that the natives of the upper river are better disposed than those of the lower: according to the relation of Franchère [13] their customs are more civilized; they cover themselves decently; they speak a different language. There will be, then, fewer dangers for the missionaries and more to hope for on the side of the savages. Heaven perhaps wishes to recompense these poor Indians for their greater faithfulness to the natural law. Does it not seem as if the finger of God were there? [14]

[11] Blanchet to Signay, October 3, 1837. QAA.
[12] Signay to Blanchet, March 31, 1838. QAA.
[13] Gabriel Franchère, *Narrative of a Voyage to the Northwest Coast of America in the Years 1811, 1812, 1813, and 1814* in Reuben G. Thwaites, *Early Western Travels, 1748-1846*, VI (Cleveland, 1904).
[14] Blanchet to Signay, March 25, 1838. QAA.

As to his own inclinations, he wrote:

> My Lord, my sacrifice was made last year: I am ready to renew it now, if you judge me fitted for a work of this importance. The Bishop of Montreal told me last year that I should obey the voice of God and be prepared to depart. My willingness to obey has not changed: not that I depend on my own powers but because I shall put my confidence in the all-powerful God who will assist this unworthy instrument to work for His glory.[15]

On March 31, 1838 Bishop Signay sent to Blanchet the happy news that Governor Simpson's reply had come and that he had acceded to all their requests. In accordance with instructions forwarded by James Keith, the Company agent at Lachine, the missionary should be at Montreal about April 25, ready to leave at any time after that date. A young priest, Joseph Mayrand, recently ordained at Quebec, would be there to accompany him to Red River. The latter would not continue to the Columbia but would be replaced by Modeste Demers,[16] who had had some experience in missionary work and who was then at Red River with Bishop Provencher.

All things were finally ready and the travelers gathered at Lachine on the morning of May 3. The missionary is silent about those last hours and he says nothing about the cost of the sacrifice of leaving his beloved Canada. Perhaps the great excitement of the leave-taking, the prospect of the adventuresome journey ahead, the glory of the final goal helped to stifle emotions that must have been present as the last canoe was loaded and the final preparations for the westward journey completed.

The departure of the Hudson's Bay Company's canoes was always a colorful ceremony. It took place from Lachine, a prettily situated village on the banks of the St. Lawrence, eight or nine miles above Montreal, in May, when the rivers and lakes were nearly free from ice. The weather was apt still to be cold and unsteady and patches of snow were likely to be seen around but the natural gaiety of the

---

[15] *Ibid.*

[16] Modeste Demers, first bishop of Vancouver, was born at St. Nicholas, diocese of Quebec, October 11, 1809, ordained priest in 1836. Nominated bishop by Pius IX. Received episcopal consecration November 30, 1847, at the hands of Archbishop Blanchet.

voyageurs, their shouts and songs, centered attention on them rather than on the inclemencies of the weather. At last, all things were ready, the canoes were loaded and launched and circled about on the river, waiting for the signal of the head steersman. It was given. The voyageurs said their customary prayer to St. Anne, struck up one of their traditional ditties and the canoes were pushed off amid the cheers and adieus of the assembled friends. The westward journey had begun.[17]

For six long months the travel continued. In all sorts of weather, through all kinds of country, with all manner of men, the missionary pressed on to the Oregon country. Up the Ottawa River they journeyed for nearly 400 miles, against a swift current and the obstacles of numerous rapids, cascades and falls; into the Mattawan, which flowed through a country wild and cheerless; across Lake Nipissing and down French River to Lake Huron and Sault Ste. Marie. From this point, Blanchet sent a report to his superior at Quebec:

> We arrived this morning at Sault Ste. Marie about seven o'clock; I hasten to make use of several hours to give your Lordship my news. My health is good in spite of the cold, the rain, the damp nights. . . . The light canoe loses no time. We leave about half past one or two in the morning and travel until about eight. Then, after breakfast, for which is allowed half an hour, we depart and the men row until dinner, which is eaten about two or three in the afternoon. No more than half an hour is allowed for dinner. Again, we go on. We stop to make camp about eight in the evening. The engagés make the fire, eat and are asleep soon after, much fatigued.[18]

It was a hard pace but the missionary was grateful that thus far they had progressed without accident; he had learned now that

---

[17] There are a number of interesting accounts of overland travel with the Hudson's Bay Company, e. g., Frederick Merk (ed.), *Fur Trade and Empire* (Cambridge, 1931); George Simpson, *Narrative of a Journey Round the World during the Years 1841 and 1842* (London, 1847); Alexander McDonald, *Peace River; A canoe voyage, Hudson's Bay to the Pacific by the late Sir George Simpson in 1828* (Ottawa, 1872); Edward Ermatinger's York Factory Journal, being a Record of journeys made between Fort Vancouver and Hudson Bay in the Years 1827-1828 in *Transactions* Royal Society Canada, Section II (1912).

[18] Blanchet to Signay, May 16, 1838. QAA.

travel by canoe was at once perilous and wearisome. From Sault Ste. Marie, they followed the northern shore of Lake Superior to Fort William, at one time the principal post of the North West Company; from Fort William they continued up the Tiministigouia River and then, by means of portages and the waters of many small rivers they came to Fort Frances, where Blanchet had the happiness of meeting Abbé George Belcourt [19] who was on a missionary tour among the Sauteux Indians. After a short rest there, the brigade of canoes continued its course. Three days were spent in descending Rivière la Pluie and two more in crossing Lac des Bois; then, three days more on the Winnipeg River; another on the Red River of the North, which brought them on the evening of June 6 to Fort Garry at the Red River Settlement, the residence of the bishop of Juliopolis.

Bishop Provencer had been in the Red River district since 1818. In answer to an appeal from the Canadian settlers, Bishop Plessis of Quebec had sent Father Joseph Norbert Provencher and Father Severus Joseph Dumoulin. Two years later Provencher was named Bishop of Juliopolis, suffragan and auxiliary to the bishop of Quebec and vicar apostolic for the district of the Northwest. Due to controversy over the possession of the territory, the first mission at Pembina was abandoned and Father Dumoulin returned to Montreal but Provencher continued his work and by this time (1838) had been joined by Fathers George Belcourt, John Thibault, Charles Poiré and Modeste Demers, who with the bishop welcomed Blanchet and Mayrand.[20] As the missionary later remarked, " It is easier to feel than to express the joys and emotions, the souvenirs and hopes caused by the meeting of these zealous laborers in the vineyard of the Lord. This was the most numerous gathering of priests ever

[19] George Belcourt was ordained in 1827 and sent as missionary to Red River in 1831; returned to Lévis (1838) but the following year was again at Red River, where he spent the next twenty years. He was the first Canadian missionary to make a special study of the Sauteux language and was the author of a dictionary and grammar of that language.—Cyprien Tanguay, *Répertoire Général du Clergé Canadien* (Quebec, 1868), 179.

[20] Joseph Mayrand, born in 1811, was ordained in 1838 just prior to his departure for Red River where he remained until 1845.—Tanguay, *op. cit.,* 202. Mayrand seems to have arrived at Red River a few days after Blanchet. The latter evidently traveled ahead of the main party in one of the light canoes.

witnessed by the inhabitants of these remote regions. The mustard-seed was beginning to appear as a vigorous tree, already shadowing a multitude of souls drawn from the darkness of idolatry and transplanted into the kingdom of God; precious fruits of the evangelical zeal animating these missionaries. Happy the prognostics of a still richer harvest to be gathered." [21]

For more than a month, Blanchet stayed at Red River, visiting the mission settlements and conferring with Bishop Provencher. The day after his arrival the latter confirmed Bishop Signay's appointment of Demers as his companion to Oregon, much to the joy of both. Blanchet wrote thus to Signay: " The Bishop of Juliopolis gave me on June 6, Modeste Demers, for a companion at the Columbia mission. His piety is eminent, his character most agreeable, his good will such, that were one the most peevish of men, one would be immediately won to him." [22] And Demers, writing from Norway House some weeks later, expressed his satisfaction: "I am enroute for the Columbia with Mr. Blanchet whom I am happy to have for my superior; he will be for me, at all times, guide and model; he is a man who will sustain me by his virtue and animate me by his zeal. I do not have to tell you that my wishes were completely fulfilled when the Bishop of Juliopolis said to me, ' Eh, bien, you are to go to the Columbia.' You know when I left last year, I dared to hope for that; I know better than anyone that I am scarcely fit for the work for which I am destined; but with the fervent prayers of so many souls who pray for this mission and for those who are charged with it, I hope to obtain from God the virtues and the requisite zeal." [23]

During this month Blanchet met for the first time, the man to whom he and all other early settlers on the Columbia owed a debt of deepest gratitude, John McLoughlin. The chief factor was on his way to Montreal and to London. From him the missionary learned with what eagerness the habitants of the Willamette were awaiting the coming of the priests. " What will be their disappointment," he wrote to Bishop Signay, " to learn that we cannot establish ourselves among them. The Bishop of Juliopolis has been obliged to

---

[21] Blanchet, *Sketches*, 12.
[22] Blanchet to Signay, June 22, 1838. QAA.
[23] Demers to Cazeau, July 25, 1838. QAA.

give in writing the assurance that the Catholic mission will not be situated on the Willamette River. Orders were express about it."[24]

The missionaries were due to leave Red River June 25, but owing to the serious indisposition of Blanchet, their departure was postponed until July 9, and again another day, when the two priests said their last good-byes to their friends. To a degree this parting must have been more painful than that of Montreal for it meant the final break with ecclesiastical superiors who, until now, had guided these pioneers on their way. Undoubtedly, as he prepared to leave, Blanchet considered seriously the step he had taken and found grave responsibility attached to it. He sent a last message to the bishop of Quebec:

> I do not know when I shall see your Lordship. I beg of you to accept my sincere gratitude for your goodness to me. I beg the Lord to grant you long life for the happiness and edification of your cherished flock. The missionaries of the Columbia are a part of that group, the sheep whom you lead. Your Lordship, I have no doubt, will pray for the poor missionaries of the far-away Columbia, so that in the midst of dangers, sufferings, discouragements and the plots of the enemy against the safety of the lambs and the sheep, their faith fail not; so that wisdom and prudence may always accompany their acts; so that perseverance may crown their good will and their works. It is with these sentiments and this hope that I confide all to the powerful arms of God, good and great, who sends us that we may advance with confidence in Him but with distrust of ourselves.[25]

On July 10 Bishop Provencher celebrated Mass in honor of St. Anne to ask God's benediction on their journey; the two missionaries received his blessing and parted from this good friend to continue on their way to Norway House,[26] a week's travel from Red River. They arrived there July 17. As was usual, " the Company treated us with the greatest regard and kindness; since we arrived here we have received the same from Mr. Donald Ross who is in charge of the Fort called Norway House. We have seen here many of the bourgeois of the Company, whom we have met with the greatest

[24] Blanchet to Signay, June 22, 1838. QAA.
[25] *Ibid.*
[26] On a channel of the Nelson River, twenty-five miles below the outlet of Lake Winnipeg. Company headquarters moved here in 1821.

pleasure." [27] Norway House was the general rendezvous of the Company where the yearly meeting of the officers took place and where the men assembled from the northern posts in order to take their places in the brigades. "They come here," wrote Demers, "from different posts or forts, bringing in their canoes the returns of the year; they will return to the sea (Hudson Bay) with merchandise and the necessities for trade with the savages. There are several among them who have not seen a priest for thirty-five or six years, since they have been always in the lands of the savages; there are some among them who are wild, you may be sure. They were here only in passing; we said Mass, which is so new to them; we preached to them; we have sown. God must give the increase." [28]

The westward journey was resumed July 26. It was the good fortune of the missionaries to have John Rowand, Esq.[29] in command of their party and Blanchet speaks with praise of his unfailing courtesy and fine efficiency. The brigade with which they traveled consisted of eleven boats laden with merchandise, a great number of hired men, women and children. With them were the English botanists, Wallace and Banks,[30] sent from England by Sir Joseph Paxton in the interests of a scientific society. For six weeks the party followed the crooked course of the Saskatchewan but at Fort Edmonton [31] they were forced to leave it, to abandon the canoes and

[27] Demers to Cazeau, July 25, 1838. QAA.
[28] *Ibid.*
[29] John Rowand was a former North West Company employee; continued with Hudson's Bay Company after the amalgamation and became a chief factor in 1825. In 1827 he was apparently placed in command of the Edmonton district. Simpson in his *Narrative of a Journey Round the World*, I, 58, pays a tribute to his efficiency, "As my new road was to lie through the country of the Blackfeet Indians, I was happy to obtain for the whole way to Fort Vancouver, the escort of Mr. Rowand, who, having been in charge of the Saskatchewan for many years had great influence among the tribes of the prairies. With that gentleman's aid and the well-appointed party of eighteen or twenty men in all, we had but little to fear from any Indians that we could meet."
[30] Hubert H. Bancroft, *History of Oregon* (San Francisco, 1886), I, 316, n. 2, lists among those drowned in the disaster that overtook the party at the Dalles of the Dead, Wallace and wife, English tourists, Banks, a botanist, and his wife, a daughter of Sir George Simpson.
[31] Principal establishment of the Saskatchewan district and residence of the chief factor.

with a caravan of horses to travel overland—" across forests, ponds, prairies, rivers, ditches and beaver dams "— to Fort Assiniboine, a task which required five days of fatiguing and dangerous walking. On September 16 they left that post and began the ascent of the Athabasca River. Twelve days later they had their first glimpse of the Rocky Mountains and went on and on, climbing now into the very heart of the mountains. On October 10 the party approached the summit of this mighty barrier and Blanchet celebrated Mass to give thanks to the Lord for the benefits He had bestowed on them during the long journey and to consecrate to Him these sublime evidences of His handiwork. This same day, he wrote again to Bishop Signay:

> Our health is good, thanks to God, in spite of the troubles, the fatigue and the privations inseparable from a voyage so long and painful. . . . It is not for us to complain; surely priests, the ministers of the Lord, should be at least as ardent and as zealous for the salvation of souls, as the men of the world are for the riches of this savage and barbarous country. We are happy in our sacrifices and we hope that guided by such holy motives as the glory of God, priests—humble, zealous, virtuous and wise—may come in a few years to help us to cultivate the vast field of the vineyard of the Lord beyond the Rocky Mountains; the vineyard of the Lord which it is impossible for us to cultivate by ourselves, in which the enemy of salvation has already sowed bad seed for several years. . . . We expected to run into danger in ascending the rivers, in running the rapids; on horseback over the portages, where there was mire to wade, rivers to cross, hills to climb and descend, trees to chop. But we have been saved. Once our canoe caught in the current and was knocked violently against another; we thought it would go to the bottom; but the steersman alone was thrown out, and he was soon pulled from the river. We owe the unexampled favorable weather which we have enjoyed along the route to the continuous, fervent prayers of the zealous souls in Canada. This has been striking, as the voyageurs have not hesitated to remark.[32]

And then the missionary paid his tribute to the natural beauty of the western country through which they were passing. It never failed to impress him and his letters often contain references to it:

---

[32] Blanchet to Signay, October 10, 1838. QAA.

> The Rocky Mountains are sublime. They are not a high and continuous chain which rises en masse; but an infinite number of grey peaks of all shapes separated one from another; bristling with points, ridges, cones and pyramids. The first tier is covered with forests. These extend over the lower mountains which serve as bases for the other two tiers of bare peaks. We never reached the highest points but followed the valley of the river in and out of this vast sea of mountains.[33]

By October 13 the travelers had descended the western slope of the mountains and prepared to follow the course of the Columbia, which Blanchet remarks "was to offer us in its rapids, its whirlpools, its dalles, its falls, its abysses, a thousand more dangers than all the rivers we had yet navigated." The missionaries had reached the Oregon country. It was Saturday, "a day dedicated to the Immaculate Mother of God, that being at the western foot of the most lofty mountain, the two missionaries began to tread beneath their feet the long-desired land of Oregon; that portion of the vineyard allotted them for cultivation. Filled with joy they retired a short distance from the place where the caravan was resting on the bosom of a beautiful prairie, and there fell on their knees, embraced the soil, took possession of it, dedicated and consecrated their persons, souls and body, to whatever God would be pleased to require of them for the glory of His holy Name, the propagation of His kingdom and the fulfillment of His will." [34]

The boats were loaded early the following afternoon and the party sailed on down the Columbia. Two days later there occurred the only real tragedy of the journey at the Dalles of the Dead,[35] a narrow channel in which the dashing waves threatened the safety of the canoes. At Big Bend, where the travelers had stopped on October 13, the number of boats had not been large enough for the entire party to go on together, so a division had been made, Blanchet and Demers continuing with the first group to the House of the

---

[33] *Ibid.*   [34] Blanchet, *op. cit.*, 9.

[35] Forty-three miles above the town of Revelstroke. Paul Kane, *Wanderings of an Artist among the Indians of North America* (Toronto, 1925) says that the name commemorates the death of two men, who having lost their canoe, endeavored in vain to descend the river; David Douglas says that it takes its name from a " tragical occurrence " when nine persons out of ten lost their lives.

Lakes from where one of the canoes was sent back for the rest. In descending the dangerous water, the returning canoe met with disaster and twelve of the twenty-six occupants were drowned. The sorrowful remnant reached the House of the Lakes on October 24. When the day of their expected arrival had past, a foreboding of disaster had filled the hearts of those who awaited them. And, when, at last, the boat appeared, half-broken, coming in mourning, without the usual joyful chant at arriving, all ran to the shore and the missionaries witnessed the desolation of those with whom they had shared many dangers. An Indian express was at once dispatched to Fort Colville to carry the news of the disaster, while a boat was returned to The Dalles, to look for and to bring down the bodies that might be found. Only those of three children were recovered.[36]

Memorable as the place of tragedy, the House of the Lakes was to be remembered by the missionaries as the scene of their first labors in the Oregon country. Utilizing the eighteen days of their enforced stay, the priests received the Indians, who, somewhat instructed by the Canadians, eagerly listened to them and brought their children to be baptized, " to have their hearts made good." Blanchet judged them to be " of a mild, peaceable character and well-disposed to receive the words of salvation."

After a three days' journey, the canoes arrived at Fort Colville,[37] November 6. The express had announced the news that they were bringing the long-awaited missionaries so there was a gathering of the neighboring tribes as the boats came into sight. Men, women and children swarmed on the shore, hoping for an opportunity to touch the hands of the " chiefs " and to bid them welcome. Scarcely could the priests tear themselves away in order to greet Archibald MacDonald, the Hudson's Bay Company's representative. The chiefs of the five Indian nations—the Chaudières, Cinpoils, Spokans,

[36] Blanchet, *op. cit.*, 10.

[37] About 1826 the post on the Spokane River was removed to Kettle Falls on the Columbia and called Fort Colville. The site was selected by Simpson. McLoughlin hesitated to build there because the location was south of the Columbia but according to Fuller, *op. cit.*, 121, there was no alternative because it was necessary that the post be placed where agricultural possibilities would make it self-supporting. Cf. Simpson, *op. cit.*, I, 150 ff., for a description of the post.

Piskoous and Okanogans—were ready and anxious to hear. "All gathered together in a large house given to them for the occasion and waited in silence for the moment when we should speak to them. With what attentive eagerness they listened to the Word of God, which being translated to them by the chiefs, acquired a new force and additional weight. We forgot nothing that was calculated to fortify them in the principles of the Catholic religion, thus, in a short time, we have scattered some of the seed of the divine word, and we have the sweet hope, that according to God's merciful designs it will bear fruit in this portion of the human family so long neglected. We easily can see what progress Christianity would make among tribes so well disposed."[38]

But four days were all they could give to this promising field. The brigade was ready for the next part of the journey and on November 11 the priests were again traveling down the winding waters of the Columbia. At Fort Okanogan,[39] south and west of Fort Colville, the canoes stopped only twenty-four hours but during that short time, the missionaries met the Indians, of whom they formed the highest opinion. "We may say of them," wrote Demers, "what we have said of those mentioned above; to make fervent Christians of them, it would suffice to teach them the Christian doctrine. Nothing more is needed."[40]

Early Sunday morning, November 18, the party arrived at Fort Walla Walla,[41] where Peter Pambrun, Esq.[42] received the priests

[38] Blanchet, *op. cit.*, 21.

[39] Situated at the junction of the Okanogan with the Columbia. Important as a gateway to Kamloops and New Caledonia.

[40] Demers to Cazeau, March 1, 1839, quoted in Blanchet, *op. cit.*, 21.

[41] Located on the north side of Walla Walla River and east side of the Columbia, where Wallula now is. Simpson, *op. cit.*, I, 160, says, "A more dismal situation than that of this post can hardly be imagined."

[42] Peter C. Pambrun, a French Canadian, the commandant of Fort Walla Walla for several years before his death in 1841. Bancroft, *op. cit.*, II, 689, calls attention to the fact that Pambrun was among the few French Canadians to rise to a position of command. Joseph Tassé, *Les Canadiens de l'Ouest* (Montreal, 1878), II, 314, remarks his friendship with the Indians and his efforts to Christianize them, as do Clinton A. Snowden, *History of Washington: the Rise and Progress of an American State* (New York, 1909), II, 95 and Gilbert J. Garraghan, S. J., *The Jesuits of the Middle United States* (New York, 1938), II, 340.

with the greatest cordiality. This post, situated in the midst of hostile Indian tribes, was the only one to be strongly fortified. At this time the savages appear to have been friendly and Cayuses and Walla Wallas came to see the " black gowns."

The following day began the final lap of the journey,[43] the descent from Fort Walla Walla to Fort Vancouver. The last run, although not without its anxious moments as the canoes ventured through the Dalles,[44] was made without accident; from the Dalles to the Cascades navigation was quiet and pleasant on the smooth waters of the Columbia. On Friday a four mile portage was necessary but on Saturday, November 24, the canoes sped on with sail and oar, while the thoughts of all turned toward the end of the journey, Fort Vancouver.

---

[43] Blanchet mentions shortage of food on November 20 as one of their difficulties. Two horses purchased from the Indians at $10 each helped to supply the deficiency.

[44] Peter S. Ogden, *Traits of American Indian Life and Character* (London, 1853), 80, graphically describes the Dalles, " In this particular place the river is parted into a number of channels, separated from each other by insulated tongues of rock, which rise abruptly from the surface of the waters. Some of these channels are navigable, though with great risks even to the most expert boatmen, at certain periods of the year; but in the summer season when the melting of the mountain snows have swelled the flood beyond its accustomed limits, most of them become indistinguishably blended together, and the mighty waters roll along with irresistible fury."

CHAPTER II

THE FIRST MISSIONS

Late in the afternoon of November 24, the watchman at Fort Vancouver spied far up the river a line of tiny, dark specks, that could only be the long awaited express. In an instant, his warning cry, "The brigade!", was passed from one to another and soon an excited, shouting, gesticulating crowd of men, women and children covered the banks of the Columbia, in order to be at hand to give a first welcome to those, whose coming meant contact with the outside world.[1] The express was late. The accident to one of the canoes at the Dalles of the Dead, which had brought death to twelve of the

---

[1] The arrival of the company ships, bringing mail from England, was likewise an event of greatest importance. Ogden, *op. cit.*, 105-106, describes the scene, "It is not easy for me to convey an idea of the degree of excitement that attends the glad announcement of the packet from London. Shut out from the world, indeed, as we are and receiving tidings from home at yearly intervals only, it is natural that anxiety as to their probable nature should prevail among the expectants. . . . For weeks before the anticipated event, the probabilities attending it form the all-pervading topic of conversation. . . . The excitement increases from day to day, until all doubts are at length solved by the arrival of the ship, first announced by a confused murmur, and then by the noisy exclamations of the children running to and fro, delighted with the novelty and screaming at the top of their voices, 'The Packet! The Packet.' The bearers of the precious burden shortly make their appearance not a little proud of the temporary importance attached to their mission. They advance to the governor's domicile and are ushered into the presence hall, where, as they well know, a hearty welcome from the great man awaits them. All etiquette is for a while suspended. A motley group of followers throng around the doors. . . . Letters are doled forth to their expectant owners. . . . As may be supposed, an event so long looked for and so interesting to all connected with the establishment deranges for a while its settled routine; every one, in short, being so engrossed with the perusal of his letters, that a general silence supplants the ordinary buzz of business. At length, the sound of the dinner bell renews the social compact. . . . Even the ladies share in the general excitement for besides the familiar topics in which they may be presumed to have an interest, they have their own special curiosity to satisfy, noting the domestic supplies shipped for them, the gowns, the bonnets, the shawls. . . . So passes the day; another sun appears, and again all is regularity and order."

The First Missions 19

party and to the saddended survivors weary delay at the House of the Lakes, had likewise caused anxiety at the fort. But necessary readjustments had been made and in the joyous excitement of reaching the end of the long journey, the sorrows of past days seem to have been forgotten, for Blanchet tells us that the boatmen followed their traditional custom of putting ashore a few miles above Fort Vancouver, so that each might lay aside his work-day dress and don his best, thus to appear at the western post in his gayest attire.[2] Then, each man in his finest, hats decorated with feathers or bunches of bright ribbon, gay colored shirts, brilliant sashes from which dangled beaded Indian pouches, the brigade swept down the river. As the boats drew nearer and nearer, the chorus of song from the voyageurs swelled louder and louder, broken now, by the shouts of welcome from the shore. When the canoes had been brought opposite the fort, still in the middle of the river, they wheeled in perfect line and came, side by side, in toward the bank. Once there, order was gone, for as the oarsmen stepped to the shore, they were swallowed up in the crowd that was waiting.

In that throng stood James Douglas, Esq., chief factor, member of the Hudson's Bay Company, and in the absence of McLoughlin, commander of Fort Vancouver.[3] Not far from him, must have been the three representatives of the Canadians of Willamette Valley, Joseph Gervais,[4] Stephen Lucier[5] and Peter Beleque,[6] who had

---

[2] Blanchet to Signay, March 17, 1839, quoted in Blanchet, *Sketches*, 18; Simpson, *Narrative of a Journey*, I, 172, calls attention to this custom, " Being anxious to approach headquarters in proper style, our men here exchanged the oar for the paddle, which besides being more orthodox in itself, was better adapted to the quick notes of the voyageur songs."

[3] James Douglas began his service in the fur trade with the North West Company at Fort William under the tutelage of John McLoughlin in 1819. The two men were long associated and worked together on the Columbia until McLoughlin's resignation in 1846.

[4] Joseph Gervais, a member of Hunt's party in 1812, became a free trapper after Astor's Company had been transferred to the North West Company in 1813 and for a time was employed by the Hudson's Bay. He was one of the original claimants in the Champoeg vicinity, where he built a house in 1821.

[5] Stephen Lucier, also one of Hunt's party and later a trapper for Hudson's Bay. In 1828 with McLoughlin's assistance he established a claim on the east bank of the Willamette and later moved to French Prairie.

[6] Peter Beleque, one of the first settlers in the vicinity of Champoeg.

been waiting long hours to pay their tribute to the priests whose coming they had petitioned three years before. Almost the whole group of settlers had come from French Prairie but they had been obliged to return to their homes before the arrival of the brigade.

Blanchet found nothing lacking in the kindly welcome of the chief factor, "he received us and treated us with great kindness and courtesy." Conducting them to the fort, Douglas ushered them into apartments prepared for them, appointed a servant to wait on them, and in every way showed his delight at their arrival.[7]

The day following, Sunday, November 25, the vicar general celebrated the first Mass in lower Oregon. The schoolhouse, prepared for the service, proved much too small for the crowd of those from the fort and from the village outside, who were anxious to attend. A High Mass of thanksgiving was sung by the missionary who also gave an instruction suitable for the occasion. Vespers were chanted in the afternoon. Deep must have been the emotion which filled the hearts of those, who, for the first time in ten, fifteen, or even twenty years had an opportunity to assist at divine services.[8]

Blanchet kept a careful account of the first activities of the missionaries. After but two days of rest, they began on the fourth the work they had come to do. On Monday, November 25, Governor[9] Douglas invited them to inspect the stores and depots of the company and to visit the clerk's office and the houses of the bourgeois, the clerks and their families. On Tuesday, he accompanied them to the village outside the fort, in which were the

[7] Blanchet to Signay, March 1, 1839. QAA.

[8] Blanchet, *op. cit.*, 23; John G. Shea, *History of the Catholic Church in the United States* (New York, 1888-1892), IV, 311.

[9] Douglas' title of governor was more or less honorary; he was at this time chief factor. Bancroft, *Northwest Coast*, II, 491, says, "It would seem that there was a dearth of words signifying dominance in those days, the term governor being applied to the highest in authority everywhere. He who presided at the London board was governor supreme; the commanding officer in America was governor-in-chief of the Hudson's Bay Territories; then there were governors of districts, governors of forts, a governor of Rupert Land, a governor of Assiniboine, and sometimes a double governor, as in the case of Douglas at Vancouver Island, who was at once Hudson's Bay Company governor and colonial governor."

houses of the servants. The census, taken at that time, showed seventy-six Catholics—Canadians and Iroquois. The Indian population on the shore of the Columbia was estimated at 300 souls. Douglas undoubtedly added to their store of information regarding the Oregon country and helped them to form some idea of the task before them. Blanchet summed up conditions as he found them:

> The Indian tribes were numerous, scattered all over the country, speaking a multitude of divers and difficult tongues, and addicted to poligamy and all the vices of paganism. The servants of the Hudson's Bay Company, in active service in its twenty-eight forts for the fur trade, were in great majority Catholics; so also were the four families settled in Cowlitz, and the twenty-six established in the Willamette Valley with their wives and children. Many of the servants and settlers had forgotten their prayers and the religious principles they had received in their youth. The women they had taken for their wives were pagans, or baptized without sufficient knowledge. Their children were raised in ignorance. One may well imagine that in many places disorders, rudeness of morals and indecency of practices, answered to that state of ignorance.[10]

Blanchet noted the presence and the activity of the Protestant missionaries who had settled, even in the Willamette Valley in the midst of the French Canadians. The Methodists [11] had two missions; the Presbyterians [12] were at Waiilatpu among the Walla Wallas and at Lapwai among the Nez Percés and on the Spokane River. Besides these the Company had had its own Anglican chaplain [13] at Fort Vancouver for two years. These men were zealous to make converts and had succeeded in some cases in winning the confidence of the ill-instructed Canadians. The priests had work ahead of them. The vicar general thus outlined the task:

---

[10] Blanchet, op. cit., 23.

[11] The first group of Methodist missionaries who came with Jason Lee in 1834 had been strengthened by the arrival of others in May and September, 1837.

[12] The directors of Presbyterian work were Marcus Whitman and H. H. Spalding.

[13] Rev. Herbert Beaver was sent by the London authorities of Hudson's Bay to Oregon in 1836. He stayed at Fort Vancouver two years but found conditions little to his liking. His criticisms of primitive living and of the domestic relations of the employees of the company soon brought him into conflict with McLoughlin.

... it is easy to understand what the missionaries had to do. They were to warn their flock against the dangers of seduction, to destroy the false impressions already received, to enlighten and confirm the faith of the wavering and deceived consciences, to bring back to the practice of religion and virtue all who had forsaken them for long years, or who, raised in infidelity, had never known nor practised any of them. They were to teach the men their duties, the women and children their prayers and catechism, to baptize them, bless their unions, and establish good order and holiness of life everywhere. In a word, they were to run after the sheep when they were in danger. Hence their passing so often from one post to another—for neither the whites nor the Indians claimed their assistance in vain.[14]

The ministry was begun at Fort Vancouver. On Tuesday evening, November 27, the missionaries gathered together their flock in the fort and from that day on held regular meetings. These assemblies proved popular and attracted on many occasions the officers, the clerks and their families. Nor were the Indians indifferent. They attended in large numbers; sometimes as many as seventy and one hundred. On February 20, there were 140 assisting at evening prayer.[15]

On the morning of November 28 classes were begun for the women and children. The afternoon was reserved for teaching the prayers and truths of religion to the Indian women and children of the village in order to prepare them for baptism. This was a difficult task; prayers had to be learned in French and this was only done by constant repetition, sometimes for weeks and even for months. Sixty women and girls and eighteen little boys came to this catechism. Father Demers set himself the task of learning the Chinook jargon,[16] which he succeeded in mastering after a few

[14] Blanchet, *op. cit.*, 24.   [15] *Ibid.*

[16] The Chinook jargon was for long supposedly invented by the employees of the Hudson's Bay Company to make possible communication with the Indian tribes. But it seems to have been in use many years before the arrival of the company on the coast. The jargon is based on the language of the Chinooks, the most widespread of the Northwest tongues, to which were added French and English words. Its vocabulary is very small, about 500 words, but it was most useful to both Indians and whites and is now in use by nearly all the Indians of the Pacific Northwest. Cf. Charles Carey, *History of Oregon* (Chicago, 1922), 57-61.

weeks. In one of his letters he wrote, " I have found here [at Fort Vancouver] some consolation; God has given me the grace to learn the Chinook language in a short time. It is in this jargon that I instruct the women and children of the white settlers and the savages [17] who come to see from far and near." [18] The missionary translated the Sign of the Cross, the Our Father and the Hail Mary into the dialect and taught them to the Indians, who, according to Father Blanchet, were much pleased to learn them. In February, 1840 Demers succeeded in composing some hymns in the same dialect, which the Indians, as well as the white men, women and children, chanted in the church with the greatest delight.[19]

The people of Fort Vancouver were closest at hand and so received the first attention of the missionaries but it was not intended that their principal establishment should be at the company's headquarters. In accordance with the agreement between Bishop Provencher and Governor Simpson, the instructions of the missionaries cautioned them to fix their place of residence on the Cowlitz River, which flows into the Columbia on the north side of the latter.[20] In

---

[17] In the use of the word, *savage*, to designate the Indians of the Northwest, a caution, suggested by Carey, *op. cit.*, 51, should be borne in mind, " While the Indians of the Oregon Country may be properly classified as savages, it is to be understood that this term is to be taken in its ethnological sense, for they had many admirable traits and showed themselves capable of feeling and conduct which might well put their more fortunate white brethren to shame."

[18] Demers to Blanchet, January 23, 1839. QAA.

[19] Blanchet, *op. cit.*, 25; Demers to Blanchet, January 17, 1839. QAA.

[20] Instructions for Messrs. Francis Norbert Blanchet and Modeste Demers, Priests, Missionaries named for that part of the Diocese of Quebec which is situated between the Pacific Ocean and the Rocky Mountains.

1. They shall consider their first object to be to regain from barbarism and its disorders, the savage tribes scattered over that country.
2. Their second object shall be to extend their help to the poor Christians who have adopted the customs of the savages and live in license and forgetfulness of their duties.
3. Persuaded that the preaching of the Gospel is the best way to obtain these happy results, they will not lose a single opportunity to inculcate its principles and maxims either in their private conversation or their public discourses.
4. In order to be as useful as possible to the natives of the country, they shall apply themselves as soon as they arrive to the study of the

order, therefore, to show his willingness to carry out that plan, Blanchet with his servant, Augustine Rochon, set out from Fort

>   language of the savages and shall try after some years of residence to publish a grammar.
> 5. They shall prepare for baptism as soon as possible the women who live in concubinage with Christians, so as to be able to substitute legitimate marriages for these irregular unions.
> 6. They shall give special attention to the Christian education of the children, establishing to that end schools and catechism classes in all the villages which they may have occasion to visit.
> 7. In all principal places they shall erect a large cross in order to take possession of these places in the name of the Catholic religion.
> 8. They shall often repeat to the people among whom they are sent, that this religion enjoins peace and obedience to the laws of both State and Church and they shall not fail to show, as much by their example as by their words, the respect and fidelity due to our gracious Sovereign, addressing to God their prayers for her prosperity and that of her empire.
> 9. The territory especially assigned to them is that between the Rocky Mountains on the east, the Pacific Ocean on the west, the Russian possessions on the north and the territory of the United States to the south. It is only in this territory that they shall establish missions; and it is particularly recommended that they do not establish any mission on land, the possession of which is contested by the United States. They may, however, according to the Indult of the Holy See, February 20, 1836, of which a copy accompanies this, exercise their powers at need in the Russian possessions as well as that part of American territory which adjoins their mission. As to this territory, it is not likely that it belongs to any diocese of the United States; but if the missionaries learn that it does, they must abstain from exercising there any act of jurisdiction, in obedience to the Indult cited, at least until they be authorized by the bishop of that diocese.
> 10. They shall fix their principal place of residence on the river Cowlitz, which flows into the Columbia on the north side of the latter river. On their arrival at Fort Vancouver they shall present themselves to the representative of the Hudson's Bay Company and consult him as to the precise situation of their establishment.
> 11. It is recommended that they have all possible regard for the members and employees of the Hudson's Bay Company with whom it is most important for the good of the work with which they are charged that they be on friendly terms.
> 12. Since they cannot depend entirely on the resources of the Associa-

Vancouver on December 12. Father Demers continued the mission at the fort.

Blanchet reached the Cowlitz settlement early in the morning of

---

tion of the Propagation of Faith, established in the diocese a year ago, to provide for their maintenance and for the building of chapels and houses at their different missions, they shall insist that the colonists and natives of the country contribute, as much as their means allow.

13. They shall not fail to give us an account of their work each year, information on all that retards or favors the progress of their mission. They shall take care to send details of such sort that they may be published for the edification and encouragement of the faithful, who as members of the Association for the Propagation of the Faith, contributed by their alms to the establishment and upkeep of this new mission.

14. The territory in which this mission is to be established having been annexed by the Indult of February 28, 1836 to the territory of the North West, whose spiritual government is confided to the Bishop of Juliopolis, the new missionaries shall correspond as regularly as possible with this prelate so that he will know the state of their mission and they shall receive his orders and wishes with submission and respect.

15. Due to the impossibility of transporting across the Rockies more than is strictly necessary in the way of ornaments and furnishings for the church the new mission may find itself at first in great need. But the zeal with which the Association of the Propagation of the Faith established at Lyons has come to the aid of the missions of Canada in the last years, give hope that it will extend its benefactions, and by way of England, will send in the vessels of the Hudson's Bay Company what may be needed. We recommend that you ask the Bishop of Juliopolis to interest himself in this and to secure help from the friends he made during his sojourn in France.

16. They may evercise the powers which have been delegated to them in all the territory of the Northwest when they pass through it on their return to the river Cowlitz, or when they return to Canada, except when in the presence of the Bishop of Juliopolis, then they may not except at the invitation of his Lordship.

. . . .

21. In the case of the death of the head of the mission, or of his serious illness, which God prevent, his colleague is authorized to exercise all his powers.

Given at Quebec the 17th of April 1838.

(Signed) Jos. Bish. of Quebec. QAA.

December 16 and offered Mass in the house of Simon Plamondon.[21] The settlers and their families welcomed the missionary and eagerly accompanied him on his visitation. Blanchet baptized seven, gave the necessary instructions to the men, and recommended that Mr. Fagnant, one of the farmers who was able to read, teach the prayers and catechism to the women and children. Before his departure on Tuesday, December 20, the vicar general chose for the mission 640 acres of clear prairie land.[22]

The Catholics of the Willamette Valley had sent (1834, 1835) appeals to Bishop Provencher for a missionary and they were anxious to see among them at least one of the priests who had come from Canada. There seemed, in 1839, no possibility of establishing a permanent mission but Father Blanchet found nothing in his agreement to prevent his visiting the Willamette settlement. Thus, on January 3, Stephen Lucier and Peter Beleque came with two large canoes to escort the missionary from Fort Vancouver. Two days later the party reached the Campement de Sable. The four miles from there to the church,[23] which had been built in 1836, were made on horseback. On the way, they stopped at the homes of Lucier and Beleque, whose families seem to have considered it a privilege to be the first to see the priest at Willamette.[24]

The actual date of the foundation of this settlement is doubtful but it evidently began about 1829.[25] Joseph Gervais and Stephen Lucier were among the first and gradually there gathered around them a colony of twenty-six families, mostly French Canadians, nearly all former servants of the Hudson's Bay Company. Frederick Holman describes the conditions under which they lived and concludes that to them they must have seemed almost ideal:

> The French Canadians had been in the wilderness for many years, where they had trapped, paddled the canoes for many a

[21] Simon Plamondon was the first free farmer in the locality. He had been sixteen years in the employ of the Hudson's Bay Company. On his retirement he was advised by McLoughlin to go to Cowlitz Prairie to farm.

[22] O'Hara, *op. cit.*, 31.

[23] This church, the first erected in Oregon, was a log structure, 30 by 70 feet. It had been built in 1836, as soon as the settlers received Provencher's assurance that missionaries would be sent to them.

[24] Blanchet, *op. cit.*, 28-29.

[25] Robert C. Clark, *History of Willamette Valley* (Chicago, 1927), I, 226.

weary mile each year, and carried the heavy packages over the portages. They had been subject to discipline and to the exercise of authority by their superior in the Hudson's Bay Company. They were old, or becoming so, from age and by reason of hardships suffered. Their gentle dispositions caused them to take kindly to retirement and an easy way of living. Their Indian consorts were patient, obedient, and were constant workers. Their children were contented. They were under the protection of the Hudson's Bay Company and of Dr. John McLoughlin whom to obey was a pleasurable duty. All their wheat was taken by the Company at a good and constant price. They purchased their goods at prices which gave the Company a very moderate profit. Their fields and their gardens supplied them in abundance. The streams were full of trout, and game, especially deer was plentiful. They had priests of their religious faith. . . . They paid no taxes. They, their families and their properties were safe from assault or other dangers. The Indians were peaceable and not to be feared. . . . What more could they ask? [26]

The picture is an attractive one and seems to have been a true one, at least many writers of the period comment favorably on these first Catholics of Oregon and the settlement they made in the Willamette Valley. There is one discordant note when Robert Clark hints that in some cases the retirement from the Company of such men as Gervais and his fellow Astorians may have been welcomed by the officers. These men were sometimes characterized as " undisciplined, impertinent, ill-behaved vagabonds, devoid of that sense of subordination which our [the fur] business requires." [27] The chief traders in the Snake country had trouble with them but found them necessary and made many concessions in order to keep them from going to the Americans. In general, however, the French Canadian was a devoted servant of the Company and the officers agreed with Lord Durham, when he said of them that " they are mild and kindly, frugal, industrious and honest, very sociable, cheerful and hospitable, and distinguished for a courtesy and real politeness." [28] Life in the fur trade had not fitted them to become

[26] Frederick V. Holman, " A Brief History of the Oregon Provisional Government and What Caused Its Formation," *Oregon Historical Quarterly*, henceforth cited at *OHQ*, XIII (1912), 99.

[27] Clark, *op. cit.*, I, 189.

[28] Report of Lord Durham, 1838, quoted by Clark, " How British and

masters of industry; life in the Willamette was easy and did not require too much expenditure of energy, so these farmers kept their flocks and herds and dabbled a little in tillage, but only a little, since painstaking and laborious attention to detail was not much to the liking of men of the roving type.[29] The missionaries were to find their love of comfort and of pleasure difficult to control; were to be troubled by the lightness of their characters and the ease with which they were influenced. But at the first meeting, January 5, 1839, there was only joy.

The afternoon of that day was spent in receiving visits, since all, especially the women and the half-breed children, were anxious to see the priest, so long announced and expected. Sunday, January 6, the feast of the Epiphany of our Lord, the tiny church, that had been waiting for more than two years, was blessed under the patronage of St. Paul. During the Mass which followed, Father Blanchet read to the people the short pastoral letter of Bishop Signay:

> To our very dear children—Greetings and Benediction of our Savior.
>
> Since the Bishop of Juliopolis told us of the desire you manifested to him to have among you priests, who would interest themselves in your spiritual concerns, we have not ceased to pray that the Lord would give us the means of procuring for you an advantage so precious. Your desires and ours have been rewarded. The members of the Honorable Company of Hudson's Bay have had the liberality to offer a passage in one of their canoes to two priests whom we propose to send to you, and we accepted their offer with gratitude.
>
> Thank God, our very dear children, for the acquisition you have made in these generous missionaires, who have separated themselves from their friends, their families, from all hopes and consolations which they would have found in Canada, so that they might live to devote themselves to the salvation of your souls and those of your brothers who are still unhappily enveloped in the shadows of paganism. Sweeten their ministry among you by your docility, obedience and zeal to profit by their instruction and good example. Look upon them as your spiritual fathers, charged with speaking to you of God and of

American Subjects United in a Constitutional Government for Oregon Territory in 1844," *OHQ*, XIII (1912), 142.

[29] Carey, *op. cit.*, 791.

speaking to God for you. They will count their weariness, their labors as nothing, if they find in the flock confided to them this desire of knowing the true religion, of practising it and of honoring it, which without doubt has been the motive of your reiterated demands for a priest to live among you. This, our very dear children, is what we hope to have the consolation of learning from the first news we shall receive from them after their arrival at their destination.[30]

Commenting on it later, the missionary wrote, " The reading of the pastoral letter touched them; they have recognized in it the voice of the first pastor; they are full of gratitude for the interest of your Lordship in their salvation." [31] After it, came an explanation of the commandments of God and of the Church, and the rules to be observed during the mission, the reception of which pleased the vicar general, if we may judge from his remarks:

> All terminated with reflections and advices which were very touching on both sides. All went home happy and willing to obey the Church, even in regard to the separation from their wives until their unions would be blessed. . . . So great was their desire to have their wives and children instructed and to lose nothing of the instructions given, that they brought them from home to live in tents around the church. The men would not do less; those living the nearest came every day to hear Mass and passed the whole day at the church, returning home in time to attend to their business and prevent the wasting of their crops by their hired men and slave Indians.[32]

The mission continued until February 4. The exercises began every day by the celebration of Mass with an instruction. During the morning, there followed the recitation of prayers in French, the explanation of the Apostles' Creed and the most important truths of religion, interspersed with the singing of hymns. This was the program for three weeks. During the fourth the missionary took the opportunity to rest a little. He went around the whole establishment to visit the settlers, who received him with the greatest demonstrations of joy and thanks to God for the consolations of religion they had received. Before leaving, Blanchet took possession

---

[30] Signay to the people of Cowlitz, April 16, 1838. QAA.
[31] Blanchet to Signay, March 1, 1839. QAA.
[32] Blanchet, *op. cit.*, 29.

of a tract of 640 acres for the mission, in the hope that the prohibition against a permanent settlement might soon be raised. The vicar general returned to Fort Vancouver on February 5 well pleased with the results of this month's work, which he estimated as follows:

> The fruits of the mission were consoling; for many of the Indian women and a number of grown up boys and girls and young children had learned to make the Sign of the Cross, the offering of the heart to God, the Lord's prayer, the Hail Mary, the Apostles' Creed, and some of the Acts; twenty-five Indian women were baptized in excellent dispositions and their unions with their husbands blessed by the Church; forty-seven other baptisms of children were made, to which, if we add those of an old Indian man and of a young Indian girl, both sick, who soon died, and were the first to be buried in the new cemetery, we will have seventy-four baptisms and twenty-five marriages.[33]

The departure of the spring express on March 5 gave the missionaries their first opportunity to send an account of their progress to the bishop of Quebec. The journey from Montreal and the travels and contacts of the first four months impressed the priests with the magnitude of the task they had undertaken and gave them some knowledge of the difficulties and problems which were likely to confront them. Although Blanchet did not minimize the needs of the Columbia country, the picture he sent is not a dark one and he found cause for rejoicing in what had already been done. His letter to Signay summed up the work accomplished and called attention to the demands of the future:

> I do not hide from you that we are incapable of doing everything. The work is great; it is bound to increase. . . . The mission of Vancouver could occupy the whole attention of one priest. We can give a short time only to each mission. I spent a month at Willamette, leaving Father Demers at Vancouver, so that we might not lose what had been begun in that place. I shall go to Cowlitz for a month. Father Demers will continue at Vancouver. The natives of Bay St. George want to see us, but when can we go? There is a large camp of Chinooks at Fort George, who do not seem indifferent; they ought to be visited: I do not know when it can be done. After the mission

---

[33] *Ibid.*, 29-30.

at Cowlitz, I shall return to spend Easter at Willamette; this will not be more than a month; I shall return at the beginning of June. I must spend some time at Vancouver during the sojourn of the brigade of the men from the north, so as to prevent disorder, trouble among the baptized, and to instruct those men and encourage good feeling. After the departure of this brigade, we must go to visit the savages of Walla Walla, Okanogan, Colville, who anxiously await our coming.[34]

Blanchet and Demers could already see the results of their ministry and found occasion to thank God who had blessed their labors. In the letter cited above, the vicar general wrote:

We have much for which to thank the Lord who does not cease to favor us and to do away with obstacles, which we meet to the good that we would do in our mission. All goes well. There are still bad Christians but vice has diminished; the good is begun; progress is visible. . . . I have found the men of the Willamette and of Cowlitz very well disposed; they received the missionary with respect, they listened to him with attention. . . . Never have people seemed more grateful than these poor men when I visited them and gave them a month of mission. . . . I can assure your Lordship that the presence of priests on the Columbia has given them new life.[35]

As for the Indians, the missionary said, "The Lord promises an abundant harvest of souls among the savages of the Columbia; they already have the faith."[36] And in a letter to Bishop Turgeon, the coadjutor of Quebec, Blanchet made this comment, "It seems to me that the savages of this country, for the most part, are disposed to receive the faith."[37] On account of the facility with which he learned the Chinook jargon, Demers had greater success in dealing with the natives and became deeply interested in their welfare. In March, 1839 he sent an account of the Indian tribes of the neighborhood to Father Charles Cazeau, secretary to the bishop of Quebec. The missionary cautioned against the acceptance of these first judgments as final but much of what he said proved to be correct. His estimate of the tribes living near Fort Vancouver was not favorable:

---

[34] Blanchet to Signay, March 1, 1839. QAA.
[35] *Ibid.*
[36] *Ibid.*   [37] Blanchet to Turgeon, March 13, 1839. QAA.

> The Chinook Indians are scattered along the Columbia River from this Fort down to the Pacific Ocean. Before the year 1830, they were the most numerous tribe inhabiting the banks of this river. This rendered them proud and haughty. Besides this they were rich; but about this time came the disastrous malady known by the name of fever-and-ague which carried a great many to their graves.... This calamity which God sent these Indians on account of their abominable lives, came to visit them every year, and always made some of them its victims. We are told they reformed their lives except those who lived near the fort, who are wicked and demoralized on account of their communication with the whites. They make a shameful traffic in crime; they have female slaves whom they hire at a price to the first who asks them. They have seen us and see us yet with an indifference that makes us regret the good Indians of the upper river; but the part of the tribe situated not far from Fort George (now Astoria) down the river, is not as depraved, which gives us hope of being able to Christianize them.[38]

He hoped to accomplish more with some of the other tribes. Demers believed that the Indians of Cowlitz gave promise of becoming real Christians:

> The Cowlitz Indians love with reverence the missionaries who are established among them. They have a language of their own, different from that of the Chinook Indians. They are tolerably numerous but poor. They give us hopes of their conversion.... Several of them came to see the missionaries at Vancouver, and expressed the most ardent desire to have them come and remain with them.[39]

[38] Demers to Cazeau, March 1, 1839, quoted in Blanchet, *op. cit.*, 21; Blanchet to Turgeon, March 13, 1839. QAA., describes conditions among the Indians around Fort Vancouver; H. E. Tobie, *The Willamette Valley before the Great Immigrations* (unpub. M. A. thesis, University of Oregon, 1927), after an examination of the records of early visitors to the Pacific coast concludes that all sources point to the physical inferiority of the coast tribes to "their hard-riding brethren of the prairies." Contact with the white traders was disastrous. When the first ship entered the river it was noticed that the "men at Columbia River are straight limbed, finelooking fellows, and the women are very pretty." The Astorians found the same Indians "flabby and shapeless and revolting because of coarse sensuality."

[39] Demers to Blanchet, January 17, 1839. QAA.; Demers to Cazeau, March 1, 1839, quoted in Blanchet, *op. cit.*, 22.

Conditions among the Willamette tribes were not promising and the missionary's report indicated that he expected their conversion would come only after repeated efforts:

> The vicar general who passed a month among the Canadians established on this river, could not speak highly of the Indians he had seen—the Kalapooias. They were very numerous before the fevers,[40] but are now reduced to a small number, which keeps decreasing every day. They are poor and lazy; thieving may be considered their predominant passion. They wish to keep away from the missionaries as much as the Cowlitz Indians wish to be near them. Hardly any of them were seen by the vicar general at the chapel assisting at the instructions. But it seems we might succeed better among the different tribes of this nation who are settled on the tributaries of the Upper Willamette. From these they take their different names.[41]

[40] Tobie, *op. cit.*, 46, quotes Alexander Henry to the effect that the Calipooias were a "wretched tribe, diminutive in size." Between 1824 and 1829 many of the Indiens were carried off by epidemics the exact nature of which is unknown; Ogden, *op. cit.*, 68-69, gives a picture of the desolation caused by these visitations, "In close contiguity with our clearance was a village containing about sixty families of Indians; a few miles lower down was a second of at least equal population. These villages before the fell visitation I have mentioned [1830] resounded with the hum of voices; smiling on the shores of the magnificent Columbia, they refreshed the eyes of the lone traveller, wearied with the unbroken monotony of woods and waters. . . . In this sequestered spot, seated on some rude turfy knoll was it a matter of pleasant contemplation to witness the evening pastimes of the simple villagers. The lively gambols of the children; the more stirring games of the youths; the sober gravity of manhood and the doting garrulity of old age; . . . Such was the scene I had often witnessed when visiting these hamlets. A short month had passed away: the shadow of death on the wing had just fallen upon our little community and passed by; and now, as I drew near the well-remembered lodges, how different were the feelings I experienced! . . . Silence reigned where erst the din of population resounded loud and lively . . . where are they who not long since peopled this deserted spot? . . . Let these unburied carcasses resolve the question. . . . The death-like silence around me, the fell vestiges of a sad calamity which I descry, the loathsome remains of mortality which alone indicate what was once the scene of life and vigor are my only answer. These speak louder than words . . . they tell me with awful distinctness that here, where the voice of laughter and the rude Indian chant have so often made my heart glad, the fever ghoul has wrecked his most dire vengeance; to the utter destruction of every human inhabitant."

[41] Demers to Cazeau, March 1, 1839, quoted in Blanchet, *op. cit.*, 22.

Demers, as well as Blanchet, seems to have been struck by the insufficiency of their efforts, in the face of the needs of the country, " What can two missionaries do among so many tribes but desire that the Lord may send missionary priests to show them the way to heaven, for which they had been created, and to tell them that their souls are the price of the blood of the Saviour."

However, the missionaries made their plans and looked forward to possible development. Blanchet, in a letter to Bishop Signay, wrote of the missions he hoped to establish in order to reach, as quickly as possible, the greatest number of Indians. The ideal situation, of which he often spoke, would have been the isolation of the tribesmen from the whites in settlements where they might learn and practise the principles of Christianity. That was never practicable but at the beginning the priests hoped that it might become so when additional helpers had been sent to them. Hence Blanchet presented and urged their needs:

> I have three missions in view: the first at Colville, the second at Yakima across the river from the Nez Percés, and the third on the Upper Willamette. They tell me that the savages will come in crowds from the surrounding country to be instructed in these places—peoples of many tribes. They have spoken to me of Nisqually on the Bay St. George, as a district most populous in native tribes; this will be a place for a fourth mission. We may add to this number Fort George; the savages around there are Chinooks in great number; this will be the place for the fifth mission; several chiefs of these savages have come up with their families to see the great chiefs of the French; one can do what one wishes with them after their language has been learned.[42]

Both Blanchet and Demers learned soon that the first demonstrations of interest on the part of the Indians meant little and that they were easily drawn away by any passing distraction. Consequently, to insure the effectiveness of the work priests should be constantly with them to instruct and guide. According to Blanchet's reasoning, " The difficulty of communication and the distances between these places, as appears from the map, show the necessity of having priests for each of these posts." And then he

[42] Blanchet to Signay, March 1, 1839. QAA.

suggested another step, " with the aid which we will obtain from France, we can establish far from the settlements of the whites, missions like those in California." That ideal could not be accomplished until priests " virtuous and filled by God with zeal for the salvation of souls " had come to assist them. Meanwhile he and Demers would do all that two men could. They had many obstacles to overcome but they had some advantages as well: " The favorable impressions given by the Canadians in favor of the priests, celibacy, the Sign of the Cross, the Mass, images, etc., the ties formed by the whites with the women of all nations and in all parts of the country; all this and more, much more the help of grace, draws and attracts the tribes." In fact the missionary felt certain " that the Columbia would make a great Catholic country."

After the departure of the express on March 5 Blanchet returned to the group at Cowlitz, where he remained for more than a month (March 17–May 1), continuing his work with the whites—the four families of French Canadians and a large number of servants, employed on the farms of the Hudson's Bay Company. The news of the arrival of the missionary at Cowlitz caused numerous delegations of Indians to come from distances to hear and see the Frenchmen's chief. Among these was one led by Chief Tsla-lakum, whose tribe lived on Whidby Island, Puget Sound, 150 miles away. After a journey in canoes to Fort Nisqually and a hard march of three days on foot across streams and rivers and along a rough trail, they reached Cowlitz with bleeding feet. Their object was to see the " black-gown " and to hear him speak of the Great Spirit. The priest had much difficulty in explaining the truths of religion to these primitive people, a difficulty which led finally to the adoption of the device, known as the " Catholic Ladder." [43]

[43] A device designed to Blanchet to assist in the explanation of Catholic history and doctrine to the Indians. In his *Sketches*, 31, Blanchet says, " the great difficulty was to give them an idea of religion so plain and simple as to command their attention, and which they could retain in their minds and carry back with them to their tribe. In looking for a plan the vicar general imagined that by representing on a square stick, the forty centuries before Christ by 40 marks; the thirty-three years of our Lord by 33 points, followed by a cross; and the eighteen centuries and thirty-nine years since, by 18 marks and 39 points, would pretty well answer his purpose, in giving him a chance to show the beginning of the

During the mission at Cowlitz, Reverend Daniel Lee,[44] the Methodist minister, stopped at the settlement and disclosed his plan of establishing a post among the Indians around Fort Nisqually. This news so stirred Father Blanchet that he immediately sent an Indian messenger to Demers, urging him to leave Vancouver and to go at once to the northern fort, in order to meet the natives there before the arrival of the Protestant worker.[45] Father Demers lost no time in following the suggestion. After a journey of six days, he reached the fort on April 1, where he received a warm welcome from Mr. William Kitson, the commander. The following day he wrote from Nisqually to give an account of the time since his departure from Vancouver:

> We arrived here only yesterday, due to the roads, which I found very bad and the mare which Cottenoir lent us; I do not think much of her. I thought the condition of the portage could easily rival that of the mountains; it rained continuously Friday and Saturday. . . . In the river Nisqually, one of the largest I had to cross, the horse carrying our packs lost the road, fell and everything was drenched. Nothing escaped being spoiled. As a result of this accident, I could not say Mass yesterday. A short distance from the fort I saw several savages who seemed to be satisfied with me . . . all came, one after the other, to shake hands; even the women, carrying their children in their arms, brought them to press my hands;

world, the creation, the fall of angels, of Adam, the promise of a Savior, the time of His birth, and His death upon the cross, as well as the mission of the apostles. The plan was a great success." A copy of the "Ladder" may be seen in Clarence B. Bagley, *Early Catholic Missions in Old Oregon* (Seattle, 1932), I, 119, and in *Rapport sur les Missions du Diocese de Quebec* (Quebec, 1843), 136. A description of it with an explanation of its use was published under the title, *A Key to the Catholic Ladder* (New York, 1859).

[44] Daniel Lee traveled to Oregon with his uncle, Jason Lee. In 1827 he was converted to Methodism and in 1831 was ordained deacon. In 1834 he received elder's orders and in the same year came to Willamette. In 1838 he was at The Dalles. In 1844 he travelled to New York with J. H. Frost with whom he wrote *Ten Years in Oregon*.

[45] Blanchet feared the extension of the influence of the Methodist ministers and the possible monopoly of them of the best places for missions. He wrote to Signay, " This may surprise you but if priests do not take them first, there will soon remain no suitable places for Catholic missions."

others that I saw followed us to the fort; I was obliged to moderate my pace so as not to fatigue them too much. In less than three hours there were perhaps 150 assembled from all sides to see the chief who had finally arrived.[46]

The Indians came from different tribes and Mr. Kitson feared that trouble might result from the gathering together of so many, but the ten days passed peacefully and Father Demers felt that he had accomplished real good in teaching the prayers, administering baptism to the children, explaining the dogmatic and moral truths of religion to the Indians, hearing the confessions of the Canadians. On April 29 the missionary had the happiness of receiving Mrs. Kitson into the Church. She was of great assistance in the work of instructing the natives and often acted as interpreter. The following day the priest left for Vancouver, stopping en route at Cowlitz. From there Blanchet accompanied him to the Company headquarters. Both were anxious to be at Vancouver when the brigades from the north and the south came in.

Three of these expeditions were sent out at regular intervals: one to New Caledonia, which travelled between Fort Vancouver and Fort Alexandria on the Fraser, by way of Okanogan and Fort Thompson; another to the Snake country east of the Cascades; and the third, to the Umpqua region, by way of the Columbia, south to the Sacramento River and on into the Spanish territory. These companies were perhaps the most picturesque feature of the fur business, combining according to Clark, "the excitement of the hunt, the difficulties of travel, apprehensions of danger, endurance of privation, and the fascination of novel scenes with the prosaic business being transacted."[47] And Chittenden, speaking of the trappers, the voyageurs, is of the opinion that they were "beyond comparison the most interesting and picturesque personalities in the trapping fraternity. Mild in disposition, mercurial in temper, obedient, willing and contented, ever ready to undergo the most severe hardship, and altogether a most useful and indispensable character in the business of the fur trade."[48]

[46] Demers to Blanchet, April 22, 1839. QAA.
[47] Clark, *Willamette Valley*, I, 182.
[48] Hiram F. Chittenden, *The American Fur Trade of the Far West* (New York, 1902), I, 58.

The Hudson's Bay Company recruited its voyageurs and laborers largely from the French Canadians and half-breeds, with some Orkneymen, Indians and Hawaiians.[49] The Canadians were favorites with the officers. Merk describes them as a "docile, happy, lovable, shiftless, irresponsible class, capable of great exertion while on the voyage, of rowing, paddling, and portaging sixteen hours a day for months, and then living over extended periods in thriftless idleness."[50] Clark notes that they prided themselves on their ability to row all day without a murmur, or clear a path through dripping tangles of underbrush, or spend days of loneliness, toil and deprivation as they trapped for the merest pittance in spots most isolated and exposed to danger. One who complained of hardships, hunger or even extreme misery, was treated with jovial disdain and termed a "mangeur de lard" or pork eater, as green menials were designated.[51]

Willing and ready for any hardship while on the march, the voyageur tried to forget once the brigade arrived in camp and sought compensation for the privations he had been forced to endure. He became "wholly interested in overwhelming the cares that might be oppressive by recklessly indulging every source of present joyousness." The fort was likely to become the scene of revelry and extravagance where every freak of prodigality was indulged to its fullest extent.

For the missionaries the return of the voyageurs was a time of anxiety. The men, released from the restraint of the discipline of the hunt, made up for the restrictions of the year's work by filling the two or three weeks at the post with every kind of excess. It was in an attempt to forestall some of this that Blanchet, accompanied by Demers, returned in May to Fort Vancouver.

The brigade from the north arrived on June 6. It consisted of a flotilla of nine barges manned by fifty-seven men under the com-

---

[49] There was a considerable number of Sandwich Islanders in the employ of the company. Nellie B. Pipes in "Indian Conditions in 1836-1838," *OHQ*, XXXII (1931), 332-343, edits a letter of Rev. Herbert Beaver in which he describes the situation. Beaver says the condition of these imported workers was little better than slavery and that they were often subjected to flogging and imprisonment. But Beaver found little to his liking at Fort Vancouver.

[50] Merk, *op. cit.*, xvii.   [51] Clark, *op. cit.*, I, 188.

mand of chief factors Peter Skene Ogden and Samuel Black. The two weeks of its stay at the fort were evidently unusually quiet. " The brigade of porteurs (so-called because not having horses, they carry all their goods on their back), coming from the north by the river Okanogan," wrote Father Blanchet, " was better comported than usual; they have merited praise." [52] On June 22 it left again for the north. A passage in the canoes was offered to one of the missionaries as far as Fort Walla Walla. Demers gladly availed himself of the opportunity to visit again the Indians of the upper country, who had been promised a priest.

The brigade of the south under the command of Michel La Framboise [53] reached Vancouver on June 15 laden with furs. It remained until July 13, leaving that day with horses packed with provisions and goods for the trade of the following year. Blanchet had both consolation and disappointment to record when he wrote to Demers: " I performed twelve marriages in the brigade of Michel and that of Mr. Joseph McLoughlin,[54] which made thirteen. . . . There were forty-four baptisms, thirteen marriages in the said brigade. I was content. . . ." But " several met with disaster before leaving the post: much drinking, quarrels, battles, blasphemy. I have lost a part of my harvest." [55]

Father Demers' trip up the Columbia with the brigade was not without interest. His letter written from the Dalles on June 26 told of the progress made thus far and chronicled his meeting with Mr. H. K. W. Perkins, one of the Methodist ministers, who with Daniel Lee had established a station among the Indians in 1838. Demers also saw many savages who seemed " to regard me favorably but I do not count too much on these passing demonstrations."

He wrote again on July 3 after his arrival at Walla Walla. Many of the natives were absent on the hunt but he hoped to see them on his return. Demers procured a guide at Walla Walla and expected to make the journey to Fort Colville in six days; in this, however,

[52] Blanchet to Turgeon, August 24, 1839. QAA.
[53] Michel La Framboise came to the Pacific coast in the *Tonquin* in 1811 and became an interpreter at Fort George.
[54] Joseph McLoughlin, eldest son of the chief factor. Nothing is known of his mother except that she was of Indian blood.
[55] Blanchet to Demers, August 27, 1839. QAA.

he was doomed to disappointment, for the man proved treacherous and left him. This necessitated sending back for another and resulted in the loss of fourteen days. At Fort Colville the missionary began a series of instructions and religious exercises which lasted for a month and proved advantageous for the employees of the Hudson's Bay Company, as well as for the numerous Indians who gathered around the fort. His efforts among the whites were impeded by the attitude of the officers of the Company. Chief factor McDonald, the commandant, said bluntly that "the missionaries had nothing to do with the employees of the Company." The trouble came over conditions which were laid down for the marriages of the men; conditions which made it almost impossible for them to marry and establish families. On his return, Demers stopped for an eight day mission at Okanogan and spent two weeks at Walla Walla, to the great joy of the assembled Indians and the few whites employed around the fort.

Blanchet had returned to Cowlitz on July 20 after the departure of the brigade. He found that some progress had been made in his absence. A log house had been erected on the mission land which was used as a chapel and residence for the priest until 1842. A barn had also been constructed and was ready to receive the crop of six bushels of wheat and nine of peas which had been planted in the spring. Augustine Rochon had fenced in twenty-four acres of land and ploughed fifteen others to be sown in the fall; so that, Blanchet says, the missionaries were assured of their daily bread. As soon as the harvest was over the missionary gathered together his flock and under the patronage of St. Francis Xavier [56] began a daily exposition of the truths of religion. Here for the first time was used the "Catholic Ladder."

In August Blanchet visited Fort Nisqually in order to give a mission and to further the work that Demers had begun in April. There were five families at the fort, including that of Mr. Kitson and his servants, numbering in all thirty-six souls. The men attended Mass in the morning and had other exercises in the evening. The woman and children of the fort received instruction in the morning; the Indians, who were few in the beginning but

[56] Blanchet seems to have been a great admirer of the work of the Jesuit saint.

continued to arrive in canoes every day until they numbered at least three hundred, had their turn in the afternoon. Among these latter was Chief Tsla-lakum, one of the twelve who had traveled from Whidby Island to Cowlitz in April.

The vicar general returned to Cowlitz on Saturday, September 14, where he blessed and planted a high cross.[57] He went on to Fort Vancouver four days later, where he was joined by Demers, returning from his mission to the upper Columbia. The joy of this reunion was increased by the good news that the Company had raised its prohibition against the establishment of a mission south of the Willamette. Blanchet hastened to announce the change to superiors in Quebec:

> Divine Providence has manifested itself in regard to the habitants of the Willamette. I propose to go there next week. The chief factor has made a proposition which has surprised me. He has announced that he has no further objection to seeing me established at the Willamette, and on my representation that I should like to have a paper signed by him, authorizing me to go there and charging himself with the consequence and blame of acting contrary to the conditions which the Committee and Governor of Hudson's Bay Company laid down for our passage, he answered he would do it and free me from any chance of reproach! That this permission came to him from England by the vessel which arrived last spring, or that he took it upon himself, does not matter; I do not hesitate to profit by it.[58]

But, being human, Blanchet could not refrain from speculation about the cause of the change. There had lately been some unpleasantness with the officers of the Company and the missionaries could not be blamed if they wondered at the motive behind the permission which would take them away from Vancouver. " Does he [Douglas] desire to see us leave Vancouver? Does he fear that the Canadians of Willamette will mingle too much with the Americans? Is it because of the smallness of the field at Cowlitz where live only three or four habitants that they want to offer us a place where there is a greater number who will be able to help us? Is it because they hope to keep possession of the Willamette and of the

[57] This was in accord with instructions received from Signay.
[58] Blanchet to Turgeon, October 5, 1839. QAA.

land this side of the Mexican possessions? Is it, etc. . . . No matter, I shall go." [59]

The missionaries were ready to leave on October 10. They bade adieu to their Vancouver congregation, to the ladies and gentlemen of the fort, to Governor Douglas, tendering him their warmest thanks for the generous hospitality they had received. Then, starting in different canoes, they sailed down the Columbia—Father Demers, to Cowlitz; the vicar general, to Willamette. Great was the joy of the people of the two missions.

By the end of the first year, the missionaries had laid the foundations for their work: they had visited the principal posts of the Hudson's Bay Company with the exception of those in New Caledonia; they had established missions at Cowlitz and Willamette and were not unknown to the people at Forts Vancouver, Nisqually, Walla Walla, Colville, Okanogan and George; they had met the officers of the Company, including McLoughlin who had returned from the east in October; they knew what they might expect from them and had had an opportunity to judge the methods of the fur trade monopoly; they had seen representatives of most of the Indian tribes and had formed some notion of the possibility of working among them.

Their efforts had not been free from difficulty; vexatious trials and petty persecution of one kind and another had annoyed and held them back. Hoping perhaps to have the field for themselves, they had found the Methodist ministers well-established and gaining converts even among the French Canadians. There was never any sympathy between the two groups of missionaries and frequently their rivalry was shown with much bitterness on both sides. The Protestants, some of them at least, brought from eastern backgrounds an intense distrust of "Jesuitical popery" and wished heartily to prevent its spread. The Catholic priests, seeing their flock led astray by false teaching, could leave nothing undone to bring them back. From the beginning the ministers showed their animosity and Blanchet and Demers felt the strength of their opposition.[60] In one of his earliest letters, Blanchet wrote to Bishop

[59] *Ibid.*; at Blanchet's request, Douglas gave in writing the assurance that the company had no longer any objection to the missionaries being established south of the Columbia. Cf. Blanchet, *op. cit.*, 37.

[60] Harvey K. Hines, *History of Washington* (Chicago, 1893), 83-84,

Turgeon, " The Protestant ministers have complained to Mr. Douglas, that I have re-baptized and re-married after them. . . . It is most necessary to have prudence and to speak without making allusion to these gentlemen in treating with the savages. . . . These gentlemen said to some one that they feared the arrival of the Catholic priests in the country." [61]

Already the country was infected with evil literature, which it was necessary to replace. Copies of *Maria Monk* [62] had been circulated in the forts and Blanchet complained that his light-of-mind Canadians read and believed the tale. He began a counter-campaign by distributing Catholic literature but his supply was limited. He appealed for more to Bishop Signay, " It is remarkable the great number of bad books that we find among the families—the truncated Bible is the first. I wish I could replace these books by others in English and French. We need above all many catechisms . . . the children who can read English will soon learn to read French; but we lack the books. I have given little catechisms along the route

attempts to explain this antagonism, " Of course the original basis of the controversy was theological, churchy,—Romanism vs. Protestantism,—which is true and which is false? This we do not debate, but it was the core of the trouble. Out of the convictions of either party and both parties on this subject came their intense zeal and bitterness against each other.

The Protestant mission and missionaries on the whole took too much counsel of their prejudices and desires. They did not sufficiently consider that the Romish priests had the same rights in the country, either religiously or politically, as they had. Their being first gave them no preemptive right to control the religion of the people. To a very great degree they forgot or ignored this very obvious and fundamental principle of human freedom: consequently they met the priests with protests against their presence and probably a somewhat acrimonious denunciation of their teachings if not of themselves. . . . On the other hand, the priests made it a special purpose to break down and destroy the Protestant missions. Instead of opening new fields to any considerable extent, they established their missions almost by the very doors of the Protestant missions. They declared it to be their purpose to antagonize and destroy them." The statement is true though it should be borne in mind that the priests came to and established themselves at Willamette at the invitation of the majority of the settlers there.

[61] Blanchet to Turgeon, March 13, 1839. QAA.

[62] Ray A. Billington, *The Protestant Crusade, 1800-1860* (New York, 1938), 99-108, discusses the influence of this publication.

but we have no more. I have none to give to those who ask for them." [63]

In contrast to the ill-will of the American ministers and the spread of anti-Catholic literature there was trouble from an excess of zeal from none other than the wife of the chief factor, Mme. McLoughlin.[64] This lady had done much for the missionaries and Blanchet mentioned her more than once in his letters, " Mme. McLoughlin and several other ladies give us consolation: the faith of this lady, the first at the fort, is great; her example is strong and powerful; " [65] and again, " Mme. McLoughlin is a very fervent Catholic, never misses a prayer, an office." But, " in an excess of zeal, she has turned from her home, her daughter, Mme. Rae. That has caused a stir. Mr. Rae thought the inspiration came from me; things have been patched up. But the daughter does not come to our services; her husband has forbidden it without doubt." [66] Returning to the subject again, Blanchet continued, " We do not argue; nothing has been done secretly. . . . But the situation of Mme. McLoughlin with regard to her daughter is painful."

On the whole Blanchet seemed well satisfied with the results of the first year, " Since the departure of the express in the month of March last, the missionaries have well advanced their work. They have left Vancouver for the mission of the Willamette. Things are about to begin. Since that time, they have begun to build the little house at Cowlitz; Father Demers went in April to Fort Nisqually after having visited Cowlitz. From there, we went to Willamette— I for a second and Father Demers for the first time. There has been more than one tribulation . . . but soon the God of mercies will deliver us." [67] The first letters contain a record of consistent hard work. But although Blanchet never suggested that the life was easy, he was usually hopeful in the early years, and sincerely believed that the Columbia would eventually become a great Catholic country.

[63] Blanchet to Signay, March 1, 1839. QAA.
[64] In 1811 or 1812 McLoughlin, married Margaret McKay, the widow of Alexander McKay. She was of Indian blood and proved a loyal and devoted companion until McLoughlin's death in 1857.
[65] Blanchet to Signay, March 1, 1839. QAA.
[66] Blanchet to Turgeon, March 13, 1839. QAA.
[67] Blanchet to Turgeon, August 24, 1839. QAA.

CHAPTER III

PIONEER PRIESTS AND MISSIONARIES

During the twelve months after their arrival in Oregon, Blanchet and his companion, Demers, learned much concerning the Columbia basin. Traveling in the Hudson's Bay Company's canoes, they explored the country and discovered the extent of their mission, while their contacts with white and Indian brought a knowledge and realization of the number and needs of those for whom they had come to labor. Their conclusion at the close of this year of initiation was a logical one. If the western land, where possibilities for good were so great, was to become the great Catholic center that it should, it was essential that they have help. It was impossible for two men to attend to everything, to visit and instruct all who appealed for counsel. In order that the mission prosper, a priest should be stationed permanently at each important point so as to direct the work; an annual visitation would not suffice. The faith was strange, not only to the Indians, but to the Canadians as well, since these had been five, ten or even twenty years away from all contact with it. Both groups needed daily guidance.

As has been seen, the priests in October, 1839 had established two permanent stations: one at Willamette, where Father Blanchet had his headquarters; the other at Cowlitz, which was the home of Father Demers. From these as centers, the missionaries extended their work north and south, east and west. But from the beginning the demands were greater than they could possibly meet and the first report (March, 1839), that Blanchet sent to his superior, the bishop of Quebec, had called attention to the needs of the new mission. A year later the spring express carried a letter to Bishop Pierre Turgeon, coadjutor to Bishop Signay, which detailed their plans for the summer months and closed with a further appeal: "We shall continue to sow, to work. Father Demers will go to Colville next summer. As for me, I shall remain in the lower country, visiting Vancouver, Willamette, Cowlitz, Nisqually, the fort on the lower Fraser River. We shall do all we can while awaiting help."[1]

The problem of sending assistance to the Oregon missions evidently caused a good deal of concern to the bishop of Quebec and there is evidence that he made numerous attempts to secure it. But deep as may have been his interest in and his sympathy for his far-away priests, the obstacles which prevented him from relieving their needs, for several years proved insurmountable. In the spring of 1840 he wrote to Blanchet to explain the situation:

> I am deeply sorry that it is not possible to secure co-workers to help you to gather your harvest. You will see from the enclosed copy of a letter that I received from Governor Simpson that the Honourable Company of Hudson Bay is not disposed to favor the extension of the Catholic missions on the Columbia before being better informed as to the progress which you have made there. I do not know whether we should regard this response as a kind of defiance on the part of the Company to the extension of the Catholic religion in this part of its possessions. But, always, we must await its good pleasure before sending you help. While I awaited the answer of Simpson, a young priest was preparing to go to join you. This refusal has paralyzed his good will; he must wait another year in order to put it into effect. We must not think for the present of French priests against whom the Company seems to have some prejudice. Perhaps it will be dispelled with time. Meanwhile, you will be crushed with your burden. However, you know that I have few priests at my disposal; that among these, there are not many who have the vocation to consecrate themselves to the missions, and that of this small number, there are some who must be eliminated on account of lack of talents and capacities needed for a work of such importance as yours. All together, I can think of but one subject in your favor. God willing, next year I shall find some one who will join you.[2]

Blanchet had asked, not only for priests, but for men and women trained to teach, to take charge of the schools he would have liked to establish. Signay's reply to this was:

> The same reason which prevents me from sending you co-laborers, prevents me also from sending school-masters and

---

[1] Blanchet to Turgeon, March 19, 1840. QAA.
[2] Signay to Blanchet, April 13, 1840. QAA.

mistresses, even if it were possible to find those who would be willing to undertake such a long journey. It is difficult enough to select priests who are ready to sacrifice their love of parents and their country to follow your example; it is still harder to get lay persons. In order to secure priests and school teachers, it would be necessary to suggest the project to the Company. Perhaps the good Dr. McLoughlin who did so much for religion on the Columbia before your arrival, would add his influence to yours in order to secure help. I know well that unless such a thing be recommended by those who are at the head of the establishment of the Company in the country that there would be no way to advance it. Speak to the excellent gentleman.[3]

In the same letter the prudent superior cautioned the missionaries against extending their activities too much. It seemed the common sense attitude to take, but the postponement of the fulfilment of their plans for so long a time must have been a blow to the zealous priests. Signay wrote:

Since you will be alone with Father Demers to bear the heat of the day for at least another year and a half, it would perhaps be better for you to limit yourselves to the good you have already begun. Too much expansion will dissipate your forces.

[3] *Ibid.*; McLoughlin's interest and assistance were a mainstay to the missionaries. The chief factor had definite ideas and plans for the spread of Catholicism in the Oregon country. Cf. Hiram M. Chittenden and Alfred T. Richardson, *Life, Letters and Travels of Father Pierre-Jean De Smet, S.J., 1801-1873* (New York, 1905), IV, 1553-1558, for his letters to De Smet. On September 27, 1841, he wrote: "... I can only observe that after mature consideration for these several years I am fully convinced that the most effectual mode to diffuse the doctrines of the Roman Catholic Church in this part of the work is by establishing it on a good foundation in the Willamette and Cowlitz among the settlers—as the Indians will form themselves on what they see done by the whites the Reverend Messrs. Blanchette and Demers have done and are doing an incalculable amount of good among the whites and Indians, but they are too few indeed there is more than sufficient employment for you all in this quarter . . . if one of you with one or two of the lay brothers could come to assist Messrs. Blanchette and Demers till their reinforcement come from Canada it would be an immense benefit to religion and the only apology I can give for thus obtruding my opinion is that from my long residence in the country I have a right to claim some knowledge of it. . . . " On October 14, 1844, McLoughlin wrote to point out advantageous situations for missions in the country between Oregon and California.

Perhaps it would be well for you to care only for the Canadians of Vancouver, Willamette and Cowlitz, and for the savages who live around these posts.[4]

However, in spite of these early discouragements, the Canadian bishop continued his efforts, as is evident from the correspondence on the subject of missionary work in the far west which passed between him and the governor of the Hudson's Bay Company. So strongly intrenched was the powerful monopoly and so complete its control over every type of activity, that there seemed at the time no other way of handling the matter except through the officers of the company. At least no other occurred to the bishop of Quebec. The situation was unsatisfactory at best. The Hudson's Bay Company was not a missionary society; and while many of its employees were Catholic, those in control of its policy were with few exceptions Protestant. It could hardly be expected that they should consider the advancement of Catholicism of primary importance. The great interest of George Simpson, since 1824 governor of the Company in North America, was the advancement of a profitable fur trade. He did little to encourage his subordinates to make any attempt to train the natives to other than the roving life of the hunter. The missionary was not always favorable to this policy and sometimes merited the hostility of the Company officers by interference in matters which the latter judged not to come under his jurisdiction.[5] However, at the time of his famous journey of 1824-1825 [6] Simpson seems to have considered the possibilities of missionary work in the Columbia country and is said to have suggested suitable sites for prospective mission centers. He even estimated the probable cost of maintaining such establishments.[7] Douglas McKay notes that the Hudson's Bay Company, under the direction of Simpson, contributed an annual stipend to the Red River mission and that similar amounts went to the support of religious work on

[4] Signay to Blanchet, April 134, 1840. QAA.

[5] George Bryce, *The Remarkable History of the Hudson's Bay Company* (London, 1910), 428; Demers to Blanchet, July 31, 1839. QAA., describes some of his difficulties in reaching a satisfactory arrangement with company authorities in regard to the marriages of the servants.

[6] For an interesting account of this voyage see Merk, *op. cit.*

[7] Robert C. Johnson, *John McLoughlin* (Portland, 1935), 105.

the Columbia.⁸ The missionaries often spoke of their indebtedness to the company; surely the free passage on the company ships and canoes was of the greatest importance to them, for they could hardly have carried on their work without such assistance.

When Bishop Signay made arrangements for the first Oregon missionaries, Simpson had been friendly and had graciously acceded to the request for places in the canoes for Blanchet and Demers, but for some reason ⁹ not too clear, his attitude changed and when new

⁸ MacKay, *op. cit.*, 266; MacKay makes clear the change in attitude of Simpson. In 1822 he thought little of the mission school plan for the education of Indian children; it was his opinion that an educated Indian meant an indolent fellow and the only benefit to follow the establishment of schools would be in " filling the pockets and bellies of some hungry missionaries and schoolmasters." He made it clear that while the missionary might be a worthy, well-meaning man, he should keep his fingers out of the company's trade affairs and not expect to be transported freely about the country in the company canoes which should be loaded to capacity with trade goods or furs. By 1832 Simpson had become an active supporter of native schools and was a contributor to the missions. Merk, *op. cit.*, xvi, says that about 1824 partly for commercial reasons and partly for altruistic, the founding of missions among the Columbia River Indians was recommended to the London office. Snowden, *op. cit.*, II, 165, quotes a letter from McLoughlin to Blanchet," I am instructed to place £100 sterling to the credit of your mission as an acknowledgement of the eminent services you and your pious colleagues are rendering the people of this country." Adrien G. Morice, O.M.I., *The History of the Northern Interior of British Columbia, 1660-1880* (London, 1906), 227, tells of a collection made among the Hudson's Bay Company employees. Peter S. Ogden on November 15, 1841 issued the following circular for the benefit of the missions of New Caledonia: " Messrs. Blanchet and Demers, the Catholic missionaries on the Columbia, requested me, prior to taking my departure from Vancouver last summer, to ask the inland servants of the district to contribute towards their mission, and I have to request that you will make application accordingly." There follows a list of the contributors with the amounts promised or subscribed. But in spite of the continued benefactions the missions were not, as has been assumed by some writers, a company affair. Assistance, while authorized from London, came rather as a result of the interest of individuals and the promotion and spread of Catholicism were never a company objective.

⁹ It would seem that the Rev. Mr. Beaver on his return to London represented conditions at Fort Vancouver as being in a deplorable state; the letter of Blanchet to Signay, November 27, 1841. QAA., gives this impression.

appeals were made in 1839, the governor refused to consider the matter. In spite of that Signay, in January 1840 sent another appeal to the Hudson's Bay official:

> Since I had the pleasure of seeing you, I have come to feel more and more that I am incapable of caring for the needs of that new mission on the Columbia, which, according to the report of Rev. Mr. Blanchet, needs the presence of six priests, not counting the two who are already there, and that I can do nothing but appeal to the zeal of the French clergy who are more numerous than are the clergy of my diocese. I do not forget the repugnance of the Company toward the admission into its territory of other than Canadian missionaries in the fear that they may cause it some trouble. But I do not hesitate to assure you that if it consents to allow French priests to come to the territory of the Columbia, that it will not find less to praise in them than in the Canadian priests who exercise their ministry in its other possessions of North America. I will be freed from a great distress, if I learn that the Gentlemen of the Committee at London have been moved to answer favorably to the request that has been made to them on this subject. In case the response of the Gentlemen is not favorable, I shall count at least on their willingness to grant a passage in one of the canoes which will leave next spring for the interior, to a young Canadian priest who desires to consecrate himself to the services of the missions on the Columbia and who is the only one I can send at the moment.[10]

This letter was forwarded to London for the consideration of the governor and general committee. We know the answer already from Bishop Signay's letter to Blanchet; it was an uncompromising refusal. Governor Simpson forwarded the decision to the bishop:

> I have read your Lordship's letter before the Governor and Committee, and.... I am instructed to say that the Governor and the Committee do not feel disposed to facilitate the extension of the Roman Catholic missions on the river Columbia until they receive further information in reference to the progress that has been made by the Revd. Mr. Blanchet and his colleague in that quarter.[11]

Signay's letter, bringing news of this rebuff, evidently reached Blanchet with the fall brigade. He answered in November:

[10] Signay to Simpson, January 7, 1840. QAA.
[11] Simpson to Signay, February 17, 1840. QAA.

What an afflicting and desolating refusal on the part of the Hudson's Bay Company! It is sad to have it said by Protestant layman, that they must know the progress of the mission of Mr. B. before they can accord passage to new missionaries! I fear it will happen that the Methodists and Presbyterians will attract the savages, contrary to the interests of the Honourable Company. If the Honourable Company only knew the efforts and misdeeds of some of our fellow citizens, the passage would soon be given. But perhaps the missions constrain them, or perhaps, they are jealous of our progress. That is something that must be considered.[12]

Bishop Signay tried again to secure favorable action during the year of 1840, but the reply of Simpson was far from friendly:

The Governor and Committee are not at all satisfied that the measures which have recently been adopted under your Lordship's direction for the purpose of advancing religious instrution on the west side of the mountains, have been attended with the benefits so earnestly desired. . . . Until they receive my report on the state of the missions after my arrival in the Columbia next year, I am instructed to say that the Governor and Committee are unwilling to comply with your Lordship's request in reference to a passage for a missionary thither by the spring canoes.[13]

Blanchet could not yet have heard of this refusal, when he wrote in March to Bishop Turgeon, but he had already reached the conclusion that it was time for the missionaries to become independent and to seek some other means of obtaining the necessary men and supplies for their work. To him, the dependence was such an obvious handicap, that he could see no valid reason for not throwing it to one side. Probably before this time (March, 1841) he had heard of the coming of Father De Smet to the western country [14] and that, together with the arrival of the Americans who were beginning to come into the Oregon territory,[15] led him to believe that priests might follow along the same route. The apparent ease

[12] Blanchet to Signay, November 9, 1840. QAA.
[13] Simpson to Signay, December 20, 1840. QAA.
[14] De Smet came from St. Louis in 1840.
[15] The numbers until 1842 were small but American settlers were constantly coming. The "great immigration" of 1843 was the first to bring any considerable number.

with which others found their way across the mountains, undoubtedly contributed to his dissatisfaction and prompted these questions: " Must we always wait until a society of Protestants holds out its hands to offer us passage on its vessels? Is it not time to disembarrass ourselves of this dependence? Our Governor [16] said: and why do not the priests come by way of St. Louis? the thing is so easy." [17]

Shortly after this, Governor Simpson appears to have reconsidered, or at least to have decided that there might have been some unfairness in the attitude of the company toward the Catholic missionaries. Before beginning his long voyage of 1841-1842,[18] he sent this message to Bishop Signay:

> I am now entering upon a very extended tour, in the course of which I hope to see the Gentlemen in charge of the Roman Catholic missions, both at Red River Settlement and the Columbia River, and your Lordship may rest assured that my report to the Governor and Committee, in reference to those missions, will be strictly impartial.[19]

Signay was undoubtedly discouraged though he probably had not yet received the letter from Simpson when he wrote to tell his vicar general of his proposed appeal to the Holy See that the Oregon missions be placed under the jurisdiction of another bishop:

> I have planned to ask the Holy See that the territory of the Columbia be placed under the care either of the bishop of St.

---

[16] McLoughlin.

[17] Blanchet to Turgeon, March 18, 1841. QAA. In a letter, Blanchet to Signay, March 1, 1839. QAA., the writer calls attention to different ways of reaching Oregon: " There are three ways of coming to this country: that by which we came; that by way of England in the vessels of the Hudson's Bay Company; the third, that from St. Louis with the groups of Americans. To this last there might be objections since some of the Americans are little favorable to the coming of Catholic priests to oppose their compatriots, etc.; . . . The voyage by ship is wearisome and the bar of the Columbia is dangerous for the ships. The route through the interior also has its dangers and sufferings: . . . There is a fourth way to come to this country: that by way of Boston or New York in American vessels which stop at the Sandwich Islands. We are told the ships leave about the month of December."

[18] Simpson's travels took him around the world.

[19] Simpson to Signay, April 15, 1841. QAA.

> Louis who is nearer, or the bishop of Nicopolis (Msgr. Rouchouse) who is still better placed, at least in so far that the Association of Lyons will be interested then in sending priests and will procure the help which will be necessary for them.[20]

However, he did not give up all hope. Although he had not heard from Simpson, Signay evidently knew of his plan to visit the west, for the same day on which he wrote to Blanchet, he wrote also to John McLoughlin:

> I must express to you my gratitude for the services you have rendered to religion on the Columbia, both before and since the coming of our missionaries, and for the favor and protection which these gentlemen have received from you since your return from your voyage in Europe and Canada. I pray God to recompense you in this world and in the other for your constant goodness.
> Sir [21] George Simpson is going to visit the establishments of the Company on the Columbia and on the way to examine whether it be well to encourage the increase of the number of missionaries. I urged Mr. Blanchet to see this gentleman and plead the cause of the work to which he is devoted. I do not doubt that your influence will serve much to corroborate the pleading of Mr. B. and to dissipate certain prejudices which I fear prevent the Company from showing favor to our Catholic missions, not only in the Columbia but in other places where they have been begun. I dare, then, to ask you to add to all the titles which you already have to our gratitude, that of seconding my good vicar general in the request which he will make to Sir George to obtain the continued protection of the Company over the missions on the Columbia. If success does not come to our hopes, we shall be forced with the help of Divine Providence in order to secure all the extension of which it is capable, to have recourse to the charity of the church in France, whose zeal has done so much for the good of missions.[22]

In November, 1841, perhaps at the suggestion of McLoughlin, Blanchet addressed a long memorandum to Governor Simpson, in which he tried to explain the position of the priests and to answer

[20] Signay to Blanchet, April 17, 1841. QAA.

[21] Simpson was knighted by Queen Victoria in 1841, probably on account of his support of the crown during the Papineau Rebellion (1837) and his assistance to a series of Arctic expeditions.

[22] Signay to McLoughlin, April 17, 1841. QAA.

any charges that might have been made against them. That was a difficult task, since he does not seem to have known exactly where the trouble lay; nor what objection the officers of the company had against them; nor where they had failed to live up to the demands that the company made of missionaries. But he described the situation as it appeared to him: with regard to the employees, the savages, the Catholic priests, the Protestant ministers and the company itself. Finally he appealed to Sir George's sense of justice and referred him to the chief factors, John McLoughlin and James Douglas, should he care to check his estimate of affairs:

> It will not be difficult, Sir George, to show under the headings which I shall mention that the Rev. Mr. Demers and I have been successful, thanks to God, in our evangelical ministry in this country; that the work there is greater than we can attend to and that the matter of an increase in the number of priests here is not a useless question.
>
> 1. The servants of the Company. The great majority of the workers are and have always been Canadian and Catholic. They have done and continue to do the most difficult and fatiguing work with a capacity without equal perhaps, even in the experience of their employees. Exposed to the heat of the day, to the rain, to cold and to the rigor of all the seasons of the year, they spend the best years of their lives in the service; they use them and lose them sometimes in that state. Many have grown old in this humble condition and become more or less the charge of the families. One finds among them the old and infirm, widows, orphans of both sexes in danger of falling again into a state of barbarism. They are scattered over a vast territory. There are sixty on the Willamette and six at Cowlitz who, having obtained a discharge from the service, have settled in these places with their families along with others who have come from Red River or who are in active service.
>
> These old and new servants know the duties they have to fulfil toward God, toward men, toward their equals, toward themselves. Their wishes are expressed in their requests of July 3, 1834, of February 23, 1835, and of March 14, 1838. In writing to their bishops at such great distance, they have been influenced by the desire of their hearts. As for those who have acknowledged signing a request, asking that they might keep the Rev. Mr. Beaver for their minister, they acknowledge also that they were fooled and let themselves be deceived.

Whatever helps of religion may be secured to these workers, both old and new, in the person of their priests, will serve to attach them, to make them more faithful and to alleviate their painful condition. To refuse them this consolation and deprive them of it is a policy which, sooner or later, will not fail to have disastrous results. Would it be just and proper for the Honourable Company to refuse its workers that which must be advantageous to itself and will procure for its people the consolations and joys of life? This act of justice was understood, I think, when two priests obtained a passage for the Columbia in 1838. Their arrival in this country was greeted with tears of joy. They were sought after from all sides. They had to overcome obstacles of routes, the distance, the difficulty and diversity of languages, to fulfil all the duties of their ministry. In spite of all, they instructed, baptized, blessed marriages. Now, prayers are recited, the catechism is learned, the holy law of God has taken its empire, the moral code is put into force, decency reigns, vice is diminished. This, Sir George, is the good which the two priests have begun to accomplish on the Columbia among the old and new servants of the Honourable Company and among their wives and children.

2. The savages. It seems to me that here also we have made some progress. The natives have had a part of our time; we know that the Savior's time of mercy has come for these poor infidels, in whom lies the desire to know, praise and serve the Master of life. The conflict of opinions, it is true, has led them to live indifferently for some time, but the moment has come when the impartial observer can easily see that the savages have finally decided to range themselves on our side. We have visited them from Colville to Fort George; from the valley of the Willamette even to the river Fraser. Everywhere we have found the same; everywhere Catholic principles have taken root, in spite of the few temporal advantages that we have been able to offer and despite the promises and numerous favors our opponents offer them. The savages of the Willamette Falls and the Clackamas held out to us their arms and refused to listen to their old masters. These last and those of the Cascades on the Columbia recite our prayers in their language, sing our hymns and know in great part our holy religion. To these I can add those of Colville, Okanogan, Cowlitz, Nisqually and Puget Sound who follow our teachings and sing our hymns in proportion to the time we have been able to give them. . . . This, Sir George, is what we have begun to

do among the savages and in the vast field which remains to us to cultivate.

3. The Catholic missionaries. Under this heading, the question of priests does not seem to me indifferent. Instead of being detrimental to the Honourable Company, their contact with the workers could be useful and advantageous, based as it is on gratitude and religion. What fruits could we not produce in hearts by motives as powerful as these? Those who gave to James Douglas, Esq., notice of a request addressed to a strange government and which contained things contrary to the character and interest of the Company and its workers are well known. It is also known who retarded and prevented the project of establishing among the colonists a local government. It is evident, besides, that the Catholic missionaries, in drawing the savages to them, show in the interest of the Company a greater interest than those individuals, whose politics and views are entirely different. There, Sir George, is one way of considering the question of the priests.

4. The American Protestant ministers. I do not want to expose myself to the charge of prejudice in treating the question of the utility of the ministers over that of the priests in this country. I refer you to the officers of the Honourable Company. Their progress has been confined to their establishments at Willamette, Fort George, Nisqually, Grand Dalles, Walla Walla and the country about the Columbia. It is for these gentlemen to declare where are their proselytes among the savages outside their missions; what has become of Campeau, Gendron, their followers the the savages of the Willamette Falls and of the village of Clackamas. Who drew up and signed the request of 1840 addressed to the American congress; by whom was begun and carried through the project of establishing at Willamette a local government; and by whom, was it decided on which side to throw the balance.

5. The Honourable Company. I say frankly, that if there are no servants without masters, neither are there masters without servants, without reciprocal obligations. The Holy Spirit, who has said: *Servants, be obedient to them that are your lords,* has by the same word, impressed on masters their obligations toward their servants. "*And he,*" says St. Paul, "*who cares not for his own, and especially for his servants, he has lost the faith and is worse than an infidel.*" There is no doubt but that the obligation of masters towards their

servants extends to the care of body and of soul and it follows that this latter should be much more the object of the solicitude of the masters, something that they value infinitely more than the body, since it is created to the image of God and bought at the price of the blood of His Son. Then, making allowance for liberty of conscience, masters ought to procure for their servants the means of attaining their salvation. The Hudson's Bay Company was moved without doubt by the force of this religious conviction when in 1838 it so generously accorded a free passage to two priests: it seems that this number is not proportioned to the need of the country; should it refuse to accord new help? There, Sir George, is my way of seeing the question of the priests on the Columbia.

I have proved that the Rev. Mr. Demers and I have made progress among the servants and the savages of the country; the reports made against us then are false. It is evident that two priests do not suffice for the needs of their flock: I am then right in begging their lordships, the bishops, to ask for new passages; my demands and theirs are founded on justice. I have worked in the interest of and for the glory of the Honourable Company; I have served better than those who have worked to [. . .] the source of these precious and glorious advantages.

When I consider, on one side, what remains to be done in order to continue, increase and finish the good which has been begun in the Columbia: our savages to visit, to instruct and civilize; the benefits of instruction and of industry to spread among the Canadian families; the schools and industrial plants to be built; the old, the infirm, the widows and orphans to be cared for; and on the other, when I reflect on these words, drawn from your correspondence, Sir George: "Many reports have reached them (the Governor and Committee of the Honourable Company at London) in regard to the causes that have operated against their (the two priests') success," I am led to believe that the authors of these reports have not had in view the lack of priests, the few facilities and means, which have operated against our success. But, it is not by closing but by opening the favors of the Honourable Company, which will remedy the evil and cause to disappear those things which form the object of their complaints.

In a word, our cause is that of the Honourable Company; it is that of the zealous, faithful and courageous servants; that of their wives, of their children, of their widows and

of their orphans, that of its officers and clerks, of their
ladies and of their Catholic families; that finally, of the
savages who remain attached to them. All of these persons
have opened to us their arms, we have hastened to their
assistance and we turn our regard toward the great and
Honourable Company of the Hudson Bay.[23]

The above memorandum must have been presented to Governor
Simpson during his stay in the Oregon country, and have received
a favorable reaction from him, for, writing a few days later to
Bishop Signay, Blanchet said:

From this time on priests will not be lacking on the Columbia.
I have made application to Sir George to obtain passage for four
farmers, four servants, four workers, four priests, four school
teachers, four teachers for an industrial school and four religious.
He has granted that for ten persons: two farmers,
two servants, two workers, two priests and two women for the
industrial school who are to come in the canoes in the spring
of 1843. Thus, my Lord, please give it your consideration.
We should have old priests among the young. The pastor of
The Cedars is one I take the liberty to recommend strongly.[24]

Blanchet had gained his point and the helpers for whom Simpson
promised to provide passage arrived in due time. The fur company
official was undoubtedly convinced that the work of the priests was

[23] Blanchet to Simpson, November 15, 1841. QAA.
[24] Blanchet to Signay, November 27, 1841. QAA. The pastor of The
Cedars was Blanchet's brother, Augustine, later bishop of Walla Walla. A
letter in QAA., from Augustine Blanchet to Cazeau, January 11, 1841 indicates
his interest in the Columbia and also his conviction that missionaries
should be sent independently of the company. Three letters of 1842 show
that the company continued its good offices. Keith to Signay, August 11,
1842. QAA., says that he has instructions from London to further the
passage of additional helpers in the spring of 1843. Signay to Blanchet,
November 14, 1842. Portland Archdiocesan Archives, henceforth PAA.,
writes that Keith has communicated to him the decision from London which
must be a result of the representations of Simpson. The bishop is faced
with the difficulty of finding priests and religious. "The Ursulines will
not do because they are cloistered and in your country where Methodist
fanaticism will seize upon anything Catholic, we must sent only those whose
actions will be open to the eyes of men . . . I shall make some efforts
here, in France and in the United States but I do not expect much success
for the demands are great." Provencher to Blanchet, June 20, 1842. PAA.,
writes of the satisfaction of Simpson in the missionaries' endeavors.

worthwhile although the possibility that missionaries might come from other sources than Canada may have had more weight with him than had the needs of the Indians or even the employees of the company. As Blanchet remarked, " Dr. McLoughlin did not hide from him that priests could come from St. Louis. He knows that obstacles to the increase of the number of Canadian priests in the country will result in the mission falling into the hands of the bishop of St. Louis or of eastern Oceania; that would not please him." [25]

No priests came with this group. Signay had hoped to be able to send Father Augustine Blanchet, the brother of the Oregon missionary, but the bishop of Montreal refused to grant him leave. He offered another priest in his stead but the latter finally decided that the requirements were too great for him and withdrew his offer. The bishop of Quebec was thus thrown on the resources of his own diocese which " consisted of young ecclesiastics, ready, it is true, to finish at the seminary, but lacking that experience and tried virtue which the missionary, often alone in difficult and embarrassing circumstances should have." [26] And so he decided not to send priests " unless they had the requisite qualities for missionaries." Perhaps in another year there would be someone.

In 1842, however, two Canadian priests had arrived at the Oregon mission. The first recruits started after all independently of the Hudson's Bay Company. Bishop Signay selected two young men, Anthony Langlois [27] and John Baptist Zachary Bolduc [28] and made arrangements for their passage on the ship, *Douglas*, sailing from Boston in September, 1841. Both were later to return to Canada but they share with Blanchet and Demers the honor of being among the first missionaries to work in the Pacific northwest. A complete year passed before they arrived at Vancouver. The Boston vessel carried them around Cape Horn and north to the Sandwich Islands, where they disembarked to wait for a ship that would take

[25] Blanchet to Signay, November 27, 1841. QAA.
[26] Signay to Blanchet, April 19, 1843. QAA.
[27] Langlois, born 1812, ordained at Quebec in 1838; 1841 sent as missionary to the Columbia where he remained until 1854, when he went to California; in 1859 he returned to Canada.
[28] Bolduc, born 1818, ordained in 1841; traveled with Langlois to Oregon where he remained until 1850, returning then to Canada.

them to the Columbia. Father Bolduc has left us a graphic and detailed account of the voyage. In his *Journal* he described the anxiety with which he and Father Langlois awaited the coming of a vessel (they were forced to spend several months in Honolulu) and the joy, with which they greeted the *Cowlitz* when she finally put into port:

> In the afternoon of July 28 [1842] a sail was seen some distance from Honolulu; but as the wind would not permit the vessel to enter, she spent the time running from north to south and vice versa, until the next day. However, a small boat came to land and about eight o'clock in the evening a servant of Mr. Pelly, the agent of the Company of Hudson's Bay, brought to Father Maigret, prefect apostolic of the Sandwich Islands, a letter from Father Blanchet. I could scarcely keep from shouting for joy. Father Langlois, several days before, had wished to embark on a ship which took sail for California, hoping that from there he could reach the Columbia. I had need of all my powers of eloquence to prevent this hazardous enterprise; and in spite of all, he would not have remained had not the prefect apostolic added his counsel to mine. The dear confrere! He was happy. The letter from Father Blanchet told us that we had been anxiously awaited for several months.[29]

The *Cowlitz* carried the missionaries to Vancouver where on September 15 McLoughlin received them with his customary kindness. They learned at the fort that Blanchet was at St. Paul and that Demers had not yet returned from New Caledonia.[30] The next morning after Mass they proceeded on their way by canoe. And toward the end of the day (September 17, 1842) they reached the mission. Bolduc commented on the rejoicing that followed their arrival, particularly that of the vicar general, " I cannot tell you the surprise and joy of Father Blanchet; he could not have shown more!" Blanchet expressed his satisfaction at the arrival of the priests in a letter to Signay and told him of the immediate plans for their work—plans of consolidation rather than of extension:

> The good missionaries, Fathers Langlois and Bolduc, announced and awaited so long, finally arrived at St. Paul of the

[29] Journal of Bolduc in *Rapport sur les Missions du Diocese de Québec* (Quebec, 1845), 4.
[30] Demers went to New Caledonia in 1842. *Infra*, 122.

Willamette at a moment when I did not expect them; they have given me your letter of last year. What can I say about the first interview, so filled with emotions of joy, of hope, of rejoicing, of complete happiness! The *Te Deum* sung that day at the foot of the altar and that of the following day at the solemn Mass, chanted with deacon and subdeacon [31] were but a feeble expression of the gratitude of our hearts. The news of their arrival had spread the evening before and the chapel was filled; Father Langlois preached with his sweet persuasive manner. Ready to work the next day, the two missionaries have for several days been trying to learn the Chinook jargon. Their progress has been rapid. Father Langlois, in his zeal and thirst for the salvation of souls, wished to fly toward the mountains to the aid of the poor pagans, there to choose at once a beautiful site surrounded by numerous peoples, far from the places where reign physical and moral contagion. I praised his zeal, I wish I might further it; but since Father Demers is absent, he is spending the winter in Caledonia, I am alone to minister to the wants of Willamette, Vancouver, the catechumens and neophytes from the river Columbia, from the Falls, from Clackamas, etc.; whereupon, having returned to Vancouver, the question was decided thus: *the conversion and reform of the whites first, that of the savages will follow naturally.*[32]

In this same year (1842) Blanchet and Demers met for the first time that indefatigable worker, Peter John De Smet.[33] The Jesuit had been in the Oregon country since 1840, but his activity had thus far been confined to the Indian tribes of the eastern section. He was the first of that zealous band who worked long and successfully among the savages of the west. Hoping to be able to satisfy the appeals for missionaries, which came from the Flathead Indians,

---

[31] Bolduc adds this comment: " The next day being Sunday, a high Mass was sung by the Vicar General and his two new co-workers assisted him as deacon and sub-deacon. The faithful of Willamette opened their eyes wide at this spectacle. " Three priests to say Mass! never before had they seen such a thing," *Rapport* (1845), 6-7.

[32] Blanchet to Signay, October 28, 1842. QAA.

[33] De Smet is the best known of the missionaries of the Northwest. Through his writings, travels and appeals for help he was an important factor in the establishment and development of the Oregon missions. The most extensive account of his life and work is found in Chittenden and Richardson, *op. cit.* Cf. also, Garraghan, *op. cit.*, II and III.

Bishop Joseph Rosati of St. Louis had written in 1839 to the Jesuit General in Rome, asking for priests.[34] The matter was referred to the provincial of the Missouri Province, Peter Verhaegen, who commissioned De Smet to visit the western country and to decide on the possibilities of establishing missions among the native tribes. De Smet returned to St. Louis in 1841 and submitted a report to Bishop Rosati and Father Verhaegen in which he strongly urged that work among the Flatheads begin at once. Accordingly plans were made to send priests to the western field.[35]

In April, 1841, De Smet with Fathers Gregory Mengarini and Nicholas Point, and Brothers Charles Huet, William Claessens and Joseph Specht were westward bound. On August 14 they reached Fort Hall where they were welcomed by Francis Ermatinger, the commandant for the Hudson's Bay Company, and where they met the representatives of the Flatheads who had come 800 miles to welcome them. On September 4, 1841, they reached their journey's end on the Bitter Root River. It was here they set up St. Mary's mission among the Flatheads. A short month after his arrival at St. Mary's, De Smet left his companions to continue the work there, while he journeyed to Fort Colville on the Columbia to secure supplies for the mission. In the spring of 1842 provisions again ran short. Unable this time to obtain them from Fort Colville, Father De Smet traveled on to Fort Vancouver, where he arrived on June 8 and where to his great joy, he found Fathers Blanchet and Demers.[36] "A scene here ensued so affecting and so edifying," writes Archbishop Seghers, "that it drew tears from the eyes of the only witness present, Father Demers, from whose lips we received the moving narrative. No sooner had Father De Smet descried the Vicar General than he ran to prostrate himself at his feet, imploring his blessing; and no sooner had the Very Rev. Blanchet caught sight of the valiant missionary than he also fell on his knees, imploring the blessing of the saintly Jesuit. Admirable struggle, where the last place, not the first, was the object of the contes-

---

[34] Rosati's interest was stimulated by the visit of four Indians to St. Louis to ask for Catholic missionaries. For an account of this pilgrimage and the literature pertaining to it cf. Garraghan, *op. cit.*, II, 243-244.

[35] *Ibid.*, II, 248.

[36] Chittenden and Richardson, *op. cit.*, I, 41.

tants!"[37] Blanchet in his *Historical Sketches* simply mentions this meeting, which was destined to play such a part in the religious future of the Oregon country:

> Rev. M. Demers returned to Vancouver in the middle of May, to attend to the wants of the mission and those of the brigades of the North and South. He had been there but a few weeks, when Father De Smet arrived at Vancouver from Colville, which he had reached in the early spring.... Rev. M. Demers brought him to St. Paul; he spent eight days with the Vicar General, sung high Mass on Sunday, addressed words of exhortation to the congregation and expressed himself much pleased with the solemnity of the Mass and vespers services, especially with the singing.... Here he returned to Vancouver with Father Demers; the Vicar General soon rejoined them to deliberate on the interests of the great mission of the Pacific Coast.[38]

De Smet's own account of the meeting is not without interest:

> We arrived at Fort Vancouver on the morning of the 8th of June. I enjoyed the happiness and great consolation of meeting in these distant parts two respectable Canadian priests— the Reverend Mr. Blanchet, grand vicar of all the country west of the mountains, claimed by the British crown, and the Reverend Mr. Demers. They are laboring in these regions for the same object we are trying to accomplish in the Rocky Mountains. The kindness and benevolence with which these reverend gentlemen received me are proofs of the pure zeal which actuates them for the salvation of these savages. They assured me that immense good might be done in the extensive regions that border on the Pacific, if a greater number of missionaries, with means at their command, were stationed in these regions; and they urged me very strongly to obtain from my superiors some of our Fathers.... The Governor of the honorable Company of Hudson Bay, Dr. McLoughlin, who resides at Fort Vancouver, after having given me every possible proof of interest, as a good Catholic, advised me to do everything in my power to gratify the wishes of the Canadian missionaries. His principal reason is, that if Catholicity was rapidly planted in these tracts where civilization begins to

---

[37] Lawrence B. Palladino, S.J., *Indian and White in the Northwest* (Baltimore, 1894), 39.

[38] Blanchet, *op. cit.*, 49.

dawn, it would be more quickly introduced thence into the interior.³⁹

During the few days that De Smet remained at Vancouver, the three missionaries made a careful survey of the situation, with the result that De Smet decided to open in the Willamette Valley a house of the Society of Jesus to serve as headquarters for the Jesuit missions of Oregon. To secure the approval of the vice-provincial (Verhaegen) for this new establishment, as well as to ask permission for a trip to Europe so that he might seek help for the missions in the Pacific northwest, De Smet again traveled to St. Louis.⁴⁰

Before he could return, the missionaries were to experience a period of deepest discouragement. Although Blanchet had reason to believe that the plans for the erection of a diocese in Oregon were being favorably considered,⁴¹ affairs in the Columbia country were far from satisfactory. A scarcity of workers still delayed progress and the development that the priests wished for their missions. The arrival of De Smet with men and money was an event, anticipated with the greatest eagerness. As the months passed and no word was received from the Jesuit, Blanchet and Demers grew weary of waiting but they had no means with which to relieve the difficult situation. Blanchet's discouragement is evident in the letter he wrote to Bishop Signay in November, 1843 when he complained that " We have done nothing for a year but hold our old position. Our efforts to extend the reign of Jesus Christ among the savages have failed. . . . We await the arrival of Reverend Father De Smet who has not yet returned. Two reverend fathers ⁴² have come with an American party of 500 souls; but they are too far away to assist us." ⁴³

Demers too was tired of the delay but he looked forward to the time when the Jesuits would come to assist them. He had been obliged to give up his missions in the north to attend to pressing

---

³⁹ Chittenden and Richardson, *op. cit.*, I, 387.

⁴⁰ Garraghan, *op. cit.*, II, 277.

⁴¹ Blanchet had written to Signay and Rosati before De Smet's departure for the east to urge them to push the establishment of a bishopric in Oregon.

⁴² Fathers Peter De Vos and Adrian Hoecken traveled west with the " great immigration " of 1843.

⁴³ Blanchet to Signay, November 6, 1843. QAA.

demands nearer home, but he never abandoned the hope of continuing his work with the Indians after the return of De Smet. He wrote to the Jesuit to give him an account of the mission, " so that he would know the number of priests who will be required, and to direct him in the plans which he will form for this far distant and difficult mission, where the means of communication are slow and laborious. It demands men, capable of making sacrifices and willing to suffer great privations. But of what are not the Jesuits capable, these men so zealous and so filled with the desire for the salvation of souls." [44]

John McLoughlin had never been indifferent to the success of the missionaries and they owed him much for his practical assistance during the first years. In this period of waiting, which all found trying, he was generous as he had ever been but he realized as perhaps no other could, the changes that were taking place in the Oregon territory and the need there was of taking cognizance of them in plans for the development of the church. In a letter to Bishop Signay he pays a tribute of praise to the work of Blanchet and Demers, at the same time stressing the desirability of sending English-speaking priests who would be able to approach the Americans:

> I have the honor to acknowledge the receipt of your valued favor of the 31 August, 1841 by the Rev. Missioners Langlois and Bolduc, whom I hope you will do me the Justice to Believe I was extremely happy to see as certain the Rev. Messrs. Blanchette and Demers had too much to do to attend to all the calls made on them. Yet with the reinforcement of these two Gentlemen there is a vast field for many more. But of this I presume you are sufficiently informed by my respectable friend the Rev. Mr. Blanchette who I am happy to say has with his most worthy colleagues done a vast deal of good among our countrymen, the Aborigines, and also among the protestants who have all been benefited by their instruction and edified by the piety and zeal with which these Reverend Gentlemen labour in their sacred avocations and of which even now they begin to reap the reward in the immense reform they have operated among our countrymen and in the respect and esteem of all who have the happiness of their acquaintance and if I may presume to give an opinion as we know that men in general

[44] Demers to Signay, February 7, 1844. QAA.

are so weak as to allow themselves to be led by national feelings. . . . I would beg to take the liberty to suggest that when your Lordship has the goodness to send us a reinforcement it would be desirable you sent us some American, Scotch, Irish or English Roman Catholic priests as we see people in general respond to a clergyman when he is their countryman. There is a fine field here at present among the Americans and others for a couple of American and an Irish, English or Scotch priest. As to do good and even to establish the Catholic religion in an Indian country is in the first place to convert the whites. The Indians will follow as a matter of course. And it should be kept in mind that though the majority at present may be Canadians in this country most probably ultimately it will be Americans.[45]

Signay perhaps decided to leave all such matters as additional priests to the bishop of the western territory, whose appointment was expected shortly, or he may have thought that De Smet would return from Europe with a sufficient number of recruits. No more missionaries were sent from Canada, and none came to the Columbia until De Smet's arrival in July, 1844. The Jesuit's voyage to Europe was indeed fruitful and when he returned to Oregon he brought with him priests and nuns, ready to devote themselves to the diffcult task. Blanchet was elated at this success:

Father De Smet went to Europe and was not idle. He visited England, France, Italy, Belgium; he obtained from the Reverend Father General at Rome, three Jesuit Fathers who went first to St. Louis, left there in May, 1844 and arrived among the Flatheads in the September following. He obtained four other fathers who sailed with him, January 19, 1844. Leaving Belgium with six sisters of Notre Dame de Namur, whom he had obtained with difficulty,[46] he rounded Cape Horn, where the vessel was in grave danger. He sailed from Valparaiso to Lima; and by all the Fathers and sisters were received with the greatest respect, with real joy. They would have kept them in this last city. The Belgian captain made his way to the Columbia without having secured a map of the entrance.

[45] McLoughlin to Signay, March 20, 1843. QAA.
[46] The first religious to come to Oregon were: Sisters Loyola, Marie Cornelie, Mary Catherine, Mary Aloysia, Norbertine and Mary Albine. Their story is told by a member of the congregation in *In Harvest Fields by Sunset Shores* (San Francisco, 1926).

Arrived at the latitude of this river, he waited three days before being able to discover the entrance. . . . The fourth day, he made a fresh attempt to find the passage, to cross the bar, not without grave misgivings. The wind and the sea accomodated him. . . . The waves . . . carried him over. . . . It was July 31, day of the feast of the patron saint of the Company of Jesus, St. Ignatius, to whom the fathers had addressed fervent prayers, the sisters, also, etc. And heaven heard their prayers, and let them enter without shipwreck, these holy missionaries and the courageous sisters who had made such great sacrifices to come to work for the conversion of the savages. In a short time, the ship was in calm water and docked at Fort George. Father De Smet went ahead in a canoe; he arrived August 4, Sunday morning, at Vancouver to the great surprise of everyone. Having waited in vain in the spring and since, he was no longer expected except by way of St. Louis. While the priest said his Mass Dr. McLoughlin sent an express with a letter for Mr. Blanchet and two others sent from Namur. That of Mr. Demers and of Sister Loyola were forgotten. That of McLoughlin was left at the Falls, or Oregon City. Mr. Blanchet did not receive at Willamette any except the letters from Belgium which said nothing of the arrival of the ship. The week passed in uneasiness. Finally, August 10, Mr. Demers wrote and gave the official news. Mr. B. left that night, August 10, and reached Vancouver the next day. . . . A good number of colonists had abandoned their harvest to go see the sisters; a ship and three or four canoes formed an escort, which left Vancouver, August 14. The 15th they camped at Oregon City; the 16th they arrived at St. Paul of the Willamette.[47]

---

[47] This letter, not signed, is in the hand of Blanchet, n. d., QAA. De Smet brought with him: Fathers John Nobili, Michael Accolti, Anthony Ravalli, **Louis Vercruysse.**

CHAPTER IV

DISSENSIONS AND PROBLEMS

The year 1839 had closed auspiciously for the Catholic missionaries. Blanchet had settled at Willamette in October, where a chapel had been begun and completed before the first enthusiasm of the French Canadians had worn away—completed even as to altar, benches, a lodging for the missionary, " a rarety for these places." The priest was glad to move into it for he was beginning to feel the inclemencies of the weather. He and his parishioners had celebrated the feast of Christmas "with a solemnity that the habitants of these places will long remember." An eighty-four pound bell, the first to be heard in the district of the Willamette, had been blessed with appropriate ceremonies and now called the faithful to divine services.[1]

North of the Columbia at Cowlitz, Demers was well established. His church was erected and in it, he and his people, white and Indian, met daily for prayer and instruction. " At midnight Mass on the festival of Christmas, they were able," he wrote to Cazeau, " by means of repeated exercises, to honor the birth of our Savior, by uniting their voices to those of the angels in the Gloria in excelsis." [2]

But there was already some evidence of the struggle for power that was to trouble the next few years. The Oregon country in 1838 was Hudson's Bay territory; it was that in 1840; even in 1843. But during these years influences were constantly growing which foreboded the end of the British régime. They were disturbing forces—alarming to the officers of the Honourable Company; disquieting to the Americans—traders, settlers, missionaries; disastrous to the Catholic missions and missionaries.

Had McLoughlin looked out over the Columbia region in 1838 he might have taken considerable pride in the organization he had

---

[1] *Rapport sur les Missions du Diocese de Quebec* (Quebec, 1840), 78.
[2] Blanchet, *Sketches*, 38.

effected. Under his direction the agents of the Hudson's Bay Company had spread over the northwest until there was little of it that had not been explored and trapped for furs, which were brought to the general headquarters, Fort Vancouver. This was a frontier settlement and like the frontier rough in many ways. But the travelers who visited there and who were entertained at the table of John McLoughlin never forgot the experience. Many are the descriptions that have been written of this north Pacific post, tiny in comparison with the cities of the world, but, in its time, unique in the interest that was directed toward it.

It was established in 1824 [3] to be the focal point of commercial operations in Oregon. The American lawyer, Thomas J. Farnham,[4] who was in the northwest in 1839, has left a description, true enough in most of its details. According to his account, Fort Vancouver

> is situated in a beautiful plain on the north bank of the Columbia, ninety miles from the sea. . . . The noble river below it is 1675 yards wide and five to seven fathoms in depth; the whole surrounding country is covered with forests of pine, cedar, and fir, etc. interspersed here and there with small open spots; all overlooked by the vast snowy pyramids of the President's Range,[5] thirty-five miles in the east.
> The fort itself is an oblong square 250 yards in length by 150 in breadth, enclosed by pickets twenty feet in height. The area within is divided into two courts, around which are store-

---

[3] One of the first steps taken after the arrival of McLoughlin in Oregon was the establishment of new headquarters. T. C. Elliott credits Simpson with the selection of the site. Cf. "Sir George Simpson's Place in the History of the 'Old Oregon' country," *Washington Historical Quarterly*, XX (1929), 33-35.

[4] The leader of the "Peoria party" which started from Illinois in 1839. Only a few of the group arrived in Oregon. Farnham later published the story of his adventures, *Travels in the Great Western Prairies, the Anahuac and Rocky Mountains, and in the Oregon Territory* (Poughkeepsie, 1841). Bancroft, *Northwest Coast*, II, 608, makes this comment, "One thing shall be said of Farnham in his first book, he speaks well of everybody, missionaries and settlers, fur-hunters and sailors, Catholic and Protestant, English and American, an exceedingly rare accomplishment in those disputatious days of early Oregon."

[5] Bancroft, *op. cit.*, II, 556, says that Hall J. Kelley gave this name to the range of mountains dividing eastern from western Oregon.

> houses for furs, goods and grains; and as workshops for carpenters, blacksmiths, coopers, tinners, wheelwrights, etc. One building near the rear gate is occupied as a school house; and a brick structure as a powder magazine. . . .

Outside the fort is another settlement where the servants of the Company have their homes; beyond these lay the farm:

> Six hundred yards below the fort, and on the bank of the river, is a village of thirty-five wooden houses, generally constructed like those within the pickets. In these live the Company's servants. Among them is a hospital, in which those who become diseased are humanely treated. At the back, and a little east of the fort, is a barn containing a mammoth threshing machine; and near this are a number of long sheds, used for storing grain in the sheaf. And behold the Vancouver farm, stretching up and down the river (3000 acres, fenced into beautiful fields) sprinkled with dairy houses, and herdsmen and shepherds' cottages! A busy place.

It is a busy place, one of ceaseless activity from early morning until late evening:

> The farmer at break of day summons one hundred half-breeds and Iroquois Indians from their cabins to the fields. Twenty or thirty ploughs tear open the generous soil; the sowers follow with their seed and pressing on them come a dozen harrows to cover it; and thus thirty or forty acres are planted in a day, till the immense farm is under crop. The season passes on, teeming with daily industry, until the harvest waves on all these fields. . . . The saw mill, too, is a scene of constant toil. Thirty or forty Sandwich Islanders are felling the pines and dragging them to the mill. . . . The grist mill is not idle. It must furnish bread stuff for the posts, and the Russian market in the north-west. . . . We will now enter the fort. . . . Listen to the voices of those children from the schoolhouse.[6] They are the half-breed offspring of the gentlemen and servants of the Company, educated at the Company's expense, preparatory to their being apprenticed to trades in Canada. . . .

Farnham then describes the great dining room where McLoughlin presided and dispensed hospitality:

---

[6] McLoughlin established the first school in 1832 with an English division for the children of the officials and another in which prayers and canticles were taught in French. John Ball, a lawyer, who came west with Wyeth was first schoolmaster.

Dissensions and Problems 71

The bell rings for dinner. . . . The dining hall is a spacious room on the second floor of the "Hall" ceiled with pine above and at the sides. In the southwest corner of it is a large closed stove giving out sufficient caloric to make it comfortable.

At the end of a table twenty feet in length stands Governor McLoughlin, directing guests and gentlemen from neighboring posts to their places; and chief traders, traders, the physician, clerks, and the farmer, slide respectfully to their places, at distances from the Governor corresponding to the dignity of their rank in the service. Thanks are given to God, and all are seated. Roast beef and pork, boiled mutton, baked salmon, boiled ham; beets, carrots, turnips, cabbage and potatoes, and wheaten bread, are tastefully distributed over the table among a dinner set of elegant queen's ware, burnished with glittering glasses and decanters of various coloured Italian wines. Course after course goes round, and the Governor fills to his guests and friends; and each gentleman in turn vies with him in diffusing around the board a most generous allowance of viands, wines, and warm fellow-feeling. The cloth and wines are removed together, cigars are lighted, and a strolling smoke about the premises, enlivened by a courteous discussion of some mooted point of natural history or politics, closes the ceremonies of the dinner hour at Fort Vancouver.[7]

Here McLoughlin reigned supreme and his rule, through his efficient subordinates, extended far and wide: to the north into New Caledonia, east to the Rockies, south to California. The Indians had long since learned the wisdom of submitting to the White Headed Eagle and except for an occasional outburst, the Hudson's Bay men were successful in dealing with the savages. There seems to have been little objection to the monarchical privileges that McLoughlin exercised. "Trappers and Indians," remarks Caughey, "thought none the less of him for his assumption of dictatorial powers. To the Indians it appeared perfectly proper; the Gallic voyageurs saw no traditions violated; the Scotch traders commended

---

[7] Farnham, *Travels in the Great Western Prairies, etc.*, in Thwaites, *Early Western Travels* (Cleveland, 1906), XXIX, 63-66; for other descriptions of Fort Vancouver cf. John K. Townsend, *Narrative of a Journey across the Rocky Mountains to the Columbia River* and Joel Palmer, *Journal of Travels over the Rocky Mountains, to the Mouth of the Columbia River; made during the Years 1845 and 1846* in Thwaites, XXI and XXX.

it as business efficiency. The only criticism came considerably later from an English chaplain and from anti-monarchical Americans." [8]

The latter except for an occasional trader, were represented first by the missionary group who arived in 1834, when Jason Lee and his nephew, Daniel Lee, made their appearance at Fort Vancouver.[9] These men, sent by the Mission Board of the New England Methodists, were ambitious to establish themselves among the Flatheads [10] but McLoughlin advised against it and following his directions they settled in the Willamette Valley, not far from the French Canadians.

Their first necessity was a mission house, the construction of which consumed most of the winter months. Thirty acres of land were seeded in the spring and the missionaries were soon producing the greater part of the foodstuffs required by their numbers. A school was begun and three Indian children came to live at the mission. Their number was gradually increased and by the third winter Cyrus Shepard was teaching nineteen Indians. Theirs was

[8] John W. Caughey, *History of the Pacific Coast of North America* (New York, 1938), 214.

[9] Jason Lee was superintendent of the Methodist mission from 1834 to 1843 and the first missionary to enter the Oregon country. To aid in the work for the Christianization of the Indians he was influential in securing three new groups of workers, two in 1837 and a third in 1840. Lee carried the memorial of 1838 across the continent to Senator Linn who caused it to be printed in the Congressional Globe. He also lectured extensively throughout the east stimulating interest in Oregon. Two accounts of his work have been written, John M. Canse, *Pilgrim and Pioneer* (New York, 1930) and Cornelius J. Brosnan, *Jason Lee, Prophet of New Oregon* (New York, 1932).

[10] Daniel Lee and Joseph H. Frost, *Ten Years in Oregon* (New York, 1844), 127, give four reasons for not settling among the Indians:

1. The means of subsistence in a region so remote and so difficult of access were, to say the least, very doubtful. . . .

2. The smallness of their numbers. . . .

3. Their vicinity to the Blackfeet, as well the White man's enemy as theirs, and who would fall upon the abettors of their foes with signal revenge;

4. A larger field of usefulness was contemplated as the object of the mission than the benefiting of a single tribe. The wants of the whole country, present and prospective, so far as they could be, were taken into account. . . .

Dissensions and Problems

a boarding school, in which the teacher gave instruction in sewing, cooking, farm and mechanical work with some of the elements of English and religion. But progress was slow and the natives were easily frightened away. Only a few of those not actually at the school had any contact with the mission and almost from the beginning its work seems to have been much more vital to the settlers in the valley than to the tribesmen of the surrounding country.

Even this interest was replaced shortly. Jason Lee was soon convinced that the future of the mission lay with the in-coming Americans rather than with the Indians or the French Canadians. In answer to his appeal two groups of assistants had arrived in 1837 [11] but in his view of the situation a still greater number was necessary and he determined to return to the east to make a personal representation of their needs. The result was that the Mission Board sent out the "great re-inforcement" of 1840, consisting of fifty-one persons.[12] This made possible the establishment of stations at Nisqually on Puget Sound, at Clatsop at the mouth of the Columbia, at the Dalles, and at the Falls.

In 1836 the Presbyterians established three missions: Waiilatpu about twenty-five miles distant from Walla Walla, Clearwater, ninety miles east of Waiilatpu and Spokane, still farther inland. McLoughlin received them cordially and assisted them generously as he had the Methodists but their stations were too far away from Fort Vancouver for them to share in the life there. The Presbyterians followed the same general plan as the Methodists in the organization of their missions and because the interior Indians were superior to those on the coast their work seemed likely to have a greater chance for success. The tribesmen, however, were wanderers and the missionaries found them difficult to assemble. They discovered that their interest in religion seemed largely conditioned by the material gifts they received and the number of conversions was small.[13]

Into the western field in 1838 came the Catholic priests in answer

---

[11] In May Dr. and Mrs. Elijah White with several others came; in September Rev. and Mrs. David Leslie, Rev. H. K. W. Perkins and Miss Margaret Smith.

[12] This group came to Oregon with Lee on the ship, *Lausanne*.

[13] Caughey, op. cit., 232.

to the appeal of the French Canadians. As has already been stated, they began their work at Fort Vancouver, then established themselves at Cowlitz, and a year later, took possession of a section in the Willamette Valley which was thereafter the center of their activity. They were full of zeal for the conversion of both white and red. They regarded the Protestant ministers as the "emissaries of Satan" who had encroached upon the field of Catholic endeavor, hence there was little chance for friendly relations between the rival groups of missionaries. Blanchet acknowledged the hostility when he outlined the task awaiting him and Demers:

> . . . it is easy to understand what the missionaries had to do. They were to warn their flock against the dangers of seduction, to destroy the false impressions already received, to enlighten and confirm the faith of the wavering and deceived consciences, to bring back to the practice of religion and virtue all who had forsaken them for long years, or who, raised in infidelity, had never known nor practised any of them.[14]

There was to be no compromise. The forces of Protestantism had been allowed too long a sway over this country; they must be resisted and conquered. Early training and personal conviction forbade any intimacy between the Catholic missionaries and those of Methodism. Convinced that the Methodist ministers were wrong, that they were ruining the lives of the French Canadians, that they were spreading false belief among the Indians, it was to be expected that the Catholic priests should use every means in their power to prevent the extension of this influence. As for the ministers, since they saw in the work of the priests an attempt of some shrewd popish schemer to establish domination over the northwest and to second British ambition to deprive the United States of any share of the Columbia territory, it is not surprising that their attitude should have been one of suspicion, as the newcomers, frankly antagonistic, proposed to destroy whatever influence they had gained.[15]

[14] Blanchet, *op. cit.*, 24.

[15] Fuller, *op. cit.*, 123, claims that the Catholic missionaries from Canada were regarded as British re-inforcements as well as ecclesiastical competitors by American ministers. J. Orin Oliphant, "Presbyterian Advance into Oregon," *WHQ*, XXVI (1935), 123-128, says that a potent argument with Protestant home missions for establishments in Oregon was that which

The presence of religious and political animosity was soon felt and scenes of bickering and of strife among the Columbia colonists were not unusual. American settlers questioned and resented the supremacy and rule of the Hudson's Bay Company and the Catholic priests whose close friendship with John McLoughlin was apparent to all, shared in their antagonism. As Bancroft points out, " The immediate effect of the arrival of Blanchet and Demers was to unite the French settlers in a community by themselves and thus weaken the power of the Methodist mission as a political body. . . . It increased the hostility of the latter toward the fur company and especially toward McLoughlin to whose jealousy of them the Methodists attributed the action of the company in allowing, or as they believed in inviting, the Catholics to settle in the territory." [16]

stressed the need of arresting the spread of Roman Catholicism. That the shadow of Rome might not completely darken the land, it was necessary to make haste to disseminate the light of the " true gospel." The spread of undefiled Christianity was necessary for the preservation of American institutions.

The attitude of the ministers is revealed here: "There are about 200 French Canadians in the settlement, all of whom are papists of the most ignorant and bigoted type; the Roman Catholic priests in the country domineer over them to their entire satisfaction, consequently there is but little probability that any protestant influence that can be exerted upon them will ever convert them from their vain system of relics and image worship, to the true principles of the gospel. These Frenchmen all having Indian wives, the most of them have families of half-breed children that they are bringing up in the consummate ignorance and barbarity. A few of the adult French understand a smattering of the English language, while their children are generally quite ignorant of it which renders it impossible to communicate with them to an extent without a thorough knowledge of the French language. Besides this, they are taught by their priests to have nothing to do with the "hereticks" not even to permit them to pray in their houses, and indeed it seems that every avenue that was formerly open to convey religious truth to this abominable mass of ignorance, by the arrival of the priests less ignorant perhaps, but equally bigoted and less sincere, has been effectually closed against all protestant encroachment."— Copy of Rev. Gustavus Hines' communication to Methodist Board, given in Robert M. Gatke, " A Document of Mission History, 1833-1843," *OHQ*, XXVI (1935), 178.

[16] *Oregon*, I, 321. This is shown, he says, by the fact that the first two petitions of the settlers to the United States congress were signed equally by French and Americans, but the subsequent memorials by Americans only.

In 1837 the Methodists had established a temperance society to which some of the Canadians belonged. It was Blanchet's belief that this was being used in order to spread anti-Catholic propaganda and hence membership in it came under his condemnation. It is quite evident that ill-feeling was rife before the priests had been present a year; there seems no other way to explain the prohibition to attend the funeral of Cyrus Shepard, the Methodist schoolmaster who died in December, 1839. Blanchet discussed the matter in a letter to Demers:

> Mr. Shepard, schoolmaster of the Methodist mission, suffered the amputation of his leg above the knee last December 18 and died on the 31; he was buried January 2. An invitation was extended to the Canadians to be present; the missionary being consulted, forbade it. Great goings-on, great reproaches, loud cries on the part of Mr. Leslie and his band. But heaven inspired the decision to break off all religious communication with this dangerous sect, so anxious to recapture the French who have entirely escaped them. This was a last way to seek to indoctrinate them. Two Irish, ignorant of my prohibition, went and had there the pleasure of hearing the minister harangue against the crucifix, images, etc.[17]

Evidently sensing that his decision in this matter might bring censure, Blanchet took the precaution of writing to James Douglas, then at Fort Vancouver, to assure him that he had acted thus through "very strong reasons and not from a lack of liberality, which had been charged." Mr. Douglas replied promptly:

> The progress you are making in the great object of your mission must be a subject of joy to every friend of mankind. I hope your congregation will not decline in attention to their religious duties, nor permit others to shake their faith or diminish the confidence with which they have hitherto received the counsels and teachings of their excellent pastor. On this subject I feel a degree of uneasiness which I cannot dispel; a bad feeling has been excited among the Americans by the refusal of your flock to attend the funeral of the late Mr. Shepard, which is now directed solely against you, in consequence of the pusillanimous conduct of the Canadians, who throw the odium on their spiritual guide, whereas in justice, they ought to have shielded you from the storm, by declaring with manly frankness that

[17] Blanchet to Demers, January 13, 1840. QAA.

they were influenced in that instance by the rules and essential doctrines of their church.[18]

This letter disturbed Father Blanchet so much, that he wrote again to Douglas, to explain his position. His reply reveals the petty disagreements which were fast separating the settlers into two hostile groups:

> The American citizens lack a proper regard for everyone but they do not wish anyone to disregard them. In declaring in public against the Catholics, in threatening them with what will happen when they [the Americans] are a majority, they have gone too far and too fast, as they have on other occasions which they have repented or will repent soon.... The refusal of the Catholics to be present at their invitation, coming as it did from a regard for duty, should not be regarded by the Americans as a lack of consideration, still less as an act of vengeance against them.... But it is said, they could have assisted at a burial. To that I reply, it is not easy to make a distinction and since my people are poorly instructed and too confident, attendance would have put them in the way of seduction. The danger would have been augmented since our separated brethen, having few scruples as to the means of gaining their ends, could have used the ruse to attach the men whom they have never ceased to begrudge to the priests—witness the advances of Daniel Lee to Joseph Gervais, and the words of Mr. Lee before his departure for the States, when he remarked that he sufficed to serve the habitants of the Willamette, as Mr. Beaver had said with regard to the men at Vancouver.... But it is said Mr. Shepard had rendered great service to the Canadians at his mission. So be it: the services were returned a hundred times when they furnished him the necessities of life, but above all when they saved the minister's party in the spring of 1839,[19] as Mr. Wilson himself declared before me at Nisqually.[20]

Blanchet then turned to the religious side of the question: the danger of such contacts to the faith of the Canadians; contacts, which exposed them to the false doctrines that were preached—the

---

[18] Douglas to Blanchet, January 14, 1840. PAA.

[19] As a result of the punishment of an Indian for the theft of some wheat from the Methodist mission, the savages threatened to massacre the people at the mission, a tragedy averted by the intervention of the Canadians.

[20] Blanchet to Douglas, February 10, 1840. PAA.

uselessness of infant baptism, the lack of need for an infallible guide in religious matters, the imperfections in the church and its members. He evidently regarded the matter as closed for his letter ended with a word of reassurance to the doubting chief factor: " I beg of you to calm your fears as to the storm which threatens, it will not materialize. Our American fellow-citizens will open their eyes; they will realize that they must leave to each one in matters spiritual the same liberty of conscience which each individual has the right to enjoy in temporal affairs." [21]

The storm unfortunately was only beginning; the incident of the funeral service was but one. Others of more importance in their consequences followed in quick succession. When in 1838 the American settlers had gotten together a petition to the American Congress; when thirty-six of them had signed it, calling themselves the "germ of a great state" and urging congress to take steps to increase American colonization in Oregon, McLoughlin had offered no objection. The settlers were well within their rights. Jason Lee took the document east with him and in January, 1839, Senator Lewis L. Linn presented it to congress. During the course of that same year an American arrived at Fort Vancouver, Thomas J. Farnham, "travelling for his health," according to Blanchet. He looked the country over, praised its beauty, its fertility, its possibilities; consulted with his fellow Americans, and with two of them, Dr. Elijah White and Dr. William J. Bailey,[22] drew up a document in which he excoriated the Hudson's Bay Company. It was circulated among the settlers of the Willamette Valley and some of the French Canadians were induced to sign. There is little doubt that McLoughlin was angry; he had every right to be. He should have been able to expect something better from the Americans whom he had generously aided, from the Canadians who depended on him for their very livelihood. A retraction was demanded from the latter, in which they affirmed the fair treat-

---

[21] *Ibid.*

[22] Bancroft, *Oregon*, I, 234, says that Leslie, temporary superintendent of the mission, and Bailey were responsible for the memorial; though Farnham may have drawn it up. On 231, he quotes Wilkes as saying that Farnham wrote the memorial from suggestions given him by Bailey. Fuller, *op. cit.*, 195, claims that feeling against British occupation was the motive for both this and the earlier memorial.

ment they had always received from the company, in which they told how their signatures had been obtained, "they had been assured that the petition contained nothing against the company, that it was in substance the same as that of Mr. Lee in 1838, the signing of which Dr. McLoughlin had not objected to." This was another matter and it was some time before the chief factor accepted the Canadians' assurance that they had acted without malice. In March, Demers wrote to Blanchet that "it is only now that Dr. McLoughlin has been convinced of the double-dealing and lying, by which the signatures of the Canadians of Willamette were secured; his indignation is boundless."[23] However, in spite of his anger, McLoughlin's reaction was characteristically generous, "The conduct of the governor was always noble and worthy of a great soul. Farnham, he received with courtesy; the others had their share of his favors. It is thus that Dr. McLoughlin avenges himself. . . ."

Peace was temporarily restored, but only temporarily. On January 26, 1840 there came a note to Blanchet from the Methodist mission in which an invitation was extended to him to be present at the annual meeting of the temperance society. Since he had forbidden his people to have any dealings with the *société d'eau fraichi*, he could scarcely appear at such an assembly. In his opinion one line in the communication, "I hope *our little past differences* will not be further thought of, nor anything hinder our uniting as far as we conscientiously can to build up the cause and kingdom of our common Lord and Saviour," precluded a simple refusal and unfortunately he considered it necessary to detail and explain past difficulties:

> I received your note of the 28th of last month. As to the *temperance society* permit me to refer you to my response of last year, that since *the Catholics wish to have nothing to do with such a society, I do not want to force them to be a part of it*. Besides, temperance being a Christian virtue, there is more virtue in the practice of it as such than as a purely natural virtue. I think that one should be obligated by a regard for all the virtues and by a horror of the vices opposed to them rather than by the rules of a society. As for forgetting *our little past differences*, I will ask my people to forget the

[23] Demers to Blanchet, March 1, 1840. PAA.

injury done them when they were tricked into signing the last petition. I will ask them to forget the injury they received in the person of their priest, when the circulation of an infamous book, filled with atrocious calumnies, sought to degrade him, to put an end to his influence. I will ask them to forget the injury done them, when for lack of knowledge of the dogmas of their faith, they were relegated to the rank of pagans and idolaters. I will ask them to forget the injury they received when a child was struck when he said that he did not believe all that was charged against the religion of his dead Catholic father. They will forget also, the crime of a doctor who visited a woman without any great necessity, without the permission of her husband, in a manner to wound modesty, to expose himself and her to temptation, her husband to sorrow. That is not the practice in savage any more than in civilized countries, because God is everywhere. The Catholics will forget the exaggeration of the crimes mentioned in the last petition and the assertion of a newspaper of New York, that *the whites of Willamette are as savage as the Indians* who live around them. The forgetting of *these differences*, the efforts, each on his side, to maintain temperance, peace, harmony, to advance the prosperity of the little colony, these are, dear Sir, the ardent wishes of the Catholic missionary, who would come with pleasure if his conscience permitted, to the gathering of citizens of all origins.[24]

This letter was delivered and happily perhaps for the missionary, none was found who read French well enough to understand all of it. Blanchet had forwarded a copy to McLoughlin who found it severe, and to James Douglas who expressed his dismay at its lack of moderation:

> The firmness and admirable devotion to a high sense of principle displayed in your late conduct are beyond praise; yet the wisest and best of men have found it necessary to yield, at times, to the pressure of circumstances with the view of averting animosity and outrage which they had no other means of escaping. In precisely such circumstances I conceive you to be placed, and, as a friend, I take the liberty of advising the exercise of extreme caution, equally in the management of your own flock and in establishing your relations with all persons around you. Your letter to Dr. . . . is severe; the implication of criminal designs on the person of a female patient

---

[24] Blanchet to [White], February 1, 1840. PAA.

excites disgust; if proved, the moral turpitude of the act must forever stamp his character with infamy; if false the consequences will recoil with equal force upon the author of the calumny; but whether true or false, you, my dear Sir, by charging the crime to the individual, are exposed to a serious prosecution in our civil courts. Dr. . . .'s ignorance of the French language has fortunately concealed the import of your words: he wrote to Dr. Tolmie that the "Bishop" had sent him a *handsome* letter on the subject of temperance.[25]

The missionary's reaction was pitiable:

This letter was a blow to me. I was beaten; I reproached myself for my imprudence. I seemed to see Dr. . . . in fury, seeking by all possible means to recover his reputation. I would be exposed to the attacks of the one and the other, in danger of not being sustained by the man and woman who had made to me their declarations. But above all the interests of my dear mission touched me to tears; I would be obliged to quit my post, to return to the States to defend my suit; there being no one to replace me, Mr. Demers would be left alone, overwhelmed with work, trouble, chagrin, ennui. I seemed to see the sick dying without the sacraments; the children without baptism; the savages in infidelity; the Methodist mission triumphant in my absence. . . . Knowing the powerful protection of Mary, I had recourse to her: *Virgo potens, consolatrix afflictorum, priez pour moi.*[26]

And Mary heard the prayer of her missionary. After all the matter was adjusted without much difficulty, the doctor [27] satisfied, the missionary happy that his attempt to protect his flock had not reacted against him and his work.

The incident had a sequel, however. After Jason Lee returned from the east in the spring (1840) evidences of discord among the Methodist missionaries were openly acknowledged. Dr. White was charged with overstepping his authority during the absence of Lee, but the rupture became final over the question of the management of the school. Dr. White had replaced Mr. Shepard but declared he did so only until the arrival of help. He had come west to practise his profession and not to teach school. The mission head

---

[25] Douglas to Blanchet, February 26, 1840. PAA.
[26] Blanchet to A. M. Blanchet, February 8, 1841. PAA.
[27] Elijah White came to Oregon in May, 1837, as mission physician.

insisted on his continuing and when he refused to obey, an ecclesiastical process was instigated against him. He was called before a council of the chief of the mission and some laymen. The other ministers of the Columbia were not notified. After four hours of deliberation, sentence was passed: the Doctor, excommunicated, was to be no longer a part of the Church of Christ of the Mission of Oregon. In his humiliation, he turned to the Catholic priest to whom he confided his plans and of whom he asked permission to use the church building as a meeting place where he might say farewell to his friends[28]

The request, containing nothing contrary to the interests of the Catholic mission, was granted without difficulty although Blanchet did not at the time understand the nature of the proposed assembly. Much to his surprise on the day set by the doctor, the superintendent of the Oregon Methodist mission arrived accompanied by several members of his group. The Canadians and Americans had already gathered. It was only then that the priest realized the meaning of the words, *transacting a little business, taking leave of my neighbors.* As he wrote to his brother, "The poor Catholic priest, maligned by the book, *Maria Monk*, was to be the witness of the humiliation of the *saints* of the Methodist sect. The poor people, *idolatrous,* ignorant Canadians were judges along with the other inhabitants, the Americans of the Willamette."[29] The assembly arranged itself. The doctor and his wife, Mr. Lee and his helpers had seats next to the building. The others placed themselves in front on benches. The proceedings began with the doctor evidently in charge. After some preliminary considerations the accused asked

[28] A. J. Allen (comp.), *Ten Years in Oregon. Travels and Adventures of Doctor E. White and Lady* (Ithaca, N. Y., 1850), 131, " Soon after this expedition [to the Umpqua] arose a difficulty between Mr. Lee and Dr. White, which was the cause of the doctor's return home. . . . This small matter, as is unfortunately often the case, gave rise to other disagreements, in which not only sentiment, but feeling was enlisted. Dr. White resigned; and thinking it the most honorable course he could pursue, under the circumstances, resolved in a written correspondence with Mr. Lee, to state his reasons for so doing; . . . The proceeding was right, had the correspondence been carried on with a little more moderation, and less bitterness of spirit."

[29] Blanchet to A. M. Blanchet, February 8, 1841. PAA.

that Mr. Lee show the accusations, the complaints made against him. This was refused on the grounds that the rules of the church did not permit it. The doctor then demanded that he be allowed to read the charges which painted him "black as midnight." Jason Lee protested, again urging the rules of the church, but his objecsions were overruled and the request was granted. Dr. White rose to read:

List of charges preferred against Dr. . . . .
I Charge. Disobedience to the orders of the church.
1. In leaving the mission school in Oregon, Willamette station in the summer of 1840 without the consent of the superintendent of the Oregon mission.
2. In neglecting the duties of his profession in the mission by being absent nearly two weeks in the sickly part of the season of 1840, when a number of the members of the mission were in ill health.
3. By refusing to serve under the superintendent of the mission as he was pledged to do, abandoning his work, and making arrangements to leave for the states.
4. In drawing several hundred dollars at Fort Vancouver on mission account between the months of March, 1838 and February, 1839 without the permission of the superintendent.

II Charge. Dishonesty.
1. In drawing at Vancouver several hundred dollars on mission account upon which he had no claim and prejudicial to the interests of the mission without the consent or advice of the superintendent. This between March, 1838 and February, 1839.
2. In appropriating all or part of said monies to his own private purposes.

III Charge. Imprudent Conduct.
1. In assailing the character of the superintendent of the mission by uncharitable, ludicrous and abusive expressions, as per communication from Dr. . . . to the superintendent in August and September, 1840.
2. By speaking to different individuals in August and September of 1840, certain communications prejudicial to the character of the superintendent and other members of this mission.

3. By taking unwarranted liberties with several females of this mission in July, August, or September, 1840. Wall. 9 Sept. 1840. (Signed) Alex F. Waller—In behalf of the Church (30)

The doctor then took some care to explain, discuss and finally to reverse all these accusations in which he showed the feebleness, the wickedness, the malice: Mr. Lee had given him permission to accompany him to the river Umpqua; Mr. Lee, foreseeing his absence, had made an advance for the schoolmaster and the doctor; his departure for the States was the result of the unfair conduct of Mr. Lee; he had wherewithal to pay what he had overdrawn at Vancouver; his accounts were just; his conduct had been prudent; his liberties with women consisted in having embraced one. The affair was going against the Oregon mission. Sympathy was plainly with the accused. He demanded reparation for defamation of character; there was besides the question of money. Mr. Lee explained that the public had no right over the mission money. However, the assembly declared that the mission owed it to the doctor to give him such documents as he might need to defend his character and although it might have no jurisdiction over this matter, yet at the appeal of the doctor, it was pleased to vote him the character he had always enjoyed as a citizen among them, a citizen—good, honest, religious, industrious and exact in the duties of his profession.[31]

[30] Copy in PAA., dated September 9, 1840.

[31] Other estimates of White are not so favorable. Brosnan, *op. cit.*, 88, quotes Sidney W. Moss, *Narrative and Remarks*, MS in Bancroft Library, 2, "Dr. White was sycophantic, but he had some very good points. He was ready to relieve you if he knew you needed relief. You would first have to convince him of the fact. He was kind and openhearted in his way; not very bright; slow of perception, but able to jump at a conclusion." Horace S. Lyman, *History of Oregon* (New York, 1903), III, 242, "Dr. White, who bears the fame of being an intriguer and seeking personal preferment, was defeated in his designs and abruptly terminated his connection with the mission. Gray [who hated White] says: "Jason Lee soon found out the character of this wolf in sheep's clothing, and presented charges against him for his immorality and expelled him from the mission. Previous to leaving the country he called a public meeting and made his statements, and attempted to mob Mr. Lee and get from the

Thus, comments Blanchet, was the infallibility of the Methodist Mission brought into question. The doctor had attained his end, that of humiliating his chief and his followers and of obtaining a recommendation before his departure for the States. " Thus, also," wrote Blanchet, " were humiliated the enemies of the Catholic mission, and in particular those who had menaced the calm of the head of the true Church of Jesus Christ on the Willamette." So the matter was closed. The doctor left for the States to plead his cause before the American Methodist Mission Board and took with him not only a volume of the letters of Dr. Milner but the pious hope of the missionary that it, plus the affronts he had suffered, might turn him toward the Catholic religion.[32]

Two other incidents, trivial in themselves, illustrate the problems of the pioneer priests. The first was concerned with a dispute between two French Canadians over a land claim. Arbiters were appointed, the matter properly discussed, the claim adjudicated apparently to the satisfaction of all. But one of the claimants was evidently less contented than he appeared, for he later appealed to Dr. McLoughlin for justice. The Governor refused to meddle with the matter himself, but no doubt unaware that it had already been considered, suggested that a general assembly be called to look into the affair. The Canadians were notified and some of the Americans.

settlers a character, in both of which he failed, and left the country to impose upon the government at Washington as he had done upon the mission and early settlers of Oregon." Of White's later career after his appointment as Indian sub-agent in 1842, Alban W. Hoopes, *Indian Affairs and their Administration* (Philadelphia, 1932), 70, says, " Whatever else may be said of him, there can be no doubt that twice, in December 1842 and in the spring of 1843, he did much to prevent an outbreak on the part of the Cayuse and the Nez Percé Indians."

[32] White was not interested in Catholicism but his judgment of the work of the Catholic missions in his Report of 1843, given in Lyman, *op. cit.*, III, 425-426 was friendly: " The Rev. Mr. Blanchet and associates, though zealous Catholics, are peaceable, industrious, indefatigable and successful in promoting religious knowledge among the Canadian population and aborigines of this country. Their enterprise in erecting mills and other public works is very commendable, and the general industry, good order and correct habits of the portion of the population under their charge is sufficient proof that their influence over their people has been exerted for good."

Their appearance was a surprise to the priest but his feelings, when he heard that Mr. David Leslie, the Methodist minister, had also been invited, were almost beyond description:

> What, I said to myself, draw into our affairs the Protestants who despise us and let them be witness to our divisions! Call a Methodist minister to judge an affair already decided by the Catholics, and even by the priest! I wished myself a hundred miles from the place. But it seemed that I must suffer the affront. I had planned to speak in this family gathering, to complain about the inconvenience of this assembly, to harangue the instigators of this trouble and to plead fervently for the rights of the mission; I had hoped to gain something. But in the presence of the Americans how was I to speak without covering with shame ourselves and others.[38]

Mr. Leslie, however, failed to appear, and the Americans, convinced that their presence was unwelcome, gradually withdrew, leaving Blanchet to deal with his parishioners. One immediately acceded to the demands of the priest and relinquished his claim, with the suggestion that it become mission property. The second was obdurate and left the assembly, insisting on the satisfaction of his rights. Two trustees were appointed to visit him, to try to gain the release of his claims in favor of the mission. But he refused.

At the Sunday Mass Blanchet complimented the one claimant on his generosity and expressed the hope that the second would not be outdone in liberality. There was no response. And so the missionary determined on desperate measures. After Vespers, he voiced his disappointment from the steps of the altar and announced that he was about to leave with Mr. Demers; that the trustees and the parish might see to the chapel and the land of the mission, if it pleased them; that since some were so poorly disposed, they did not merit longer to have a missionary with them. The implied threat had the desired effect. All began to blame the poor unfortunate. For two days the priest did not appear. Meanwhile the recalcitrant could no longer hold out against the constant scolding of his fellow-men. He visited the priest, asking permission to remain on the land. He was received coldly, reproached for his hardness of heart. He returned a second time, completely humbled, offering to release

---

[38] Blanchet to Jerome Demers, February 11, 1841. PAA.

his pretensions in favor of the mission. His offer was made publicly while at the same time, he asked pardon for his conduct.

The second affair occurred in January, 1841 just as the missionary had begun to congratulate himself that things were going well. On the evening of January 5, Joseph Gervais stopped to tell the priest that he was returning from the upper river whence he had been asked to accompany a member of the mission. Their errand had been to investigate the report of some Indians that they had seen in the home of one of the Catholic Canadians, property belonging to the Methodist mission, which had been lost in the wreck of a canoe the previous October. The Indians' story was only too true: a stolen padlock was found on the door; gowns and linens were drawn from cases, from the bed. The goods were recognized as belonging to the mission and James L. Whitcomb, who had directed the investigation, returned triumphant. The accused was a citizen seemingly so honest, enjoying so excellent a reputation, that Blanchet could scarcely believe the charges, but since he was the head of the Catholic mission, it seemed to be his place to take action. Accordingly he wrote to Jason Lee:

> It was with indignation that I learned Tuesday evening from Mr. Gervais, that a part of the cargo which one of the members of your mission lost several months ago in a shipwreck, had been found in the home of one of my parishioners. Be assured, Sir, that if this man is found guilty of such a crime, it is not his religion which teaches him to act so; for stealing, the retention of the goods of another, are with us crimes which cannot be pardoned until entire retribution and perfect recompense have accompanied sincere repentance and a real change of heart. The holy Catholic religion teaches that one must obey the commandments of God. As an example to my flock, for your interest, my own satisfaction and the good of the accused, I have thought it proper to investigate this sad affair. Not having been able to do anything today on account of the solemnity of the feast on which Christians were called to the faith in the persons of the Magi, I shall begin tomorrow. I ask you to do me the favor and yourself the satisfaction to come with me and several members of your mission, to hear the proofs of this unhappy affair, so as to render justice where it may be due.[34]

[34] Blanchet to Lee, January 6, 1841. PAA.

Jason Lee declined the honor but he sent in his stead, James Whitcomb, who presented the following letter:

> I have been informed that Mr. Leslie was unanimously chosen justice of the peace for the settlement and he, having authorized Mr. J. L. Whitcomb to search for the lost property, if any further search is necessary, I think Mr. Whitcomb should be present, and as it is not convenient for both of us to leave, I have judged it best for him to accompany you. I agree with you that this affair should be thoroughly investigated without delay and you would have been called upon to accompany Mr. Whitcomb at first, had Mr. Gervais thought it advisable. . . .
>
> The man in whose house the property was found, belongs to the Hudson's Bay Company, and whether that Company considers that this settlement has any jurisdiction over their servants or not, I am not informed. Whether the settlers here consider that they have a right to deal with the company's servants, as they would with other settlers, I know not, but this being a point of importance, if it has not been already settled, should be without delay.[35]

The investigation of this matter and its settlement were to bring to a head some of the differences of opinion between the Canadians and the Americans, principally concerning the question of who had the power in the settlement to try and to punish the offender. There were three groups to be considered: the Hudson's Bay Company, which presumably was the only body with legally established jurisdiction;[36] the American Methodist Mission, which had for several years advocated the formation of a local government under the protection of the United States; and the Catholic mission under

---

[35] Lee to Blanchet, January 7, 1841. PAA.

[36] Carey, *op. cit.*, 255, n. 2, lists the rights and powers granted to the Hudson's Bay Company by the charter of 1670: the members of the company were authorized to hold court, "to make, ordain and constitute such and so many reasonable laws, constitutions, orders and ordinances" as should seem necessary and convenient for the good government "of the said company, and of all governors of colonies . . . and other officers employed or to be employed in any of the territories . . ."; and also to revoke or alter them. Furthermore they "shall and may lawfully impose, ordain, limit and provide such pains, penalties and punishments upon all offenders, contrary to such laws, . . ." and levy and impose fines and amercements. The charter is printed in Appendix A in R. M. Martin, *Hudson's Bay Territories and Vancouver Island* (London, 1849).

the direction of Father Blanchet. Whatever rights the priest had in the matter came simply from his position as natural leader and guide of the French Canadians in a country where the administration of law was still in a primitive stage. Blanchet and Lee differed over the manner of settling the case and from their disagreements over principles and methods in this and later cases may be seen the forces which eventually brought a realization of the necessity for a stable government in Oregon.

From the beginning Blanchet seemed determined to take into his own hands the punishment of the guilty Canadian who was quite willing to accept any terms, lest he be sent to Vancouver, where the customary penalty for the crime of theft was expulsion from the country. Lee was equally determined that unless the Hudson's Bay Company asserted its right to deal with the matter that a judge and jury should be chosen and delegated to settle the affair. There is something to be said for both points of view. Blanchet regarded the matter from the standpoint of the individual; it was his contention that since the accused had acknowledged his guilt and expressed his willingness to make amends to the injured party, nothing more was needed except the arrangement and fulfilment of the terms of the reparation. Lee was of the opinion that the affair was one for the courts; he believed the issue at hand might force the establishment of civil authority in the country. As he expressed it, " I feel but little interest, *comparatively,* in this *one* case; but I do feel deeply interested to know whether there *is* any civil power to punish crime, in this settlement or whether there is *not*; whether we are *two* communities (as I have heard stated today) or whether we are one." [37] He insisted that there were individuals in the community " duly elected and qualified " to " take cognizance of the misdemeanors of the citizens of this community." Blanchet refused to recognize their jurisdiction and had some justification for his refusal. The officers in question had been chosen by the Methodist mission group in 1839 when two of their number had been designated to act as magistrates. This was done entirely without the cooperation of the settlers although they had realized the need of some species of government and had tacitly acquiesced.[38]

[37] Lee to Blanchet, January 11, 1841. PAA.
[38] Carey, *op. cit.*, 368.

Blanchet meantime had imposed sentence upon the unhappy culprit:

1. he with his wife and daughter should assist at divine service from the door of the church during the space of a year;
2. at the end of religious services, he should receive three strokes of the discipline from the hands of his fellow citizens in the presence of the men, women and children, the savages of the settlement;
3. he should make the rounds of the settlement to ask pardon at each house for his fault and for the scandal he had given;
4. he should present himself also to the chief of the Methodist mission in order to make just reparation and to restore the damage he had caused.[39]

This arrangement of the matter was far from satisfactory to Lee who objected to such a settlement: "The punishment may indeed be 'hard and severe,' of that I express no opinion; and if the punishment inflicted is purely ecclesiastical, I object not; but if it is intended to prevent the action of civil authority or preclude the necessity of a civil process, I am at issue with the *principle*." [40]

Blanchet did not fail to reply and to protest vigorously against the attitude of the Methodist minister:

> I should have thought that you would have given me credit for having tried to keep some form of law in the affair of the trial of P. . . . But far from that, you have supposed that I was not ready to join my fellow citizens, to cooperate with them in seeking the best means to bring the guilty to justice. . . . You have supposed that I would constitute myself and name myself judge in this civil affair . . . you declare haughtily that if you had better understood the meaning of my letter you would have refused to send any member of your mission to act with me in the case. And why? because you say, if there were no civil power in the place, it would then be a case for the Hudson's Bay Company. I take notice of the desire you express of respecting an authority without which our moral force would be very small. But when I hear you say that you will refuse to take it from me, because if there is no civil power, either in our colony or in the Hudson's Bay Company, you are ready to meet your fellow citizens, to cooperate

---

[39] Blanchet to Jerome Demers, February 11, 1841. PAA.
[40] Lee to Blanchet, January 11, 1841. PAA.

with them to bring the guilty to justice, it seems to me that
this reason, far from serving you, is just that which you con-
demn in your refusal to come to assist me. For my assembly
was composed of your fellow citizens; it had for its object to
bring a guilty one to justice. Then was the time for you to
show the good will that you boast by cooperating with them to
bring the guilty to justice since all other authority was absent.
And persuaded, as you are, that I have arrogated to myself an
authority, a primacy, unjust in my assembly, was it not your
duty to come to oppose my pretensions, and fight as a good
citizen to preserve the public rights and liberties? [41]

Added to the nineteenth century antipathy between the adherents of Methodism and those of Catholicism, and to the personal antagonism between Lee and Blanchet, is evident a fundamental difference of ideas as to the organization of government in the Oregon territory. On the whole the French Canadian element of the population in the Wilamette Valley was content with the semi-feudal system and supervision of the Hudson's Bay Company; the American, on the other hand, felt itself without protection and longed for the time when the civil institutions of the United States might be established in the west. In this instance Lee apparently believed a beginning had been made toward such an establishment and that its authority extended over all; Blanchet failed to recognize that such existed. He continues his defense:

But if I prove that your suppositions against me are without
foundation, what follows? The proof is found in the simple nar-
ration of what passed during the assembly which I convoked.
Persuaded as I was that no other civil power existed in the colony and the individual at fault being a member of my church,
I felt myself obliged before God and man to take the first steps
to bring the cause to justice. An assembly was convoked. The
Methodist mission was not *shunted aside*. The assembly was
opened by the reading of the copy of the letter which had been
sent you. That of your response followed. It presented objections. According to you, there existed in the place a civil
power. But you did not know whether or not it had jurisdiction over the servants of the Hudson's Bay Company.
Several of the assembly assured us that there was such a power.
The citizen Whitcomb reviewed the rights in the present case,

[41] Blanchet to Lee, January 18, 1841. PAA.

> whose was the right to make inquiries. I had discharged before God and man the obligation of pushing the thing further. Judge by that of my ambition to seize the supreme power. . . . The citizen Whitcomb having announced that if the accused would present himself at the mission, things would be arranged, Johnson came to tell him of it in my presence; and having found him, the day for the meeting was set for Monday. Judge now Sir, as a man frank and honest, of the justice, of the impertinence of your remarks. It is a pity that the citizen Whitcomb who could in a word have told you of this, failed to do so, left you in ignorance; it is a pity that he was so unmindful of doing me justice; he might have spared you the pain of your remarks and me the disagreeable task of answering them.[42]

Blanchet's correspondence does not reveal the final settlement of this case. In itself its importance was not great but nonetheless it reveals some of the practical difficulties of "joint occupation." Blanchet's conclusion shows little of a spirit of compromise and reveals the bitterness that he felt toward the attempted domination of the Methodist group:

> To my way of thinking, your anxiety to know whether or not there is in the place a civil power is out of place, since you have already exercised the rights, the attributes and the jurisdiction of one, even over a citizen who did not perhaps come under your power. Either there is a civil power or there is not. If there is not, why exercise it? If there is, why your anxiety? When you ask me if there are here *two communities*, as someone has said to you, I answer that it is not desirable that there be, for a kingdom divided will be destroyed. But when I see a renewal among mine of plots of which they have been the victims during your absence, the time will not be far distant, when drawing ourselves to one side, we shall, while awaiting the establishment of a good government, govern ourselves under the protection of the Hudson's Bay Company, much better than you could do it for us.
> I close by remarking that it is much better to be lacking in the form than in the principles of justice. . . .[43]

It was perhaps fortunate that another problem soon absorbed the

[42] *Ibid.*
[43] *Ibid.*

interest of all. On February 15, 1841 Ewing Young,[44] pioneer of the Willamette Valley and its wealthiest independent settler, died intestate. A meeting was called at the Methodist mission to arrange for the disposition of his estate. The priest with his people was present. He questioned the legality of the assembly since some of the citizens were not represented on the committee which convened it and complained of the lack of representation in the group which had drawn up the agenda of the work to be accomplished. Nevertheless the meeting got under way.[45] Before proceeding very far, its purpose was greatly enlarged and it was proposed to appoint a committee to draw up a constitution, to formulate a code of laws, to elect a governor, a surpeme judge, a sheriff, three justices of the peace, three constables, three overseers of roads, an overseer of the poor. Blanchet expressed himself as "much astonished." And

> believing that they had already gone too far, wishing to have time to think, and disturbed as to the reaction of the Governor of Vancouver to the proposal of all these things, I suggested that the election of the officers for the different posts be delayed until the first Tuesday in June, with the exception that the nomination of a committee to draw up a constitution and the selection of a supreme judge, a sheriff and constables might be carried through. This was done. . . . Believe me it was with repugnance that I found myself obliged to meddle with civil affairs; it was only to lead my people, to look after their welfare, to prevent them from making false moves and to hinder those who would harm us. I was received with regard, was offered the presiding officer's chair which I refused so as to have the advantage of speaking. . . .[46]

Before the adjournment of the meeting over which Rev. David Leslie presided, Blanchet found himself chosen to head the committee on the new constitution. He found also an opportunity to press home a point he had tried to make in his correspondence with Lee relative to the stolen mission goods. After complimenting the assembly on the progress that had been made that day, he remarked

[44] Young came to Oregon in 1833 but due to the report that he and his party, among them Hall K. Kelley, were horse thieves, McLoughlin failed to extend his usual cordial welcome.

[45] February 18, 1841.

[46] Blanchet to Jerome Demers, February 11, 1841. PAA.

that if there were already a legally established civil power in the place—a power capable of judging the citizens—it appeared that the action of the day might be a condemnation of the acts of that tribunal. Leslie countered by replying that in other days there had been few people in the valley but since the colony was growing it seemed necessary to hold a new election to determine the wishes of all. Blanchet acknowledged that this was just but wondered if the wishes of the majority of the people had been considered at the time of the trial of one of the citizens; wondered if the court which had judged him, had had competence to judge. It had been elected by an assembly of only twelve persons who had given it no rule, no jurisdiction, no code to follow; yet it had dared to assume jurisdiction. He gravely doubted its powers and hoped to bring the matter before the next assembly. The ministers had nothing to say and an adjournment was voted until June.[47]

The difficulty of settlement of the estate of Ewing Young convinced a strong minority among the inhabitants of the Willamette Valley of the necessity of the establishment of some means of control. The American population was small as yet and made up for the most part of transitory groups—fur men, missionaries, government explorers—rather than those who planned to remain permanently in the country. In 1839 a small party, inspired by the series of lectures that Jason Lee had given in Peoria, Illinois in 1837-1838, had come over the Rockies. In 1840 Joel Walker with his wife and children had the distinction of being the first family to cross the plains with the intention of making a home in Oregon. The disruption of the American Fur Company also added to the number of settlers in the Willamette Valley when some of its members were forced to turn to agriculture to gain a livelihood. In 1841 the arrivals were chiefly from the Hudson's Bay Company's Red River settlements. The Company was anxious to settle these in the Puget Sound region so as to strengthen its claims there but they soon discovered the superior charms of the Willamette Valley and within a year or two many of them had moved there.[48] The entire population—Hudson's Bay men, French Canadians, Methodists and the so-called Independents—was not more than 500.

[47] *Ibid.* [48] Carey, *op. cit.*, 420.

These gathered on June 1, 1841 at the "new building near the Catholic Church," all interested in the proposed establishment of local governmental machinery. Blanchet sent an account of the meeting to Quebec:

> The day fixed for the election of the officers who would rule our little colony having arrived, that is the first of June, there was a general assembly of all the American citizens and Canadians in the common room of the house of my habitants. Mr. D. Leslie presided and asked the report of what had been done by the committee charged with the drawing up of a code of laws. As president of said committee charged with the drawing up of a code of laws, I arose and answered that due to lack of time and for various other reasons, the committee had not been called, that nothing had been done; if someone should receive the blame, I charged myself with it; that besides in my opinion and that of my people, the action of such a committee would have been a waste of time, since we were all opposed to the establishment of such a government; that moreover, I was of the opinion that since they had elected three magistrates, some constables and two overseers of roads was not that enough?[49]

The only procedure possible if the work was to continue was to relieve Father Blanchet of the chairmanship, appoint someone in his place and begin over again. This was done and a new date was set for a meeting in October:

> They began the day's work by excusing me and replaced my name according to my wishes. Someone proposed that the committee make report on the code of laws in the same month that they provided for the election of the officers. These two propositions were discussed. It was decided that the election should be held at another assembly when the code of laws should be presented. . . . Since the American, Commodore Wilkes, was about to visit the Columbia, an American suggested that it might be well to postpone the next assembly until the first of October so as to give time to see the Commodore and to learn his views. This counsel prevailed. . . . The committee was also ordered to consult Dr. McLoughlin and Mr. Douglas.[50]

Blanchet's attitude toward the Americans and their plans and

[49] Report of Blanchet to Quebec (unpub.), June 1–October 12, 1841. PAA.
[50] *Ibid.*

projects may seem particularly unsympathetic. It is, however, easily understood. Those most interested in promoting the local government, the group of leaders at the Methodist mission, seemed actuated by a spirit of opposition to the Hudson's Bay Company. This was obvious to Father Blanchet and however much he may have resented the restrictions placed on his activities by the prohibitions of the far-away London committee, his relations with Dr. McLoughlin had always been friendly. His dependence on the bounty of the chief factor and his gratitude to him for his constant assistance precluded any cooperation with a movement that seemed likely to interfere with his power and influence. In addition he was convinced that the attempt to set up a local government was premature and his judgment was confirmed by Commodore Wilkes. That American jurisdiction would eventually be extended over the country south of the Columbia had long been taken for granted by McLoughlin; he realized that the tiny trickle of emigrants who were making their way to the coast would soon swell to a mighty stream and that the rule of the Hudson's Bay Company would be over. When that day came McLoughlin was ready for the new régime.

CHAPTER V

THE APOSTOLATE OF THE INDIANS

Blanchet and Demers came to the Oregon country filled with zeal for the conversion of the native inhabitants. Guided by the instructions of their bishops and inspired by a magnificent ideal, both were prepared to give their best to the new land to which they had been assigned. And yet, as far as one can judge, the work of the first missionaries among the Indian tribes of the northwest was a failure. Their plan was good. Their ideal of service was high. But the difficulties were great, far too great for them to control and as month succeeded month and they were left alone to struggle against handicaps it was impossible to overcome, their reports revealed discouragement, and finally, there came the acknowledgment that the task was too big and that they could do no more.

In 1839 Blanchet had written to his Bishop: "The Lord promises an abundant harvest of souls among the savages of the Columbia; they already have the faith,"[1] and to Bishop Turgeon: "It seems to me that the savages of this country, for the most part, are disposed to receive the Faith."[2] Accordingly the missionaries made their plans. Although their first efforts were directed chiefly toward the Canadian habitants, neither priest failed to recognize that the Indians had need of them, nor were the Indians ever excluded from their ministry. They realized that they could never supply all the demands but they hoped to prepare the way for others, who, they had no doubt, would come to aid and to succeed them.

The tiny settlements of St. Paul and Cowlitz were the centers of their missionary activity. Here they received the chiefs who appealed to them, and from here they undertook journeys to the far distant points of their mission, visiting, if it were at all possible, the tribes who asked their assistance. But the days they could give to each group were far from being sufficient for the task of teaching

---

[1] Blanchet to Signay, March 1, 1839. QAA.
[2] Blanchet to Turgeon, March 13, 1839. QAA.

the natives the Christian religion. They could scarcely make a beginning; there was never more than time to give a few fundamental instructions, perhaps to explain to some willing chief the "Catholic Ladder"[3] so that he might carry on the work. Then, the missionary traveled to the next tribe, promising to return, it is true, but with little hope of being able to fulfil that pledge for many months. Under the circumstances it was the best that could be done. These pioneer missionaries traveled over the Oregon country, instructing, baptizing the children, preparing the way for what they hoped would in time be permanent missions. Both soon realized that it was necessary to have a resident missionary with each tribe or group of tribes and that could not be until help was sent them. They appealed time and again for that help. It was too long in coming. And so the beginnings that promised so much came to nothing.

Blanchet and Demers first met the Indians of the northwest during the course of their journey from Red River to Fort Vancouver. At each of the Hudson's Bay Company's posts the natives had flocked to see the "French chiefs," the "blackgowns," of whom they had heard. The missionaries, with few exceptions, were favorably impressed and their conclusion was usually, "They give us hopes of their conversion." During the first mission at Fort Vancouver (November, 1838-April, 1839) the Indians were not neglected. Demers, who had learned the Chinook jargon, was their teacher and gathered them twice a day to teach them the Sign of the Cross, the Our Father and Hail Mary. Blanchet has left the note that they "were much pleased to learn them."[4]

During the mission at Cowlitz in March, 1839 Blanchet was visited by numerous delegations of Indians who came from remote distances in order to hear and see the "black gown." Among these was one group, led by Chief Tsla-lakum, whose home was Whidby

---

[3] It has been suggested that the "Catholic Ladder" might have been inspired by a study of St. Augustine's methods of teaching catechism. The latter made Bible history the basis of religious instruction. Cf. Joseph P. Christopher, *S. Aureli Augustini Hipponiensis Episcopi de Catechizandis Rudibus* (Washington, D. C., 1926). The pictorial representation seems to have been Blanchet's own contribution. It proved a successful means of instruction and received high praise from De Smet.

[4] Blanchet, *op. cit.*, 25.

Island.⁵ In April in order to forestall Rev. David Leslie, the Methodist minister, who planned to establish a mission for the Indians at Fort Nisqually, Blanchet sent Demers to that place and in August, he himself, went north in order to confirm the work begun by his colleague. Meanwhile Demers, in June, visited again the Indians of Forts Colville, Okanogan and Walla Walla.

The contacts of this first year were sufficient to enable the priests to form an estimate of the needs of the country and it was not long before Blanchet sent an appeal to Quebec, describing the possibilities and begging for more priests:

> To do good here and to carry on the instruction of the savages, we should have about ten priests, placed as follows:
> 1. Two at Colville or nearby to instruct the Kootamies, the Flatheads, the men of Colville and the Okanogans; and besides the Canadians, the women and children at Fort Colville. That is a task, even for two priests on account of the greatness of the distances;
> 2. two others at Fort Nez Percés to the south or to the north on the Yakima River—that place has been praised for the many savages, Yakimas, Nez Percés, Walla Wallas, another rich nation called the Cayuse, and for the savages forty leagues below at the falls of the Grand Dalles and those of Priest Rapids; the task will be immense;
> 3. a fifth missionary at Vancouver for the Canadians, their wives and children and the savages of the Cascades and the neighboring country;
> 4. a sixth at Willamette for the habitants and the numerous savages of the upper river, where a mission will be well placed;
> 5. a seventh on the lower Columbia near Fort George for the many savages near the sea and at the mouth of the river;
> 6. an eighth at Cowlitz for the Canadians and the savages of the place;
> 7. a ninth and tenth at Fort Nisqually, built to the south of Bay St. George, for the many tribes of savages who live in this district.⁶

⁵ *Ibid.*, 31; it was with this group that Blanchet first experimented with the plan that developed into the "Catholic Ladder." A square rule which the Indians called *Sahale stick* (stick from above) was the forerunner of the later elaborate chart.

⁶ Blanchet to Turgeon, March 13, 1839. QAA.

Had it been possible to carry out such a plan great might have been the accomplishment. But it called for ten priests. Ten priests! and they were but two. Nevertheless Blanchet and Demers made a gallant attempt in the next few years so to direct their efforts that they might be as effective as possible. Neither seems to have been able to withstand an appeal for assistance, even after they began to realize, as they did very soon, that the first enthusiastic reaction of the redmen did not mean a sincere conversion to Christianity. The obstacles to that were deep rooted. Blanchet listed the three he considered most important, "Experience has taught us that we must not count too much on the first appearances of good will from the savages. Their old customs and usages of jugglery, medicine, polygamy are the handicaps which we will overcome by the grace of God, but which retard the progress of the Gospel among them."[7] Demers confirmed the judgment of his superior:

> Experience has taught us not to rely too much on the first demonstrations of the Indians nor on the first dispositions they manifest.... Everywhere we meet the same obstacles which always retard the conversion of the Indians, namely: polygamy, their adherence to the customs of their ancestors, and still more to tamanwas, the name given to the medicines they prepare for the sick.... Hand play is also very common among them, they get excited and often end it with a quarrel. They add idolatry to infidelity. They paint on a piece of wood a rough likeness of a human being and keep it very preciously. They believe these charms have a superior power and strength, and they pray to them.... You may see that progress has been very slow among them so far; their customs and habits are so inveterate that it will take a long time for religion and the fear and knowledge of God to uproot and destroy them entirely. Polygamy is not as widely spread now as it used to be, but there is in both sexes a fearful immorality. It is kept up and often taught by the whites, who, by their scandalous conduct and boundless debaucheries, destroy the impressions made by the truths of religion.[8]

[7] Blanchet to Turgeon, March 19, 1840. QAA.

[8] Demers to Cazeault, February 5, 1840, quoted in Blanchet, *op. cit.*, 38-39; polygamy was evidently a means of strengthening political and commercial influence. Such is the opinion of Simpson, "... in order to strengthen their commercial relations men of consequence or extensive traders have sometimes as many as half a Doz Wives selected from among

However, the savages continued to come and the missionaries were encouraged in spite of obvious difficulties and made plans for their conversion.

It is not possible to follow in minute detail the story of the missionary labors during the next few years. Blanchet and Demers traveled north and south, east and west, gradually expanding their knowledge of the country and becoming acquainted with many of the tribes who inhabited the region. Roughly, there were three centers for their work: the Columbia River Valley with its numerous nations; the Puget Sound area from which came Chief Tsla-lakum; and New Caledonia, the home of the Carriers and the Atnas. With the exception of the last, the evangelization of which was begun in 1842, the missionaries at first tried to visit all the territory each year. This was soon recognized as being impracticable and as new and more pressing demands were made on their time, the visitation of the Indian nations was gradually abandoned.

It is difficult at the present time to identify and properly classify all the tribes with whom the whites came in contact during the period of exploration and settlement of the Pacific northwest. Due to the variety in the spelling of names and to the fact that many of the tribes were migratory, having come from districts far east of the Rocky Mountains, it is almost impossible to decide with accuracy the groups that were native to the Oregon country.[9] Hoopes claims

the best Families of the Neighboring tribes and each of these is entrusted with a small Outfit and sent on trading excursions to Her Friends and relatives . . . ," Merk, *op. cit.*, 98; and Demers to Blanchet, April 22, 1839. QAA. writes, " It seems, from what I can see, that this [polygamy] will be, at least for some, the greatest obstacle to their conversion. Polygamy is a political matter with them. A chief, for instance, has 4 wives, one from one nation, another from another for the sake of security with the nation of each of these wives."

[9] Carey, *op. cit.*, 48, lists the principal groups, classified with reference to linguistic stocks, referred to in Oregon history. Cf. Joel V. Berreman, *Tribal Distribution in Oregon* (Pennsylvania, 1937), Albert B. Lewis, *Tribes of the Columbia Valley and the Coast of Washington and Oregon* (Pennsylvania, 1906), Leslie Spier, *Tribal Distribution in Washington* (Menasha, Wis., 1936), H. E. Tobie, *The Willamette Valley before the Great Immigrations* (M. A. thesis, unpub., University of Oregon, 1927), George Gibbs, " Tribes of Western Washington and North Western Oregon," *U. S. Geographical and Geological Survey of the Rocky Mountain Region*, I (1877), 157-241.

that there were about sixty different tribes and bands of Indians.[10] These included representatives of the most extensive Indian families of America. The Athapascan group appears in several isolated tribes on the coast, on the Willapa and Chihalis rivers, Wapato Island and along the Oregon shore. The Blue Mountains, which lie within the Oregon country, were the home of the Shoshoneans. The local representatives of the family were the Shoshones and Bannocks. Another general name for them was Snakes. The Salishans inhabited western Montana, northern Idaho and Washington, most of the southern mainland of British Columbia and the southeastern part of Vancouver Island, as well as a strip of the northern coast of the present state of Oregon. They were most numerous on Puget Sound. The Shahaptian family formerly extended from the Rockies to the Cascades and from (including) the Yakima Valley and the Palouse country to the Blue Mountains. These tribes were intelligent and brave and generally friendly toward the whites, though jealous of encroachment upon their lands. The only move to extend their territory took place in the west, when disease depopulated the Willamette Valley and the lower Columbia region in 1829 and the Klikitats moved across the Cascades for awhile. The Chinooks held their positions on the Columbia, however, and the Shahaptian villages on the river were kept east of the Dalles. The principal tribes were the Nez Percés and the Yakimas. The Walla Wallas occupied an important position at the crossroads of travel on the lower Walla Walla River and along the east bank of the Columbia from the Snake nearly to the Umatilla. The Waiilatpuan family had two divisions, the Molalla in the Molalla Valley, Oregon, and the Cayuses in what is now Washington. The Chinooks lived on the Columbia River from its mouth to the Dalles and were long in control.[11]

Blanchet estimated the Indian population of 1838 as 110,000 but his number seems too large. It was probably around 100,000 in 1828 but in that year and several times in the decade following, an epidemic, the exact nature of which is not known, swept through the Indian villages, entirely destroying the population of many of them. Parrish claims that the Indians were reduced to 20,000;[12] Wilkes

[10] Hoopes, *op. cit.*, n. 2, 69.   [11] Fuller, *op. cit.*, 37-40.
[12] Philip A. Parrish, *Before the Covered Wagon* (Portland, 1934), 270.

gives the same number for 1841;[13] and Lane, writing to the Secretary of War in October, 1849, gives the population as 24,433.[14]

Estimates of the character of the Indian tribes vary from outright condemnation to genuine admiration. Sperlin says that his studies of the early journals show that the Indians received the strangers hospitably, that they practised a simple, unostentatious religion, that they were men of honor, of industry and of physical skill, that their government was simple but efficient, that the home embodied strong attachments, though it exhibited at times improperly apportioned burdens. Indian vices, not necessarily crimes, were such as improvidence, gambling and cruel treatment of enemies; but we cannot justly charge the race with the alleged crimes of treachery and drunkenness, nor with atheism nor idolatry.[15]

[13] Charles Wilkes, *U. S. Exploring Expedition*, V, 140; Carey, *op. cit.*, 48, says, " The estimate of Lewis and Clark was that there were some 16,000 Chinooks, and early accounts indicate that other tribes in the Oregon Country were numerous, so that the indian population at the beginning of the nineteenth century was probably near fifty thousand. But in 1824 and 1829 smallpox and what was designated as ague fever, an ailment the exact nature of which is not now recognized, swept off thousands of these people. Competent authority estimates destruction of four-fifths of the native population in a single summer." Cf. Leslie M. Scott, " Indian Diseases as Aids to Pacific Northwest Settlement," *OHQ*, XXIX (1928), 144-161.

[14] Quoted in Hoopes, *op. cit.*, n. 2, 69.

[15] O. B. Sperlin, " The Indian of the Northwest as Revealed by the Earliest Journals," *OHQ*, XVII (1916), 1; Clark, *Willamette Valley*, I, 69, remarks, " Looking at these early settlers of Oregon as nearly as possible from the Indian viewpoint, we must believe that they were succeeding in their system of life. . . . Nothing so disproves the supposed inferiority of these Indians as their well-built houses, wonderful canoes, and commissary accomplishments," but, " The Indian system of living was incompatible with that of the whites. We must concede that the Indians of the Willamette Valley were unusually peaceful, friendly, and hospitable and that they were in general more tolerant of the whites than might have been expected. We must also say for the first white settlers . . . that they adjusted themselves to the Indian system remarkably well and overlooked more exasperating shortcomings than was usual. Yet the pilfering, superstition, filth and vindictiveness made them undesirable neighbors for the whites and the business instincts of the early occupants made them willing to drive the Indian from his ancestral home or reduce him to peonage, while vices and diseases introduced by the intruder degraded and decimated

Carey thinks that "this estimate is in the main justified by the record although the presentation may be criticised as rather the brief of an advocate than the unbiased conclusion of an historian." [16] He continues, "the Indians on the Pacific Coast no doubt differed greatly in their honesty, and some tribes were more treacherous and more bloodthirsty and cruel than others."

Contact with the whites had few happy results for the Indian tribes on the coast. Fuller claims that contact with mariners and fur traders introduced temptations which disrupted the moral conventions of the natives.[17] Social diseases spread without check and increased the infant death rate, which was already high on account of unsanitary conditions and the practice of infanticide. Commercialized relations with the whites immediately relaxed all restraint within the tribe and brought despair to the missionaries who found it almost impossible to do anything for the degraded people.

According to the plan for the summer of 1840,[18] the Chinooks who lived around Fort George were the first tribe to be visited. In general, the missionaries had not been favorably impressed with this nation which lived scattered along the Columbia River from Fort Vancouver to the Pacific Ocean. Nor do the Indians, at least those who lived near the Fort, seem to have regarded the priests with approval. But in March, 1839 the group at Fort George had sent deputies, one of their chiefs with some of his men, to ask the missionaries to visit and instruct them.[19] Blanchet had written of them, "There is a large camp of Chinooks at Fort George who do not seem indifferent; they want us to visit them. No one knows

the native population. Previous to the coming of the whites the Indians had been able to maintain themselves since their chief struggle had been with nature; but they lacked protective moral customs, medical knowledge and adequate weapons with which to withstand the white invasions."

[16] Carey, *op. cit.*, 51.

[17] Fuller, *op. cit.*, 31; MacKay, *op. cit.*, 192, characterizes the coast Indians as of "amiable disposition, verminous condition, absence of chastity and prevalence of venereal disease," and nearly every writer calls attention to the disastrous effect the arrival of the whites had on conditions among the Indians. Cf. Ross Cox, *Adventures on the Columbia River* (New York, 1832), Paul Kane, *Wanderings of an Artist among the Indians of North America* (Toronto, 1925), Daniel W. Harmon, *A Journal of Voyages and Travels in the Interior of North America* (New York, 1903).

[18] *Rapport* (1842), 55 ff.   [19] Blanchet, *op. cit.*, 21.

when we will be able." [20] It was more than a year later that time was found to respond to the appeal of these savages, and it was Father Demers who gave the first mission among them. It lasted for three weeks.[21] At its close the priest returned to Vancouver so as to be there to meet the brigade of *porteurs* with whom he left toward the end of June to visit the posts along the Columbia. Three months were devoted to the peoples of Forts Colville, Okanogan and Walla Walla [22] and it was not until October and Demers rejoined Father Blanchet at St. Paul.

In March, 1840 the two priests again met at Fort Vancouver, to arrange for the work of the summer. Writing at this time to Bishop Turgeon, Blanchet gave an encouraging report of their progress among the tribesmen:

> The power of the Methodists decreases; they destroy themselves and make themselves despised, hated by all. The savages whom they gained at first by all sorts of ruses, lies and promises of presents, abandon them little by little, as they have a chance to discover the truth for themselves. Those whom we gained first are, in general, firm as rocks. Such are those of Nisqually and the Bay, some who live near Colville, at Walla Walla, at Vancouver and at Fort George. Several savages of Okanogan spent the winter near my chapel; received instructions and left this spring to return to their country. Crosses, rosaries, pictures, "Catholic Ladders" are much esteemed by these nations.[23]

But he realized that there were still many obstacles to overcome. It was difficult to get the people together; most of them lived at

[20] Blanchet to Signay, March 1, 1839. QAA.

[21] Blanchet, *op. cit.*, 42-43. It was an odd coincidence that just as Demers arrived at Fort George, the "great re-inforcement" for the Methodist mission crossed the bar of the Columbia, bringing men and help of all kinds to those whom Demers and his companion regarded as "emissaries of Satan."

[22] Demers to Blanchet, March 8, 1840. QAA.

[23] Blanchet to Turgeon, March 18, 1841. QAA. With regard to the Methodist missions, William J. Ghent, *The Road to Oregon* (New York, 1929), 35, says, "The Methodist missions had, however, by 1840 about run their course. The Indians had proved intractable, and the missionaries and their lay helpers had become more interested in business ventures and in politics than in the seemingly futile task of converting the heathen."

some distance from the chapel and found it hard to come every day for instructions: "The men are held back during the seasons of sowing and harvest and during the rainy months; and the women must look after their homes, milk their cows, etc.; they can scarcely abandon them in the good season."[24]

The month of January, 1841 was brightened by the conversion of Chief Pohpoh whose tribe, the Clackamas, lived on the banks of the Clackamas River, which flows into the Willamette about a mile from the Falls. Pohpoh was hired as a guide by Augustine Rochon, Blanchet's servant, and in that capacity first came to St. Paul. The story of his conversion is vividly told by Father Blanchet:

> . . . this chief arrived and found my instructions so much to his taste that after a few days he declared that for the two years he had been following the ministers he had been blind and deaf but that now he began to open his eyes and ears, to see and to hear. I showed him sacred vessels, chalices, the altar, rosaries, medals, etc. I spent four days instructing him. I explained the "Catholic Ladder" to him many times. He understood and remembered all remarkably. "Le chemin de travers" struck him especially. He easily accepted that Jesus Christ had instituted but one way (religion) to lead to heaven. The principal texts of Sacred Scripture, which prove the primacy of St. Peter, impressed him. He was astonished to see that after 900 years, three men had wished to trace another route to heaven, etc., etc. . . . He left joyous and resolved to reject Methodism and to make his people catholic. I promised to go to visit him when I went to Vancouver.[25]

The Indian chief returned to his home where Alvin Waller, the Methodist minister, soon learned of his defection. If we may trust Blanchet's account, he made great efforts to regain the Indian but Pohpoh refused to be influenced and began the task of spreading Catholic doctrine among his people. In February, 1841 when the missionary visited the tribe he found that the savages had been well instructed. They received him gladly. Pohpoh's conversion caused much comment among the Indians but when he tried to gain recruits among the Cascades they for a time refused to listen to him. Blanchet, however, was much encouraged by his response and

---

[24] *Rapport* (1843), 25.
[25] Blanchet to Turgeon, March 18, 1841. QAA.

planned to build a mission on his lands to serve as a center from which Catholicism might be propagated far and near.

In May he again visited this tribe. Waller was still present and came to reproach Blanchet for encroaching on his territory. Blanchet's reply was not calculated to improve the feelings between the two, "My response was that my mission in the Columbia did not except any part of the country; that not considering him a true missionary, my duty was to disabuse the savages of the false doctrine, which he taught them." [26] The Indians seem to have stood around and listened to the altercation and one of them, more enterprising than the rest, went in search of the " Evangelical Ladder " [27]

---

[26] *Rapport* (1843), 36.

[27] Mrs. Spalding, wife of the Presbyterian minister at Lapwai, designed a Protestant ladder intended to counteract the influence of Blanchet's device. A copy of this is reproduced in *OHQ*, XXXVII (1936) along with an explanatory article by Nellie B. Pipes, " The Protestant Ladder," 237-240. Miss Pipes gives a letter of Spalding to the board, February 12, 1846, in which he explains the ladder:

" Two meetings on the sabbath where I exhibited the Protestant chart which by the way I will here describe & the cause of it. The Catholics in this country have had printed (I suppose in the states) a vast No of small charts on which the Road to Heaven is exhibited & from which Luther is represented as branching off in a road that leads to hell. . . . They tell the people that Luther laid down his black gown & cross together & went off on the Road to hell after a wife & never returned & that all American preachers i e all Protestants are on the same road to destruction. To meet this attack I have planed & Mrs. S. has drawn & printed a chart about 6 feet long & 2 feet wide containing two ways one narrow & one broad. After representing briefly some of the important events of the world before the Christian era & the crucifixion of Christ I come to Paul whom I represent as pointing to one who has turned off from the narrow way where he has left his wife & children & with black gown on & a cross in his hand is just entering the Broad road. A few of Paul's prophecies concerning the man of sin are translated & printed as proceeding from his mouth such as he shall forbid to marry & after he has left his wife & entered the Broad Road he is represented as the Pope with a sword in one hand & torch or fagot in the other, a king kissing one foot & a bishop the other. Further up he is represented with 5 children by his side & again as receiving the bleeding head of Admiral Coligny who was beheaded at the great slaughter of St. Bartholomew & his head sent by Charles IX to the Pope who ordered public thanks to be given to Charles & a jubalee to be proclaimed throughout France. Boniface IX & Benedict XIII are represented as contending with deadly

of the minister and having found it, compared it with that of the priest. "The savages saw with their own eyes that the religion of this poor Mr. Waller did not begin with Jesus Christ." The minister reproached his former neophytes with their lack of constancy; threatened them with fever, sickness, death but not being able to move them, he finally took his hat and left.

His departure did not clear away all the difficulties. There were others. The chiefs of the tribe were jealous of Pohpoh. Blanchet had been giving his instruction from Pohpoh's tent. That had to be given up. New disturbances broke out when Pohpoh was commissioned to distribute provisions. The priest was on the point of losing all the fruit of his mission. So, after assuring Pohpoh that he held first place in his heart, he withdrew him from all active service and distributed the offices of honor to some of the others.[28]

After four days of instruction, Blanchet began to feel that he had gained the confidence of twelve lodges. Waller's conduct had helped. But, on the fifth, came disaster. His savages joined with the Molallas who lived at a short distance, in games of chance. It proved impossible to draw them away; religious instruction had no charms in comparison with those of the games. There was nothing for the missionary to do but to seek other fields.[29]

He returned in September, however. But in spite of the reassurances of Pohpoh, he found the lack of interest appalling. This, he acknowledged was partially the fault of the missionaries who, by staying away for so long a period of time, allowed the Indians to

weapons. Tetzel receiving a sum of money from a young man whose father has escaped hell all but one of his feet, is represented. A Nunnery is drawn from which a young priest has come out & is paying 18s to get the sin of Fornication pardoned. . . . Some of those burnt in queen Marys reign are drawn, the Burning of Bibles in the N of N y State is drawn. Luther is represented as leaving the Broad road & returning to the narrow way. The end of the Man of Sin is represented by his falling back into hell at the approach of the Lord Jesus Christ who is coming in the clouds of heaven with his holy angels. . . . "

[28] *Rapport* (1843), 37.

[29] The Indians seem to have had a passion for games of chance and according to Clark, *Willamette Valley*, I, 57, " With great recklessness and good sportmanship, the participants would risk trinkets, ornaments, clothing, wives, and even themselves as slaves."

lose touch with the instructions they had received. Blanchet visited the Clackamas a third time in December, 1841. Mr. Perkins had joined Mr. Waller and the priest was somewhat uneasy about their combined influence over his converts. But they were more faithful than he had expected and he rejoiced that the ministers could gather only a handful in contrast to his forty worshippers:

> All the chiefs were on my side. The ministers, seeing that they could gain nothing, retired after having witnessed the triumph of the cross over their cold and insignificant ceremony. They had for nothing employed all their talents and means of persuasion to entrap Pohpoh; he remained firm. " No, he answered them, " it is finished; I will not change; my eyes and my ears are opened since the priest spoke to me. Were not your fathers Catholic? Who began your way (religion) ? Was it not men like me? What right had they to change what Jesus Christ had established so long before? What right to abolish what was good? [30]

In September, 1841 Blanchet had visited the Cascades at Willamette Falls. Their chief, Tamakoun, had come to Vancouver, where he received instructions; now, he welcomed the missionary among his people. The priest erected his tent and then began the visitation of the scattered families. He found only young men in the village; the old had been destroyed by the fever. His explanations of the " Catholic Ladder " continued for several days, until it was time for the Indians to make ready for the departure for Vancouver Island, where they spent the winter, finding it less rigorous and the chase more abundant. Blanchet accompanied them to the foot of the Falls, where they remained a few days. Each day the priest visited the lodges—a task made necessary by the indifference of the natives. Fever attacked some of them and the missionary lacking the necessary remedies to care for the invalids, they applied to an old woman who claimed to have skill for cures. In the general indifference, Tamakoun was some consolation to the missionary. He spent the evenings with the priest speaking of religion. The mission ended with final instructions when the savages were ready to move on. Blanchet estimated the number as from 150 to

[30] Blanchet to Turgeon, March 18, 1841. QAA.

200. He baptized some of the children but the adults were far from ready to receive this favor.[31]

Due to the enterprising zeal of Chief Tsla-lakum who visited the missionaries at Cowlitz in the spring of 1839, the tribes of Puget Sound were among the first to share in the ministrations of the pioneer priests. Demers traveled north to Fort Nisqually in April, 1839 and a few months later in August Blanchet too made the trip in order to continue the work already begun. Great was the enthusiasm aroused and encouraged by the zeal of Mr. and Mrs. Kitson, instructions were carried on after the departure of the priest to whom good reports were sent from time to time. Demers relayed one of the messages in November, " Since I have been here, a chief of the Snohomis, whom we had not seen before, has come; he gave me the happiest news of all the savages whom we saw at Nisqually; prayers are said regularly . . . delinquents are punished severely and the women are compelled to submit to the law. . . . I gave him a chronological ladder and a picture." [32]

In the spring of 1840, when Blanchet and Demers met at Cowlitz to plan the summer's work, word was brought to the vicar general that Mr. Kitson was ill. He left immediately (May 14) for Nisqually. Two days later after a tiresome journey on horseback over dangerous roads, along mountain paths, he crossed the Nisqually River without accident and early on the evening of May 16 was at the bedside of his friend. After attending to the needs of Mr. Kitson, Blanchet began a mission for the Indians of the fort which lasted till May 27. The mornings were given to the instruction of the wives and children of the Canadians, the rest of the day to the savages. Mrs. Kitson gave valuable aid by acting as interpreter with the Nisqually and Flathead Indians. Blanchet was pleased with the "charming simplicity" of his people, to whom he taught the truths of Christianity and the prayers, "as one would little children, and God blessed this occupation by enlightening the intelligence of my poor neophytes."

---

[31] *Rapport* (1843), 43; Tobie, *op. cit.*, 109, says that the medicine men and women often had a real knowledge of medicinal herbs and effected many cures, especially of external disorders. Demers in a letter to Blanchet, April 22, 1839. QAA., describes one of the " cures " he witnessed.

[32] Demers to Blanchet, November 4, 1839. QAA.

While he was busy with the Indians of the fort, a number of chiefs from the islands of Puget Sound, hearing of his presence, came to see him with some of their people. There might have been more had it not been that civil war was being waged among the tribes. A savage had run away with his sister, the wife of a Sockwamish, and her husband had re-taken his wife and killed his brother-in-law. Such a crime could not go unpunished and the tribes prepared for war. Blanchet remarks that under the circumstances the chiefs from a distance could not profit from the benefits of his mission: " I was sensibly saddened that the demon of discord, in sowing the seeds of division among these savage people deprived them of the benefits of the mission." But on the other hand:

> . . . among all those who frequented the mission, I remarked always an impressive desire to know the way to eternal life. They came at the first sound of the bell; they gave perfect attention to my words; and after the public instruction, the young men gathered around my room, to hear again the manner of making the Sign of the Cross and of giving the heart to God. How sad it is for a missionary to have his time so limited that he must change his place before having, so to say, put his hand to the work! There are so many souls who perish that a missionary would wish to carry to all the help of his ministry; but in this vast country, he would need the wings of an angel to fly everywhere there are souls in need of his aid.[33]

The priest was preparing to bring the mission to a close on May 26 when a delegation from Whidby Island, six men and a woman, Chief Tsla-lakum's wife and men, appeared to beg the favor of a visit from the missionary. Nothing could have been more to his liking and so, having arranged for a canoe and an interpreter, the priest set out to sail over " the beautiful Puget Sound." Blanchet remarks plaintively, " I had often in other times while I was in Canada looked at this bay on the maps. I was now traveling over it, far from my dear country, alone in the midst of savages. . . . This thought was little likely to animate my courage. But the religion which goes everywhere where there are miseries to succor and tears to dry, pointed out to me souls formed to the image of God, who languish in the shadows of death, and joy so filled my

---

[33] *Rapport* (1842), 57.

heart that I found my lot a thousand times more happy than that of the great and rich of the century." [34]

The canoes sailed east skirting the coast of an island where the Snohomishs lived, ruled over by a chief named Le Français; the island of the Skewamishs, whose chief visited Demers the preceding winter at Cowlitz and who had returned well-satisfied with his reception by the "black gown;" the island of the Skagits, thirty leagues from Nisqually in the middle of the Sound, and came finally to the lands of Tsla-lakum. From there the missionary looked across to Vancouver Island, where lived the Yougletas, a fierce and barbarous nation, the terror of neighboring tribes; and toward the mouth of the Fraser, the home of the Cowitchins, as well as toward the lands of the Klalams.[35]

The task of instructing the followers of Chief Tsla-lakum was accompanied by pleasant surprises. To the joy of the missionary, the Indians knew the prayers and their chief leading them, pronounced the words "just as fervent Christians." He began a hymn to the tune, *Tu vas remplir le voeu de ta tendresse*, and all joined and continued. He began another to the Blessed Virgin, *Je mets ma confiance*, and found that the savages knew that as well. "I blessed God for the surprising progress that the Chief Tsla-lakum had made with this poor people before the arrival of the missionaries in these far-away regions. I admired the happy dispositions of these pagan people for the faith and the extraordinary means which divine Providence had taken for spreading to them its light. I congratulated myself on my good fortune, and my joy manifested itself by tears." [36]

In a short time other groups joined them. The chiefs Netlam (Skagit) and Witskalatche (Snohomish) had not been outdone by Tsla-lakum but had taught their peoples what they knew and now brought them to the missionary. Others came still later, among

---

[34] *Ibid.*, 59.

[35] Spier, *op. cit.*, has notes on the Snohomish, Skagit and Klalam Indians. Cf. Frederick W. Hodge, *Handbook of American Indians North of Mexico* (Washington, 1912), for Cowichans and Yougletas. The latter which Hodge gives under the names, Lekwiltok and Ucluelet, bore the reputation of being the most warlike tribe on the coast and were considered the terror and scourge of the others.

[36] *Rapport* (1842), 63.

them a Klalam. On Saturday, May 30, a large number arrived from various points of the island and showed themselves attentive to the instructions of the missionary. After Mass, Blanchet accompanied by some of the chiefs, visited the camps on the island noting the customs and manner of living.

Sunday, May 31, 1840 was a gala occasion. Early came the Skagits with their wives and children, the great chief, Netlam, at their head. Witskalatche, dressed as a Frenchman with trousers, shirt, under vest all decorated with porcupine quills, hat, cravatte, everything complete, appeared at the head of his people, accompanied by several lesser chiefs. Tsla-lakum brought the Sokwamishs. Each Indian, following his rank, placed himself according to a solemn ceremonial. Altogether there were more than 400 persons. The missionary was moved, " I could not control my emotion at the sight of this great assemblage so desirous for the kingdom of heaven; at the chant so pure and so expressive, whose natural accents seem to me to surpass in beauty the greatest compositions of the musical masters." Holy Mass being over, the missionary suggested dinner:

> Salmon and smoked vension were served on grass mats, and the guests seated around, joy on their faces, did honor to this splendid repast, served without other table service than that provided by nature. There followed a great smoke, sign of peace and union among the nations, and for that I was not niggardly with the tobacco. In the midst of the noisy, joyous talk of that assembly, a cry attracted the attention of all; the crowd arose. A large cross twenty four feet in length, prepared the night before, was now brought forward, majestically carried on the shoulders of several savages amid the acclamation of all the rest. They brought it to the place where it was to be planted and the missionary solemnly blessed it. Each imitated the black robe in adoring Jesus on the cross by prostrating and venerating this sacred wood which carried the price of the salvation of the human race. The air echoes the chant of the hymns, repeated by this multitude of savages, giving homage for the first time to the true God. This touching spectacle was succeeded by another. The women and children placed themselves in two lines, the rest of the crowd ranged itself at the ends, and I took my place in the middle with the chiefs and fathers of the children. I questioned; I exacted promises; I explained again the creation, the fall of Adam, the redemption, the institution of the seven medicines

(the seven sacraments) and particularly baptism. What was the attention and unanimity of faith in Jesus Christ and His holy Church! How touching must have been the cry carried by the angels to the throne of the Eternal! Yes, we believe in God who created all. . . . Yes, we believe in Jesus Christ who has redeemed us. . . . Yes, we believe that He has instituted seven medicines to sanctify us. . . . Yes, we believe that Jesus Christ made but one way to go to heaven. Yes, we promise to keep and follow the way of the black robe, which was made by Jesus Christ; and we reject those who have been made since by men. . . . Yes, we renounce the devil . . . his thoughts . . . his words . . . his actions. . . . Yes, we want to know, love and serve the great Master. Then began the ceremonies of baptism which lasted four hours during which the priest baptized 122 children.[37]

On June 2 the missionary began his return journey well satisfied with the progress that had been made. " The time I had spent in the midst of them [the savages] seemed very short to me and my weariness was repaid a hundred times." Before leaving, he promised to send them a priest as soon as possible. He encouraged the chiefs to see that their people followed his instructions and to reject all other " ways " which might be pointed out to them. He urged the resumption of peaceful relations among the tribes and had the happiness of seeing negotiations begun toward that end. Several stops were made on the way to Nisqually where Blanchet prayed and instructed the crowds of Indians who invariably assembled. They left Whidby Island finally at 3 o'clock on June 3. " The water was contrary to us, the heat stifling, the natural laziness of the savages wearying to me. But my sight was rejoiced by the beauty of the sites, reflected in the water as in a mirror. I saw in all its beauty, Mt. Rainier, which majestically raises its cone-shaped summit, always covered with snow. This peak does not seem to be a part of a chain of mountains, but as I said in another report, seated in the midst of vast forests."[38] When they arrived at Nisqually on June 4 they found to their joy that Mr. Kitson was much improved and so the missionary left immediately for Cowlitz.

In 1841 the work in the north was confided to Demers who seems at that time to have been an enthusiastic believer in the possibility

---

[37] *Ibid.*, 67-68.   [38] *Ibid.*, 71-72.

of converting the Indians. He left Cowlitz in August accompanied by an old Canadian who had begged the privilege of traveling with him. A few days only were spent at Nisqually for most of the natives were away and so the priest went on to the camp of the Sokwamishs, where he found Tsla-lakum. He would have liked to spend some time on Whidby Island where it was the custom of the savages to gather at this time—some to harvest the root, karnace; others to fish; but his ambition was to travel north to the Fraser River to meet the peoples who lived there. Real difficulty lay in the way of his plan. The Cowichans who lived on the lower Fraser had threatened to kill the priest as soon as they met him; and the Yougletas, a strong nation of cannibals, who lived near the sea, at the mouth of the Fraser, were on the point of one of their incursions.

But in spite of the danger, Chief Tsla-lakum offered to accompany the missionary and furnish him with a canoe. They stopped first with the Snohomishs who had heard Father Blanchet the year before. This tribe welcomed the missionary with universal rejoicing. " So many beautiful sentiments in a savage people at the sight of the humble representative of Jesus Christ," he wrote, "made me lament my shortcomings. Chosen by the Lord to announce the good tidings to the pagans, I had not, like the apostle, an areopagus to convert and wise men to instruct, but a poor people, docile and desirous of having their eyes opened to the light. God wished to do all by the sole power of His grace and to show man that He had no need of his work." Three chiefs asked to be allowed to accompany him for the rest of the voyage and nothing could have pleased him better. As his group climbed into the canoes and began the long trip the people gathered on the banks and shouted good wishes: " Go, our brothers, don't fear; our father the priest is with you. He will speak to the Great Chief on high (God). It is for him that you expose your life. If you lose your lives, you will be happy to have lost them for him and with our father." [39]

This was the evening of August 21. The missionary and his Indian friends judged it wise to continue their travel during the night to avoid possible attacks. Even so, they did not feel altogether secure:

[39] *Rapport* (1843), 57.

We had been wearily rowing for some hours; and sleep threatened to overpower us, when we heard from a distance a menacing cry, which made us fear we had fallen into an ambush. Soon a second, then a third cry, came from different directions. My party, alarmed, made ready for any contingency; the guns were charged and placed ready at hand; the oars dipped in and out of the water without a sound; we sailed as fast as possible in gloomy silence for four long hours, and finally fear left us; with the coming of day, we were with our friends at the fort of the Skagits.[40]

Demers received an eager welcome. Since the day was Sunday, an altar was soon set up and the Holy Sacrifice was offered for the first time in this land. There followed the usual baptism of the children, the customary distribution of presents. Late in the evening the missionary bade farewell to this group and the next morning was at the camp of the Wholerneils.[41] Two of the first men of the Skagits had now joined his party, which included seven great chiefs. According to the missionary, " This noble escort was well calculated to inspire the savages with a high idea of the distinguished character of the great chief of the French, of 'papa le prête,' as they called him."

The reception given by the Wholerneils seems to have transcended all others. Their enthusiasm was so great and seemed to Demers so sincere that he remarks, " Here they honored me as if it were my feast, and I had not to offer to the Eternal Father a single taste of the bitter chalice of which His Son, my divine Redeemer, drank." [42]

The Cowichans, whose home was but a short distance away, hearing of the arrival of the priest among their neighbors, sent one of their chiefs to assure him of their friendliness. His good dispositions " reassured me perfectly about the pretended plot to assassinate me, of which they were suspected."

A chief of the Skagits went ahead to tell the habitants of Fort Langley that the priest was on his way. Hence, when Demers and his Indian escort arived they found Mr. Yale, the commandant,

[40] *Ibid.*, 58.

[41] I have not been able to identify this tribe. It is possible that it belonged to the Skagit groups.

[42] *Rapport* (1843), 61.

with the employees of the Company and five or six hundred savages awaiting them. The flag of the fort was raised and the cannon saluted with seven rounds in honor of the occasion. The missionary found some work with the Company employees, eight Canadians, one Iroquois and some Kanaks, inhabitants of the Sandwich Islands, all having wives and children in the manner of the country. But he had come north for the savages and to them he gave his principal attention.

On his arrival they came to meet him, extending their hands with respect and a certain fear. Nearly all knew how to make the Sign of the Cross and to sing several hymns. The nations scattered through the country had taught each other what they had learned and remembered of the instructions of the previous year. Thus the missionary "found souls prepared and eager to hear of the kingdom of heaven!" Shortly after his arrival, Demers met one of the dreaded Yougletas, who, through a recent alliance had formed a friendship with the Wholerneils. Demers describes him as a man of remarkable stature and of distinguished appearance. He was constant in his attendance at the instructions and even brought one of his children to be baptized. As for himself, "I am wicked," he said, "as are those of my nation, because we do not know the great chief on high, of whom I have heard you speak for the first time. But I shall not reject the word that you have announced and I promise you that I will carry it to my people when I return among them." [43]

The assemblies were held a short distance from the fort on a clear prairie. Demers estimated the number of savages as from 1500 to 1600, all of whom listened with attention and unbelievable interest. The number was increased on September 6 to 3000; savages of many tribes, all of whom had forgotten for the time their hates and plans for vengeance in order to listen together to the word of God. Some of the injuries had not been repaired and revenge was only postponed. This was the reason, according to Demers, "why some came to the instructions filled with distrust, armed with guns, which I made them place at my feet, and then abandon entirely. It was extraordinary and an evidence of the visible protection of heaven that in an assembly so numerous, of so many nations, separated by

[43] *Ibid.*, 64.

their interests, their languages, and their customs, there was not a single altercation, a single reminder of past injuries. The presence of a minister of God calmed all aversions and united all hearts." [44]

There was still another group to be heard from. Farther up the Fraser River lived the Teits [45] who were delayed for fear of an attack by the Miskiwins. Demers was unwilling to leave before seeing them and at last sent a chief to tell them he was waiting and to urge them to come without fear. The following evening, 306 persons in forty canoes announced their arrival by numerous discharges of musketry. There were cries, songs, an enthusiasm and extraordinary eagerness. All placed themselves in line to greet the missionary who shook hands with each one, meanwhile holding his left hand high over his head. After the first greetings, the savages returned to their canoes for the gifts they had brought to the great chief. They were proffered with this explanation: " Chief, we have little to give you; but you know our poverty. If we had more, we should give it with the same good will. We offer you this little present, that you may know our heart and to express to you our joy that you have come to see us." Then each head of a family presented two dried salmon and some added a kind of cake made with pounded pears. It was then the turn of the missionary who made all sit down, distributed tobacco and assisted at the " grand smoke :"

Demers seems to have been well pleased with the success of his work. Writing to Bishop Signay, he says:

> With all the savages I met, I found an eagerness and admirable zeal for the things of heaven. . . . What good might not be done if we could find priests enough to profit by the good dispositions of the poor savages. . . . The success with which the Lord has been pleased to bless my mission on the Fraser River is more than sufficient to encourage me to return there again in June or July. Perhaps I shall go a little farther, if it is not imprudent to do so; for I know there may be danger. I have some hopes of gaining the Yougletas. Who knows if this barbarous nation may not become civilized? and what could contribute to this happy change, if not the all-powerful virtue of the word of God and the knowledge of His holy name.[46]

[44] *Ibid.*, 65.
[45] Collective name for the Cowichan tribes on the Fraser River above Nicomen and Chilliwak rivers.
[46] Demers to Signay, March 18, 1842, quoted in *Rapport* (1843), 54.

Much to the regret of both missionaries it was found impossible to visit these tribes in 1842. In June of that year the officers of the Hudson's Bay Company offered Demers a place in one of its canoes going to New Caledonia and it seemed too good an opportunity to let slip. As a result of Demers' absence Blanchet was left alone and did not feel that he could desert the home missions long enough to travel to the north. It is true that two recruits arrived in September, 1842, young men filled with zeal for the conversion of the natives. Blanchet was obliged to temper their ardor for a time until they had become a little accustomed to the country and familiar with the language of the Indians. Undoubtedly, Demers' glowing account of the good he had been able to accomplish in the north kept alive the desire to carry on in that locality. Demers himself, was anxious to return to the people. He was chosen for the New Caledonia field but plans for the other were not entirely given up. Bolduc speaks of them in his *Journal*:

> As I write there is question of establishing a mission north of Nisqually; I am destined to go to be the first to carry the light of the gospel to that land which still adores the devil. I do not know yet where my residence will be; perhaps not on the mainland. The Company plans to build a fort on Vancouver Island. Mr. Douglas, who will be commandant of the expedition, said he would be pleased to give me a passage on his steamboat. Thus, in several days I shall leave here to go to Nisqually and there join the expedition. If I do not establish my residence there, it will surely be on Whidby Island, where Blanchet has already planted a cross and where the savages have shown very good dispositions. There is not on these islands a single white man and I must go there alone. Vancouver or Quadra Island attracts me much. On going there with the Company, I shall prevent the evils which would follow the whites; and if I fix my residence there, nothing will prevent me from visiting from time to time, the island of Whidby, which is not more than about ten leagues from the new fort. There is some danger from the savages of the north who frequently come to wage war against their neighbors and to take slaves. The great tribe of the Yougletas is camped on the extreme north of Vancouver Island and causes anxiety even to well-armed ships.[47]

[47] Journal of Bolduc in *Rapport* (1845), 12. Simpson gave orders on June 25, 1835 for a survey to be made to find a suitable site for a principal

This attempt was made but nothing came of it. Blanchet, writing to Bishop Signay, simply said, " Our efforts to extend the kingdom of Jesus Christ among the savages have failed. Father Bolduc thought to make himself useful last spring by a visit to the forts of the north, but gave up and returned in a short while to Vancouver Island." [48] In May, 1843 Demers and Bolduc, after the former's return from New Caledonia, made another attempt, this time on Whidby Island. Demers gives an account of it in a letter to Cazeau:

> In May I was sent with Mr. Bolduc to establish a mission on Whidby Island; but we did not have enough help to build a house and a fort, which is necessary in that place, exposed to the incursions of savage tribes, especially the Yougotta, who, according to the reports of the savages, were on the point of making war against them and us. We gathered together some of our baggage and abandoned the post for the time. If priests come, I think someone should return there.[49]

But priests were long in coming and gradually the work that had been so bravely begun was given up and the missionaries concentrated their attention on the whites. Blanchet, writing to Bishop Signay, sums up conditions as they appeared to him:

> Aside from the general notice that I am sending, there remains little to say on the state of our mission. You will see at a glance what we have undertaken and done during the year—the mission at Whidby failed, the dearth of priests has prevented us from attempting it again and has made changes in the plans we had formed. We lack for the establishment of Indian missions, men, faithful, pious, proven. . . . The savages are, so to say, abandoned for lack of means to establish permanent missions among them and because the whites take all our time. Experience has taught us that due to the inconstancy of the savages; the little time that we can give them; the dangers which they must run; the perversion to which they are exposed;

post on Vancouver Island and wrote again on April 29, 1839 of the necessity of establishing such a post. In December, 1839 the London office sent instructions to McLoughlin to make such an establishment. Cf. Frederick Merk, "The Oregon Pioneers and the Boundary," *American Historical Review*, XXIX (1923-1924), 681-699.

[48] Blanchet to Signay, November 6, 1843. QAA.

[49] Demers to Cazeau, October 4, 1843. QAA. The Yougotta are evidently the Lekwiltok Indians.

the example of others and their own weakness; that we cannot baptise even those who seem to us the most fervent among these wandering tribes without exposing the sacraments to profanation. These poor savages are to be pitied; they plead with us not to abandon them; those of the Bay made me promise to return, saying that there was no danger. The dispositions of the natives are favorable to us, they want their children baptized. At Nisqually Dr. Richmond has made himself detested both by whites and savages, and especially by the latter, on account of the brutality of his conduct. At Fort George or with the Clatsops, Mr. Parish can do no more than his predecessors; at Grand Dalles, the savages sing and pray but their customs remain the same. Mr. Spalding who succeeded best on the River of the Nez Percés, has made himself detested by his avarice which has led him to sell all; the influence of the missons of the reverend Jesuit Fathers has made itself felt there. The savages say, *it is not thus with the priests*. A great chief has abandoned the above mentioned minister. On the River Spokane the ministers Waller and Hill do not seem to advance, any more than Dr. Whitman at Walla Walla. The minister, Waller, at the Falls does not visit the savages any more. The mission at Wallamet has come to an end. The departure of the ministers proves the truth of the reports that there was no union among them, that each wished to be at the head and seek his own interest. . . . These are the ways that Providence uses to throw all into our arms. . . . Is not the finger of God there? But the dispositions of the savages of the lower river are far from as good as those of the upper and it will be several years before the reverend fathers will enjoy the fruit of their labors. And this will not be except at great cost. The mission must be self-sustaining. There must be a band of cows and a flock of sheep, everything that is necessary for the cultivation of the land. These savages have a thousand needs and things must be provided for them; they are so spoiled here . . . that one cannot gain the good will of a chief except by gifts. It will be a real difficulty to assemble the savages of the same or of several languages from different posts, to unite and keep them around the mission, because of their attachment to their native soil. It will only be when great advantages are offered by the mission that they will come. Still more difficult will it be to detach them from the chase, the salmon, which is their favorite food. We have done little for the savages, you say, but could we have done more? ought we to have devoted our time to them to the detriment of the whites, established missions for them and abandoned the

French? Ought we to have received them before they were instructed and improved enough so that we could be without fear of their changing. . . . Does it count for nothing that we have traveled through the country, baptized the children, won the savages, arrested the progress of error, announced the tidings of salvation, given a taste for the word of God, inculcated Catholic ideas? Does it count for nothing that we have destroyed prejudice against us, meanwhile arresting the progress of error, or at least diminishing it? What of the influence that we have acquired, that holy and happy impulse toward the Catholic Church, that spirit of friendliness that the tribes in general have toward the priests? The ministers tried to establish themselves in New Caledonia, on Whidby Island at Nisqually, Cascades, Hakemar, Okanogan, Colville. What have they been able to do with their material goods and personnel, even when they lived in the midst of the tribes? What could we not have done had we been able to do likewise? This is where we are; this is what we have done; this is what we have gained among the savages. You may judge if two could have done more; and if, since we have been four, each of us, has not been well occupied at his post.[50]

The most ambitious attempt of 1842 was the evangelization of the tribes of eastern British Columbia, or as it was known at the time, New Caledonia. It was a venturesome undertaking, only to be made under difficulties: the country was rough and far distant; the travel of the day was always wearisome; the people were strange—the whites few and the Indians unknown. But several

[50] Blanchet to Signay, March 24, 1844. QAA. It had been Blanchet's ideal to establish Indian missions on the plan of the "reductions" of South America, where the tribesmen, separated from the whites, might have been taught the rudiments of civilized life as well as the principles of Christianity. Father Roothaan, the Jesuit General, perhaps encouraged by De Smet, seems to have had the same ambition. A letter of his, quoted in Garraghan, op. cit., II, 438, gives his explanation of the failure of such plans: "It seems that the idea of renewing the miracles of Paraguay amid those mountains was a Utopia. In the first place, we could not hope for the means which our Fathers received from the Crowns of Spain and Portugal. Then, it was impossible to keep the whites at a distance; then, too, the nature of the land is quite different and one cannot hope to wean the bulk of the savages from their nomadic life during a great part of the year when they are on the hunt and scattered and disbanded. . . . Impossible for the missionary to follow them. . . ."

factors favored the new establishment, the first and most powerful undoubtedly being the enthusiasm of De Smet with whom the Canadian priests had an opportunity to confer in June. Garraghan says that "Demers appears to have undertaken the venturesome trip at the instance or at least with the encouragement of Father De Smet, who gave assurance that the work would be carried on by Jesuit hands."[51] It would otherwise have been a fool-hardy attempt for the missionaries were still awaiting help from Canada and already had much more to attend to than two men could possibly handle. Blanchet in a letter to Bishop Signay mentions another motive. It had been rumored that one of the Protestant ministers, one of the Presbyterians from Walla Walla, was about to make an establishment in the northern country and Blanchet felt that any sacrifice was worthwhile in order to forestall such a happening.[52]

Demers was selected to be the first apostle of the new territory. For twenty years after the coalition of the Northwest and Hudson's Bay Companies, nothing was done to introduce Christianity into New Caledonia. The natives had heard something of it from the French Canadians and Iroquois and Mr. Peter Warren Dease, during a short stay at Stuart Lake, had done his best, but with indifferent success, to impart at least a smattering of Christian doctrine to the Indians. Some years later another evangelist, William McBean, made another attempt. But the Company had been too much interested in profits to give much consideration to the improvement of the condition of the natives and so the work lagged and little was accomplished.[53]

On June 30, 1842 Demers and De Smet took their places in one of the barges of the New Caledonia brigade commanded by the chief factor, Peter Skene Ogden, who seems to have enjoyed the company of the missionaries and to have provided for their comfort to the best of his ability. On July 11 the brigade reached Fort Walla Walla, where the priests parted: the one to go on to St. Louis and eventually to Europe in search of men and money for the western missions; the other to continue to the north.

[51] Garraghan, *op. cit.*, II, 326.
[52] Blanchet to Signay, June 24, 1842. QAA.
[53] Adrien G. Morice, *History of the Northern Interior of British Columbia* (London, 1906), 225.

Demers has left us a picture of his progress through the country, the conditions he found and the conversions he made. Both he and Blanchet had had too many contacts with the Indians to take literally their first protestations of interest and loyalty but in spite of this Demers found some whom he regarded as sincere and with them he was able to make plans for future work. The journey was slow and painful and not all the consideration of the Hudson's Bay Company officers could make pleasant the many days of travel. The missionary's description gives the details of their voyage and of the customary procedure with the brigades:

> Such caravans are composed of large crowds of men and horses, the latter packing the baggage and merchandise destined for the different parts of the north. The assemblage of men, horses and baggage naturally renders progress slow and irksome. It is nine or ten in the morning before everything can be made ready for a start. One must seek out and gather the animals let loose and scattered in all directions the previous night. After long hours of waiting, the band is finally brought in and the neighing of the horses, the yells of the engagés, the contestations of the inferiors and the orders of the leaders, result in a confused uproar not always flattering to scrupulous ears. At length, after having partaken on the grass of a meal of dried salmon, they load their horses, and at ten o'clock we are off. We must face a fiery atmosphere, an enervating sun, a suffocating dust, with sometimes a hill to climb and a ravine to cross. The first days are especially difficult. . . . Happy indeed if an unfavorable wind does not force one to breathe a thick dust which does not let one see more than a few feet ahead. A dull and monotonous sound of conversing voices is constantly drumming in one's ears, which only the crossing of a creek or a river can interrupt. Then people draw nearer to one another, the horses hesitate, the drivers shout and get angry; there follow pushings, falls, and grumblings with wrecks, which excite general merriment and furnish a theme for conversation and laughter during the rest of the day. We stop only to camp.[54]

After five days of such march, the party reached the fork of the Okanogan, where De Smet had made a stop the preceding spring. Knowing the interest of the Jesuit in the country, Demers sent him

[54] Demers to Signay, December 20, 1842, quoted in *Rapport* (1845), 14; translated in part in Morice, *op. cit.*, 230-231.

The Apostolate of the Indians

an account to tell him of the joy of the savages at the second visit of a priest. He spent a few days with these people, gave them some instructions and baptized their children. On August 24, the party crossed the river Fraser after a fatiguing journey of twenty-six days on horseback and arrived at Fort Alexandria, where Demers first met the Porteurs for whom he had made this voyage. He had intended to spend some time here but being offered a place in the brigade, he continued with Ogden to Fort George. Due to the fact that the Indians had not been warned of his visit few of them assembled and Demers does not seem to have been altogether satisfied with these few. "The savages of other places have shown better dispositions," he wrote to De Smet, "but I made use of this short space of time in pointing out the principal disorders which existed among them, and in teaching them to make the Sign of the Cross." [55]

Demers returned to Fort Alexandria October 27 where he spent the winter in the home of A. C. Anderson and had an opportunity to continue his work with the Porteurs.[56] They seem to have been less prepossessing than most of the tribes with whom the missionaries had come into contact. In a letter to Bishop Signay, Demers thus describes them:

> The men are remarkable enough for their height and their erect carriage. The women are large and corpulent, something which one does not find among the nations of the Columbia. They are also clothed with greater decency than the Columbians. . . . It is understandable that the severe eye of civilization would not be satisfied with such dress; but the degraded state of these poor creatures tends to make them disregard those things which would frighten the prudery of civilized society. If their ideas of convention do not lead them to make it the rule to cover all the body, at least they have the good habit of observing the principal rules of decency. It is not that their morals are more pure; they are, on the contrary, in

---

[55] Demers to De Smet, February 11, 1843, in *United States Catholic Magazine* (1843), 741-743.

[56] Hodge classifies this tribe as a part of the Denes nation of the Athapascan language group. Their home was around the upper branches of the Fraser River. Cf. Adrien C. Morice, "The Western Denes," *Proceedings* Canadian Institute (1893) and Alice Ravenhill, *Native Tribes of British Columbia* (Victoria, 1938).

> a shocking state of degradation. These unfortunate savages, as far as their feeble intelligence is concerned, cannot be distinguished from animals, so degraded and entirely subjugated are they to the slavery of the senses. They ignore all checks, all laws of decency which seem natural to human beings, all ties of nature and blood; the sacred laws of marriage are relaxed more than in any nation in North America; promiscuity seems a sort of public right. However, who would believe it! jealousy reigns in all its fury; a woman rejected by her husband will hang herself to a tree. Suicide, murder and a thousand other disorders are the daily consequence of this disregard for the laws of the family and the degrading vices which secretly undermine this unfortunate nation.[57]

The task of converting the Carrier nation promised to be difficult. Demers did not minimize the obstacles in the way. Continuing his account, he said:

> Even though these savages listen with pleasure to the explanation of the gospel, they are even farther from the kingdom of heaven than they are lacking in the dignity of man; for aside from the moral baseness which degrades them, their minds do not grasp even the simple notion of the existence of God. They have no idea of God or of creation, which they attribute to chance. They lack even fanciful gods, idols, fetishes, have no evil spirit like the manitou of the Columbia; have no idea of expiation or of sacrifice, seemingly no interest in their past history or their origin. They fear nothing aside from that which attacks their lives or crosses the desires of their brute appetites. It is not astonishing then, that they surpass the animals in the baseness of their actions.[58]

But the missionary did not give way to despondency. Finding that the Indians could learn, he devoted himself to the task of teaching them and encouraged himself by reporting such progress as he could. In January, 1843 Demers left the Porteurs for a time in

---

[57] *Rapport* (1845), 17.

[58] *Ibid.*, 18; Morice, *British Columbia*, 232, gives the opinion of John McLean, long an employee of the Hudson's Bay Company, on the conversion of this people: "The influence of the ' men of medicine,' who strenuously withstand a religion which exposes their delusive tricks and consequently deprives them of their gains—together with the dreadful depravity everywhere prevalent—renders the conversion of the Tekallies (Carriers) an object most difficult to accomplish."

order to visit the Atnans, situated at two days' march. They received him with "demonstrations of extraordinary joy." Their chapel was built and the old chief gave his house for the missionary's use during his stay. Demers mentions having a table, two benches, an altar—all rare luxuries in the north land. This people proved extremely devoted and the priest was generous in their instruction. He describes their interest in a letter to Bishop Signay:

> An extraordinary crowd obstructed the entrance to the chapel, so much so, that one day it was impossible for me to reach my place except by passing over the shoulders and heads of my neophytes, which I did without touching the earth from the entrance to the front of the chapel. The hours passed rapidly in the pious exercises of the mission and it was only at night that I had time for prayer, for study of the language and the translation of hymns. God blessed my labors and filled me with His divine consolations.[59]

Like the Porteurs, before their contact with the whites, the Atnans had no idea of a Supreme Being, the creator of the universe. Demers gives an interesting comparison of them with the tribes of the Columbia:

> The character of the Atnans and the Porteurs differs much and favorably compares with that of the nations of the Columbia, especially those who live near the sea. One does not find in them that lightness and inconstancy which characterize the latter. The Porteur and the Atnan are easily persuaded, confide in the whites, believe the truths of faith with sincerity and without any holding back. The Chinooks, on the contrary, and the Cowlitz agree with what seems to them to be true, even believe it; but they change easily an instant afterward, even for a blanket or a shirt; their interest is their god.[60]

However, he does not overlook the obstacles to the sincere conversion of the northern peoples:

> ... the obstacles which oppose the kingdom of God here are numerous and terrible. The greatest, the death-dealing scourge of these regions, is polygamy. It will only be a powerful grace of a merciful God that will extirpate a disorder rooted in their national customs, favoring the most dangerous of the passions,

---

[59] *Rapport* (1845), 23.   [60] *Ibid.*, 24.

and made lawful by long precedent and by practice universal and immemorial.[61]

Demers could do no more than begin the work but he had opened the field for those who were to come later.[62] He sent on his report to De Smet, giving him the details of the missions with the hope that he would realize the pressing need for missionaries and would see that they were supplied. He had intended to wait until summer to return to Vancouver but in February, 1843 Ogden was ready to return and asked the priest to accompany him. They started on horseback in three or four feet of snow from Fort Alexandria, reaching Fort Thompson on March 1; passed thirteen days at Okanogan, starving and waiting for a boat; came from there on horseback along the Columbia to the Snake River; hence by boat to Walla Walla and Vancouver.[63]

---

[61] *Ibid.*, 23.
[62] The Jesuits, Nobili and Ravalli, continued this work in 1845.
[63] Blanchet, *op. cit.*, 52.

CHAPTER VI

THE VICARIATE APOSTOLIC OF OREGON

The Church in Canada was formally established when, according to the bull of 1674, the see of Quebec was established, comprehending all the possessions of France in North America: Newfoundland, Cape Breton, Acadia, Ile St. Jean, all New France from the Atlantic to the plains of the far west, the valley of the Mississippi and Louisiana. After the peace of Paris in 1782 that territory was considerably diminished. The bishop of Quebec kept Newfoundland and somewhat more than what now forms the Dominion of Canada.

The great achievement of Joseph Plessis, who was consecrated bishop of Canthe in 1801 and presided over the diocese of Quebec from 1806 to 1825, was the organization of the Church in Canada. After the peace of Ghent in 1814 he was for the first time officially acknowledged as Catholic bishop of Quebec. Bishop Plessis obtained from Rome, besides the erection of the vicariate apostolic of Nova Scotia (1817), the appointment of bishops for Upper Canada, Montreal, New Brunswick and the North West, where Provencher and Dumoulin had begun (1818) the mission of Red River. England assented to this arrangement, but on the express condition, that these bishops would be auxiliaries and vicars-general of the bishop of Quebec. Rome conferred on Plessis the title of archbishop in 1819 with the stipulation, however, that it should not be used as long as the government objected. The organization remained the same under the successor of Plessis, Bernard Panet, who was bishop of Quebec from 1825 to 1833.

The latter was succeeded in 1833 by Joseph Signay, who was successful in securing the erection of Quebec as a metropolitan with three suffragan sees, Kingston, Montreal and Toronto (1844). Signay's jurisdiction when he became bishop extended far to the west but the exact limits of his diocese were at the time uncertain. It was during his episcopate that the Oregon missions on the Columbia were founded and became successively, vicariate apostolic and ecclesiastical province.[1]

The Church in the United States had progressed far since the days of John Carroll. Baltimore in 1838 still stood as sole province but the number of suffragans was steadily growing to meet the needs of the constantly increasing Catholic population. By 1840 the number of sees had reached fifteen. West of the Mississippi, jurisdiction was in the hands of the bishop of St. Louis.

In 1826 the diocese of Louisiana had been divided into: the diocese of New Orleans, which included the lower part of Louisiana and the territory of Mississippi; and the diocese of St. Louis, which embraced the upper part of Louisiana. In 1841 the latter diocese had been somewhat more definitely limited to include Missouri, Arkansas, the western part of Illinois and the territory now constituting Kansas, Nebraska, Indiana, Oklahoma with all the wilderness of the Rocky Mountains. Apparently, however, the bishop of St. Louis had jurisdiction over the country west of the Rockies as well.[2]

His claim to jurisdiction over the country came perhaps from the interest which William Du Bourg, Bishop of Louisiana and the Floridas, had taken in the Indian missions of the far west. As early as 1823, realizing that the natives had some claim to attention, Du Bourg urged the General of the Jesuits to send priests to his diocese to establish missions among the Indians. It was impossible at the time but eventually a Jesuit community was founded with the express purpose of caring for the savages. An agreement was drawn up between the bishop and the superior of the Jesuits by which the bishop ceded to the Jesuits forever the absolute and ex-

---

[1] Cf. Lionel St. G. Lindsay, " Centenary of the Archdiocese of Quebec," *Catholic Historical Review*, henceforth cited as *CHR*, n. s. I (1921-1922), 152-164, and Hugh J. Somers, " Legal Status of the Bishop of Quebec," *CHR*, XIX (1933-1934), 167-189.

[2] Donald C. Shearer, O.M. Cap., *Pontificia Americana: A Documentary History of the Catholic Church in the United States, 1784-1884* (Washington, 1933), 144-146; Garraghan, *op. cit.*, II, 236, calls attention to the difficulty of making a decision with regard to the limits of the jurisdiction of Rosati and Signay. Since the Oregon county was held by the United States and Great Britain together until 1846 there were no distinct American or British possessions in Oregon before that time.

clusive care of all the missions already established and which shall hereafter be established on the Missouri River and its tributary streams. This grant was confirmed and expanded by the second Provincial Council of Baltimore (1833), which recommended that the care of the Indian tribes in the entire United States be confided to the Jesuits.[3]

It is not difficult to see that there existed the possibility of an overlapping of ecclesiastical jurisdiction. Lack of precise knowledge of geography prevented a definite delimitation of boundaries, and especially in the far west where exploration and settlement were still in a pioneer stage, there was real difficulty about deciding to whom ecclesiastical authority belonged. To the jurisdiction over the Oregon territory at least two dioceses might lay claim. The first of these was Quebec, which had answered the appeal of the Canadians in the west and had been the first to send missionaries (1838). Since the people of the region at that time were so largely British subjects, Signay had taken it for granted that his jurisdiction extended over them. The *Annals of the Propagation of the Faith*, published at Lyons, had first made him aware of the possibility of another claimant to the territory. He wrote in 1842 to the bishop of St. Louis, asking whether or not he had any definite knowledge about the limits of the diocese:

> A portion of the territory in question is in dispute between the government of the United States and Great Britain as regards temporalities. I should like to know if your Grace have any reliable data to determine the limits of your jurisdiction on that side. All that I know is that my diocese extends to the Pacific ocean and comprises all the territory, north of California, which has not been aggregated to any of the dioceses of the United States.[4]

[3] Shea, *op. cit.*, III, 433; Peter Guilday, *A History of the Councils of Baltimore, 1791-1884* (New York, 1932), 106.

[4] Signay to Rosati, December 2, 1842. Translated in *Records* of American Catholic Historical Society, henceforth cited as *RACHS*, XIX (1908), 320. Lindsay, *op. cit.*, says that the Propaganda document (1819) which was instrumental in completing the division of the diocese of Quebec mentions the area west of the Rocky Mountains, as being still beyond the outposts of civilization and unorganized. There was no prospect of founding a church there at that time but it was hoped that the native tribes of the region might at no distant date be drawn into the church when neighbor-

We do not know whether Bishop Rosati had any information regarding the limits of his diocese to send to Bishop Signay. Apparently he too took it for granted that his jurisdiction extended to the Pacific, although no attempt was made to send missionaries there until 1840. In that year, the Jesuit, Father De Smet, was commissioned to explore the country and to report on its possibilities as a field for missionary labor. By that time two Canadian priests were already established there.

Offering further possibility for confusion, was the settlement that had been made at Red River under the Canadian, Father Provencher.[5] This was to become in 1844 the vicariate apostolic of the North West and comprised the entire territory west of the Great Lakes and as far north as the pole. However, although Bishop Provencher had been there with episcopal rank since 1822, his vicariate does not seem to have had any official organization since the English government objected strenuously to the establishment of any see, excepting that of Quebec. There is some confusion, however, for O'Hara says that an indult of the Holy See (February 28, 1836) annexed the Columbia country to the vicariate apostolic of Provencher at Red River.[6] It is true that the appeal of the western Canadians was made first to Bishop Provencher, and that he, unable to do anything about it, forwarded the petition to Bishop Signay at Quebec.[7]

Far from Oregon, and seemingly completely away from its affairs, lie the Sandwich Islands. And yet in spite of their distance, com-

ing tribes should be converted. The scarcity of missionaries made it impossible for the bishop of Quebec to extend his authority in this direction. Possibly either Russia or California could more easily attempt it.

[5] Provencher had been at Red River since 1818.

[6] O'Hara, "Catholic Pioneers in Oregon," *CHR*, III (1917-1918), 189; this is also mentioned in No. 14 of the instructions given by Signay to Blanchet and Demers, April 17, 1838. QAA.

[7] Signay seems to have directed the missions as first superior though the correspondence with Provencher was steady and the latter showed his interest in the undertaking in many ways. In a letter of Provencher to Blanchet, July 1, 1844. PAA., he speaks of his efforts to obtain religious and priests and expresses his dissatisfaction with Signay's administration of Oregon affairs, adding that the Councils of Lyons and Paris had furnished the money for the missions, while the Jesuits had supplied the priests.

munication frequently passed between them and Oregon, and Blanchet at one time thought his missions might come under the jurisdiction of the bishop of that region.[8] The introduction of Catholicism among the natives of the Islands was a French project which was confided to the Congregation of the Sacred Hearts of Jesus and Mary. The first group of missionaries, Fathers Alexis Bachelot, Abraham Armand and Patrick Short, arrived in 1827. Received favorably in the beginning, there developed after a time a spirit of opposition and finally of persecution against the priests and the native converts. In 1831 a formal order of banishment was issued and the missionaries were placed on board the ship, *Waverly*, and taken to California, where they remained until 1837 awaiting a favorable opportunity to return.

In 1833 the Sacred Congregation de Propaganda Fide had established the vicariate apostolic of Eastern Oceania and placed it under the care of the Congregation of the Sacred Hearts. The vicariate was divided at the equator into two prefectures. Bishop Rouchouze, vicar apostolic, was given general jurisdiction over both, with Father Bachelot as prefect apostolic over the northern half, which included the Sandwich Islands. There was no question of his authority extending as far north as Oregon in 1838 but Blanchet often expressed the opinion that were the Columbia territory to be placed under the care of the bishop of the Islands, he would be much better placed to care for its interests than was the bishop of Quebec.[9]

[8] For the history of the Church in the Islands, cf. Reginald Yzendoorn, *History of the Catholic Missions in the Hawaiian Islands* (Honolulu, 1927) and Ralph S. Kuykendall, *The Hawaiian Kingdom, 1778-1854* (Honolulu, 1938).

[9] Provencher too seems to have had this opinion and speaks of Rouchouse as Blanchet's "nearest neighbor." However, "I doubt if Bishop Rouchouse can give you priests because he has not a great number of them but you could interest him in favor of your missions through the superior of Picpus, and at least if they do not wish strange priests, as has been the case in other times, this may be a reason for the company to give passage to the Canadians, a thing which I do not count too much on, at least unless God change for the better the dispositions of those whose interest in the advancement of the kingdom of God is conditioned by whether or not that will be of advantage to them," Provencher to Blanchet, December 10, 1840. PAA.

In addition to the impossibility of finally settling the matter of jurisdiction, other equally trying problems constantly arose to vex the missionaries and to hinder and impede the progress of their work. One of the worst of these was the difficulty of bridging the distance that separated Oregon from Quebec. Whatever the mode of travel, the journey from east to west, or from west to east, was long and wearisome, often beset by real danger. Six months from Quebec to Fort Vancouver was good time for the voyage; but six months thus required for the delivery of a letter, and another six months of waiting for an answer were matters of concern. And when the lengthy accounts from the Columbia were finally placed in the hands of those for whom they were intended there was much chance that conditions represented there might be misunderstood. It was a difficult task for a churchman of Quebec to imagine the life of a missionary at Fort Vancouver. The problems of Quebec were not those of the west; and the situations there were hardly similar to those of the frontier. No one doubts the sincerity of interest on the part of Bishop Signay and his assistants; but it is a matter of speculation whether or not he could ever have come close enough to the realization of conditions to appreciate the difficulties and needs of the men he had sent into the wilderness. To him quite properly the demands of Quebec came first.

The advantages of a separate organization for the Oregon missions are readily seen. First of all, direct dependence on the Holy See would eliminate the difficulties involved in round about negotiations through a third party. Secondly, a bishop would have more chance of securing aid. Grants and gifts were made from Quebec from time to time, and Signay never seems to have complained of the demands for money which came from his vicar general but Blanchet believed that independence would be an advantage and that the societies established for the help of the missions would be favorable, were a direct appeal to be made. De Smet encouraged him in this, as did the reports that came from the Sandwich Islands and elsewhere. The greatest need, however, was not money but priests. Blanchet could never believe that it should have been impossible to secure recruits in spite of the constant protestations of his superiors. Here again he was encouraged by De Smet to think that negotiations, direct from Oregon to the sources of supply, might be more successful.

The Vicariate Apostolic of Oregon 135

Blanchet had not been long in the Oregon country before he realized that if the work were to continue with any degree of success, he and Demers would have to have help. In a letter written to Bishop Signay from Fort Vancouver in March, 1839, the missionary gave an account of conditions and stressed particularly that he and Demers could not possibly satisfy all the demands:

> Your Lordship can see from this and from other notices that we have sent, that we are unable to do all in this country; we should have six more priests who might be placed as follows with the two who are here: two at Colville or in its neighborhood for the many savages of the different rivers of this country, etc.; two at Walla Walla for the many Nez Percés, Cayuse, Yakima, etc.; two at Vancouver, one for the Canadians, their wives and children, for the ladies, etc., another for the savages, Chinooks and others; the seventh at Willamette for the Canadians and the savages; the eighth at Cowlitz for the Canadians, the savages of the place. There remain besides Bay St. George and the country to the north, in which live many tribes.[10]

In another letter, also written in March, 1839, Blanchet addressed an appeal to Bishop Turgeon, the coadjutor of Quebec. After relating some of his difficulties he made a suggestion of some significance, "we should have here Bishop Provencher with a brigade of priests." This is the first time that Blanchet has mentioned the Bishop of Juliopolis in connection with Oregon, but we find his name often hereafter. In a postscript to the letter, quoted above, he speaks again of the desirability of Provencher coming to the Oregon country:

> I return to the idea of asking his lordship, Bishop Provencher, to come and establish himself among us on the Columbia, or, at least to come and spend here several years. This idea, coming at the moment of the departure of the letters, must have been inspired from on high; I beg of you to think of this plan and to consider the advantages and the effects his presence would produce. Bishop Provencher could come by the interior with several priests and accomplish some good along the route, or by way of St. Louis, where he could gather a large number of priests, some Sisters of the Congregation, workers for the churches, masters and mistresses for the schools. . . . Send us Bishop Provencher; he can be replaced at Red River by a

[10] Blanchet to Signay, March 1, 1839. QAA.

vicar general; the post here will become more important than that of Red River.[11]

A year later, in March, 1840, Blanchet wrote again to Bishop Turgeon to give an account of the work that had been done and of plans for the future. Once more, he begged for the coming of the bishop of Red River and tried to impress the Quebec authorities with the need of a bishop in Oregon:

> I have already mentioned that it would be advantageous for the Bishop of Juliopolis to visit the Columbia. But now, I ask not only for a visit; Father Demers and I beg for the good of religion that Bishop Provencher come to live among us, to govern the mission, to direct its operations, and to give by his presence the final blow to the sectaries, which will be effected when the savages see in his person a successor of the Apostles. If his Lordship refuses, I ask that you take measures to find us a superior among Fathers Cook, Dumoulin, McGuin or Mailloux, who will come here with several priests. . . . What I ask is of the greatest importance. I have written to Bishop Provencher. He can be replaced at Red River by another superior. . . . I hope that the plan will be pleasing to our superiors. It is for the greater glory of God that I ask.[12]

Perhaps hoping to stir the ambition of the prelates at home, and to show them the good that might be accomplished under favorable conditions, the western missionary cited instances of the success of workers in other fields. Some correspondence had passed between Blanchet and Walsh,[13] the active missionary of the Sandwich

---

[11] Blanchet to Turgeon, March 13, 1839. QAA. This letter also stresses the need of priests on the Columbia. Provencher seems to have been fully in sympathy with Blanchet's planning. He had experienced some of the difficulties of the Oregon priest. Hence in Provencher to Blanchet, December 10, 1840. PAA., he writes, "I feel with you the necessity of a greater number of priests and even of the presence of a bishop who will be more independent in his actions. . . . I have also spoken to the effect that they should give some attention to securing a bishop for you but I have never been much good at pushing great affairs. . . . The cares by which I sometimes find myself surrounded, have made me ask an independent bishop or a vicar apostolic at the Columbia, which will be a great country. . . ."

[12] Blanchet to Turgeon, March 19, 1840. QAA.

[13] Robert A. Walsh, Order of the Sacred Hearts, was a British subject who arrived in the Islands in 1836. He was ordered to depart but the arrival of the French ship of war, *La Bonite*, altered the situation. His career as a missionary was evidently a successful one.

Islands. The latter rejoiced that missionaries had been sent to the northern country. To encourage their efforts, he told them of the difficulties he had encountered in the establishment of his work, but also of the success that had come to it. Blanchet was undoubtedly impressed by the methods employed in the southern field, perhaps a little envious of the number of priests and of the amount of material assistance that were devoted to it. On February 25, 1839 Father Walsh had written:

> Our mission at Gambiers Island where our bishop (Mgr. Rouchoux of Nicopolis) resides for the present, is in a most flourishing condition. In a letter dated in August last, my bishop informs me that only five or six remain unbaptized. There are missionaries (Cath.) sent to the Marquises.[14]

And a few months later in August, 1839 Walsh sent an account which may well have stimulated the zeal of Blanchet and Demers:

> Thousands crowded to our small chapel. . . . Since my last to you, I believe, our bishop has visited the Marquises Islands and established missions there. His Lordship was everywhere throughout that group well received by the inhabitants. His priests were well-treated by the Chiefs, who promised to build houses and churches for them.[15]

The Oregon missionary, writing to Bishop Turgeon, in October, 1839, quoted from the *Sandwich Island Gazette* of April 27, 1839, and relayed the good news from other missions, no doubt rejoicing with them in their success but at the same time perhaps hoping to impress far away superiors with the idea of what could be done in the Columbia territory with more effective cooperation:

> We learn from letters received per ship, *Vineyard*, Captain Silton, that the Right Rev. Dr. Rouchoux accompanied by six missionaries arrived at Vaitoo, one of the Marquisian group, the third of February last. . . . They experienced marks of kindness and attention from all whom they met. The bishop having added two priests to those previously residing on the Island, and encouraged them to persevere in their arduous duties, sailed the sixth of the same month for Nuka-Neva . . . where he founded a new mission. . . . His Lordship remained

---

[14] Walsh to Blanchet, February 25, 1839. QAA.
[15] Walsh to Blanchet, August 10, 1839. QAA.

at Nuka-Neva three days and then returned to Vaitoo, accompanied by the Revd. Mr. Caret. . . . They visited also St. Dominico and were well received there, the chiefs promised to build a house for the Catholic missionaries and solicited the bishop to send them as soon as possible.[16]

Blanchet took care that his superior should know what was being done by others. His letter of November, 1840 to Signay gave a glowing picture of the success that was being attained:

> The Bishop of Pompallis with jurisdiction over Western Oceania, has made great progress in New Zealand. The Bishop of Eastern Oceania (Rouchoux) has done wonders; all bow before the missionaries. The Marquise Islands are Catholic; there are eight priests in the Marquises; there are four in the Sandwich Islands, where the bishop returned last May. A large church has been begun; holy Mass will be celebrated there this autumn. The natives come by thousands; forty priests would not be too many for the need. Those are missions. And we, we do nothing but vegetate for lack of help.[17]

Demers had already made his appeal. His letter of March, 1840 to Father Cazeau, secretary to the bishop of Quebec, repeated what his superior had said and closed with one appealing sentence, " You see the unhappiness that is ours in being two priests only, where there should be eight or ten!"[18]

Even the news of the coming of De Smet, the Jesuit missionary, to the Oregon territory was not an unalloyed joy. True, the zealous Belgian had found the country to his liking; he had instructed and baptized a great number of savages, and he would soon return with a brigade of priests; but that would not solve the problems of the Canadian workers on the coast.

In March, 1841 Blanchet again wrote to Bishop Turgeon. He and his co-worker still awaited the coming of priests; their work lagged for lack of time and assistance; two men could do only so much. Blanchet presented the needs of the Oregon missions, especially those of the Indians, whom he had many times been forced to turn away:

[16] Blanchet to Turgeon, October 5, 1839. QAA.
[17] Blanchet to Signay, November 9, 1840. QAA.
[18] Demers to Cazeau, March 24, 1840. QAA.

It is sad to see the savages coming every day from all sides, and
not to have time to speak to them; to see that our time is given
entirely to the Canadians and to be obliged to leave Vancouver
for our respective posts without having time to do anything for
the natives. I tell you our position is that of martyrs. We are
surrounded by savages, among whom the ministers spread error.
It attacks our Indians, our Canadians, and forces us to remain
at Willamette and at Cowlitz. How long must the martyrdom
last? Could not Canada make some sacrifices and send us
priests by way of St. Louis? Can it be insensible to our misery,
our embarrassment, our sorrow? [19]

More than a year later, on June 8, 1842 De Smet arrived at Fort
Vancouver. There began then eight days of conference during
which the three missionaries, Blanchet, Demers and De Smet,
deliberated on the interests of the great mission of the Pacific coast.
The result of that meeting was momentous in Oregon church
history. The immediate outcome was the decision that Demers
should go north to open a mission in New Caledonia; Blanchet
should remain at St. Paul; while De Smet should start for St.
Louis, and providing his superiors approved, go on to Belgium in
quest of workers and material assistance. Besides the real encouragement of at last finding some one who knew Oregon, its
problems and possibilities, was the promise of assistance with the

[19] Blanchet to Turgeon, March 18, 1841. QAA. Provencher was anxious
to send help to Oregon and he made a number of appeals of his own
besides his efforts to secure more assistance through Signay. Provencher
to Blanchet, June 22, 1839. PAA., " You are already overburdened; you
must have help. You would have had it before this had it depended only
on me. I have applied to the committee at London to obtain passages but
I do not know what they will decide. Meanwhile you will have no one.
Probably it will be necessary to send help by sea or by St. Louis, or more
probable still, it will be necessary to get priests from France." And again,
Provencher to Blanchet, December 10, 1840. PAA., "I have written
strongly to Quebec to urge them to send you help by way of St. Louis. I
have recommended that they write immediately to St. Louis, to Boston,
and to have several priests ready to leave. . . ." A month earlier Signay
had written to St. Louis, asking information regarding expenses and routes
of travel. Signay to Rosati, November 20, 1840. Tr. in *RACHS*, XIX
(1908), 315. Father Verhaegen had replied with the necessary data and
the report that De Smet had just returned with a glowing account of the
country. Verhaegen to Signay, n. d. Tr. *in RACHS*, XIX (1908), 318.

opportunity of putting into practice the hopes that had been growing in spite of discouragement, since the two Canadians arrived in Oregon. De Smet approved a plan of immediate organization; undoubtedly, he saw the good that could be done; undoubtedly he too realized the impossibility of accomplishment when the work was dependent on an authority 3000 miles away.

Even before De Smet left Oregon Blanchet, his enthusiasm aroused, wrote to Bishop Rosati at St. Louis to inform him of the plans that had been made. After relating the encouragement and inspiration of De Smet's visit Blanchet outlined the glorious work lying open to the Catholic missionaries of Oregon, the great good to be done among the Indian tribes, the difficulties, coming from the opposition of the Protestant ministers, the establishments that he and Demers had made, the obstacles yet to be overcome and finally, the bold plan, proposed by De Smet and approved by Demers and himself, of appealing immediately for the erection of an independent vicariate apostolic in Oregon.[20]

A few days later, June 24, 1842, Blanchet communicated the plan to his superior, the bishop of Quebec. After praising the work of De Smet and his fellow religious, Blanchet confessed that he had written to the bishop of St. Louis and also to the provincial of the Jesuits in the hope of increasing the number of Jesuits in the Oregon country. Having been refused on all sides he had thought it wise to accept the offers that De Smet had made and hopes that the bishop will approve of what he has done. The main point of the letter is found in the lines:

> I have let myself be carried away by the plan to obtain as soon as possible an independent bishop for the territory of the Columbia, on the model of the dioceses established in the States, where even the poorest bishops have been successful in obtaining abundant help from all countries and have made rapid progress.[21]

Signay answered this communication in April, 1843. He was enthusiastic about the plan and wrote of the means he had taken to put it into immediate execution: "I received yours of June 24,

[20] Blanchet to Rosati, June 20, 1842. QAA.
[21] Blanchet to Signay, June 24, 1842. QAA.

telling me of the visit of De Smet and the project of erecting an independent diocese in the territory of the Columbia. I found it so much to my liking that I wrote at once to the Bishop of St. Louis so as to take with him the steps of carrying it out. In his absence I received a response from Bishop Kenrick, his coadjutor, to whom the proposition was agreeable. It will be submitted to the bishops of the United States when they assemble at Baltimore next month." [22]

Bishop Signay had for sometime hoped to be able to dispose of a part of his vast diocese, hence the news of the ambitious planning of his vicar general was probably welcome to the bishop of Quebec. He found it impossible to care for the Oregon country and was most willing that the task be delegated to someone else.[23] Consequently, he lost no time in writing to St. Louis.[24]

[22] Signay to Blanchet, April 19, 1843. QAA.

[23] References to this may be found in the correspondence. In Blanchet to Rosati, June 20, 1842. QAA., " Seeing the obstacles that he met with to the good that he would have accomplished in the Columbia territory, his Lordship tried to free himself of the charge of governing this part of his diocese, which he could not provide for. His hopes will perhaps be realized." And in Blanchet to Signay, June 24, 1842. QAA., "Your Lordship's plan of being free from the care of the Columbia will perhaps be effected; the bishop of Montreal who was charged with notes toward that end, having met their lordships, the bishops of the Sandwich Islands and of St. Louis, at Rome, the matter should be easily regulated." And still earlier, Provencher to Blanchet, December 13, 1841. PAA., "I do not know if you will receive help in 1842. I insisted as strongly as I could with the bishops of Quebec that they send you two priests by St. Louis. Will it be done? Will they be well-chosen? You will be the judge. . . . You know that the bishop of Quebec hopes to be relieved of your mission. I do not know how the project progresses. Who would want it? If only they would appoint a bishop, all would be well." Garraghan, *op. cit.*, II, 279, mentions a letter of Signay to Propaganda, April 17, 1841, in which he petitions that the Columbia mission be transferred to another bishop.

[24] Garraghan, *op. cit.*, II, 278-279, summarizes the letter, ". . . the principal matter discussed between Fathers Blanchet and De Smet at their meeting of June, 1842, was the ecclesiastical organization of Oregon Territory and its erection into a diocese. To interest the American prelates in this project and secure aid for the proposed diocese were, according to the Bishop of Quebec, the chief reasons that led De Smet to return to St. Louis in 1842." In addition Signay recommends the appointment of De Smet to the proposed bishopric.

Bishop Rosati was in Rome but Bishop Kenrick, his coadjutor, forwarded the correspondence to him there and also volunteered to present the matter to the bishops in council at Baltimore, when they should convene in May, 1843. In a letter February, 1843 to Bishop Signay, Kenrick said:

> I have already sent your letter to Bishop Rosati and I have spoken of your intentions to the Archbishop of Baltimore, so that at the next council which will be held in the month of May, proper measures may be taken to give a bishop to these "fideles éloignées." Before I received the letter of your Lordship, Father de Smedt had expressed to me his wishes for the erection of this new bishopric and had at the same time recommended the Revd. Mr. Blanchet as a subject, worthy of this dignity and most capable of spreading the kingdom of God among the savages of this territory.
>
> As for the Jesuits, they will not at all accept the burden of the episcopate, and, in the case that it is determined to erect the bishopric proposed, I do not think it will be possible to find a priest here to nominate. If your Lordship will consent to the nomination of Father Blanchet for this post I would like to know before Easter because I shall leave here immediately after for Baltimore, and I do not doubt of the success of this project if we can find a capable subject. Perhaps it would be better if your Lordship were to write to the Archbishop of Baltimore to recommend to him the erection of this new bishopric.[25]

After the preliminary discussion some difference of opinion was discovered as to the actual form of the new organization in the west. Bishop Signay, writing to Bishop Kenrick, in March, 1843 gave his ideas on the subject:

> I think that the proposed diocese should include all the territory between the arctic circle on the north, California on the south, the Rocky mountains on the east, and the Pacific ocean on the west; and that the bishop who is to bear the burden of it, should take his title from Vancouver, which is the headquarters of the Hudson's Bay Company's establishments beyond the Rocky Mountains and from which it is easier to hold communications with all parts of the country. However, Father De Smet who has been in those parts, may perhaps entertain a different opinion from mine of these two points, and I shall

[25] Kenrick to Signay, February 7, 1843. QAA.

be very glad if he make it known to your Lordship so that I may act accordingly in my request to the Holy See.[26]

Whether or not the influence of De Smet was responsible for the difference of opinion we do not know. At any rate the fathers of the Council decided not to follow the suggestion of the bishop of Quebec, either as to the form proposed or as to the candidate selected. Kenrick wrote to Signay after the Council to give him the results of the deliberation since Signay preferred to deal with him rather than directly with the Archbishop of Baltimore. On May 29, 1843, shortly after the close of the council, Kenrick wrote:

> In accordance with the promise I made you, in answer to Your Grace's letter of March 12th, I have the honor to inform you that the Council just closed at Baltimore recommended that the Holy See form a Vicariate Apostolic west of the Rocky Mountains, in the territory called Oregon. Three names were submitted to the Holy See for choice. They are:
>
> Father Pierre de Smedt, of the Society of Jesus.
> Father Nicholas Point, of the same Society.
> Father Pierre Verheyden, of the same Society.
>
> The motive which determined the fathers of the Council to recommend the erection of a Vicariate Apostolic rather than a bishopric was the difficulty about fixing upon a see for the new bishop, because of the differences between our two governments with regard to Oregon. They believed it best to ask the Holy See to confide the new vicariate to a Jesuit, and especially to Father de Smedt, because they considered that this mission, in order to succeed, should be entrusted principally to the Jesuits, so that these good fathers may interest themselves more and more in it and send it further aid. True it is that the Jesuits do not usually accept the episcopal dignity; but it was thought that this difficulty would not hold good when it is a question of a mission among the Indians. I hope, my Lord, that this action on the part of the Council will meet with your approval and that you will support it at Rome with the weight of your authority.[27]

---

[26] Signay to Kenrick, March 14, 1843. Tr. in *RACHS*, VIII (1907), 460. Accepting Kenrick's opinion that the Jesuits would not be available for the new diocese, Signay suggested Blanchet.

[27] Kenrick to Signay, May 29, 1843. Tr. in *RACHS*, XIX (1908), 322-323.

Bishop Signay replied on June 12, 1843:

> Although I had already forewarned Mr. Blanchet that he might expect to be burdened with the care of the diocese that there is question of erecting beyond the Rocky mountains, I nevertheless make it my duty to support the decision of the Fathers of the Baltimore Council with the Holy See, because I consider that our holy religion can but gain more advantages therefrom. Yet as I had invited my colleagues in Canada to sign testimonial letters in favor of Mr. Blanchet, I am forwarding these letters to the Holy See with a request in favor of this missionary in case it be judged not appropriate to force the Jesuit Fathers, recommended for the episcopate by the council, to accept a dignity which is almost prohibited them by the rules of their Society.
>
> Notwithstanding my deference for the plan proposed to the Holy See by the council, I have thought it my duty to recommend the erection of a regular diocese beyond the Rocky mountains rather than of a vicariate apostolic which would be less in harmony with the canonical laws; and what especially induced me to make this recommendation was that I am informed that the General of the Jesuits, who has influence as to what is to be enacted by the Holy See, is strongly opposed to the erection of vicariates apostolic. He gave expression to this in presence of Bishop Rosati in 1841 to the Bishop of Montreal when he arranged with him that the Jesuits to be established in the Montreal diocese should be directly charged with the care of that mission.
>
> I have likewise added to the request of the council, which appears to limit its solicitude to the one territory of the Columbia, that of joining the Russian possessions to that territory in erection of the new diocese. Your lordship will undoubtedly understand that it would not be just to leave still on my hands the Russian possessions which are more than 2000 miles distant from me whilst a bishop is to be found in the vicinity.
>
> Finally, as our government and yours disagree about the possession of a part of the territory on the Columbia, I have asked, that, in order to avoid all difficulty with either government, the bishop appointed shall not be dependent upon either the Archbishop of Baltimore or the Archbishop of Quebec but that he shall be subject directly to the Holy See.
>
> I beg of your lordship to rest assured that it is not through any spirit of opposition that I ask some changes in the plan proposed by Fathers of the Council but because of what I consider will effect greater good; and that as to what concerns

the bishop to whom the proposed diocese shall be confided, I shall be all the more content that the recommendation of the council be followed as Mr. Blanchet shows much opposition to the great dignity that it is desired to confer upon him.[28]

A month later in July, 1843 Bishop Turgeon, coadjutor to Bishop Signay, wrote to Blanchet to advise him of the progress made thus far:

> We wrote you in April that you might expect to be made bishop of this new diocese; that was, we told you, the desire of De Smet that you be recommended to the Holy See; and in spite of your repugnance to accept, our recommendation was drawn up and signed by the bishops of Lower and Upper Canada.
>
> The last council of Baltimore, however, occupied with this important matter, took another stand than ours; Bishop Kenrick, who first knew the desire of De Smet, informed us that the Fathers of the council had asked that a vicariate apostolic be formed west of the Rockys in place of a bishopric, because of the difficulty of fixing the see of the new bishopric, on account of the differences between the two governments. Then persuaded that the missions of Oregon ought, for success, to be confided to the Jesuits, they asked for bishop, De Smet, whose name they sent to Rome along with those of two other Jesuits. . . .
>
> We did not doubt that if De Smet or another Jesuit accepted the bishopric, that you would rejoice. . . . However, in case they refused, we decided to send our recommendation in your favor with the supplication by which we asked, with the council of Baltimore, a bishop for Oregon. . . . Our action was not to secure an end contrary to the views of the bishops of the United States, but only to assure the prompt nomination of a bishop for a country in pressing need, and we had besides, other reasons for persisting in our first design. The bishops of Montreal and Toronto were persuaded that the General of the Jesuits would not consent to the promotion of one of his.[29]

De Smet was in Rome when the matter of the Oregon bishopric was being considered and it appears that he would have been appointed bishop had it not been for the intercession of the General

---

[28] Signay to Kenrick, June 12, 1843. Tr. in *RACHS*, XIX (1908), 323-325.

[29] Turgeon to Blanchet, July 11, 1843. QAA.

of the Jesuits who evidently succeeded in bringing forward sufficient reasons to convince Pope Gregory XVI that the Society of Jesus should not be asked to make this exception to their Rule.[30] The matter was settled in September, 1843, as is evidenced by a letter, written by Cardinal Acton to Bishop Signay on the twenty-fifth, in which he congratulates the Quebec prelate on the happy conclusion of the matter and expresses the hope that it may result in much good for the Church.[31]

The official documents were issued by the Holy See, December 1, 1843: three briefs which were forwarded to Bishop Signay at Quebec: the first, which erected the territory of Oregon into a vicariate apostolic; the second, which named Blanchet bishop of Philadelphia *in partibus infidelium*; and the third, which placed

---

[30] Blanchet seems to have been convinced that De Smet should be appointed bishop and in 1842 he would not have been averse to joining the ranks of the zealous band of Jesuits in Oregon. In Blanchet to Signay, October 28, 1842. QAA., he writes, "I rejoice to see that the spiritual affairs of this country are to fall under the learned and enlightened direction of the Reverend Jesuit Fathers. . . . I am not far from becoming a member of this holy society with my confreres, so as better to secure unity of action in the spiritual government of all the missions. Reverend Father De Smet will from another side press the immediate adoption of the plans proposed. . . . Yes, assuredly, the good God will be known, loved and served in our beautiful Columbia." And in Blanchet to Signay, March 21, 1843. QAA., he writes, "That [letter] which announced to me the plans, which heaven prepared, made and accepted at Rome, when with no knowledge of them, we took measures so that Father De Smet should find all prepared here, all prove the care of Providence for this country."

[31] C. Card. Acton to Signay, September 25, 1843. QAA., "I thank your Lordship for the kindness with which you have communicated to me the interesting details concerning your vast diocese. . . . I find the moment a happy one for expressing my satisfaction because I have the consolation of knowing that the Holy See has deigned to listen to your prayers and to aid you in your apostolic labors by naming an ecclesiastic to take charge of the territory around the Columbia, and in choosing for the episcopal dignity the same whom the wisdom of your Lordship had sent to found this great mission, and who had been recommended to the Sacred Congregation by the bishops of Canada. When the documents are ready, your Lordship will receive the official news of the election of Bishop Blanchet for the Columbia, but I can assure you that His Holiness has fully approved the decision of Propaganda."

the new vicariate under the care of the bishop.[32] Signay wrote to Kenrick in February, 1844 to tell him of the receipt of the papers from Rome and of the arrangements that had been made:

> I think I should inform your Grace, that I have at last received from the Holy See, the bulls which erect a Vicariate Apostolic in the Territory of Oregon and all the territory situated to the north of that which is west of the Rocky mountains and which confide it to the care of my vicar general, Mr. Blanchet, under the title of Bishop of Philadelphia in Asia Minor. . . . I am led to believe that the Reverend Father de Smedt who returned from Rome last summer, neglected nothing to prevent him receiving the burden which it was wished to impose upon him, and that it was through his solicitation that Mr. Blanchet was substituted for him. I shall send to Mr. Blanchet the documents from the Court of Rome next spring under the care of the Hudson Bay Company.[33]

Kenrick replied the following month, expressing his satisfaction on the occasion of the promotion of M. "Bachelet," whose merit he knows perfectly through the relations of De Smet. Blanchet would have been his choice for the position and it was only through motives of prudence that the fathers of the last Council refrained from recommending him to the Holy See. He does not doubt that under the direction of this zealous ecclesiastic, now elevated to the episcopate, with the help given him by the Jesuits that religion will make real progress in that far away country.[34] It was undoubtedly

---

[32] Copies of these documents are in the Quebec Archives; on May 7, 1844, an apostolic brief was issued which, in order to avoid confusion, changed Blanchet's title from Bishop of Philadelphia to Bishop of Drasa.

[33] Signay to Kenrick, February 24, 1844. QAA.

[34] Kenrick to Signay, March 29, 1844. QAA. Garraghan, *op. cit.*, II, 283, cites a letter of Kenrick to Purcell, in which he says, " I . . . would be glad to profit by your views before expressing my own, which are favorable to the appointment of M. Blanchet. . . . " Garraghan also suggests that political conditions and uncertainties may have influenced the bishops at Baltimore who possibly considered the appointment of an American (by adoption) as more prudent under the circumstances than that of a Canadian. Provencher to Blanchet, June 8, 1843. PAA., expresses his satisfaction that action has finally been taken, " They have approved at Quebec and I approve your arrangement with Father De Smet. A bishop at the Columbia is what you have asked since your arrival in the country

a pleasant task for the bishop of Quebec to communicate the news of his appointment to the newly named bishop of Philadelphia. In April, 1844 Signay found an opportunity of forwarding the briefs and his congratulations.

and what I wished as much as you. If they had not been so timid at Quebec, this great work would have been accomplished. As late as the month of November, they could not yet see that the time had come to put a bishop at the Columbia. But finally your letter via Mexico made them act as you asked in your letters to Quebec. This future bishop should be no other than you. St. Louis and Quebec will be willing and I give you my vote. . . . You must accept without seeking to give the burden to someone else."

CHAPTER VII

THE PROVINCE OF OREGON CITY

On November 4, 1844 the news that the Columbia mission had been erected into a vicariate apostolic and that Father Blanchet had been appointed first vicar, reached Oregon, almost a year after the issuance of the briefs. The honor was one he would most willingly have shifted to other shoulders. During the time that discussion regarding such an appointment had been under way, letters had passed back and forth between Quebec and Oregon. Blanchet knew that there was question of choosing him for the office and he protested and continued to protest that he was not the man for the post. In March, 1844 he had written to Bishop Signay:

> I rejoice at the advance of the plan to establish a bishop on the Columbia for the good and general interest of religion, as long as they have regard for my repugnance, for my objections, if they select another than your poor servant. I have thought and said enough about it to make it clear that I think a priest should be chosen in Canada, who, being consecrated there and coming here accompanied, will augment our number and be ready to begin his work at once; this will exempt me or another from the trouble and the expense of leaving the country to the detriment of religion, to go to seek a place of consecration. It should be easy for the newly-promoted to gain in a month or two the requisite knowledge of the state and needs of the mission. I hope that there is still time to remedy the evil and that my superiors will assist me to revoke and to change that which has been concluded against me. The happiest kind of news would be to learn that nothing has been done in my favor. I believe that a bishop from the United States should be at the Columbia, because all the progress due to emigration and colonization, will be from the south side of the Columbia River. I shall not believe myself obliged to accept before having given my reasons for opposing such an appointment, if it be made. Heaven should wish to protect me.[1]

---

[1] Blanchet to Signay, March 24, 1844. QAA. The "great immigration" of 1843 gave the Americans an overwhelming majority on the Columbia

Again in April, he reiterated his disapproval of his appointment, this time to Bishop Turgeon:

> I have already made known to you my feelings with regard to the report that they wish to elevate me to the episcopacy. . . . I ask that before all is finished and done the thing may be examined, considered and weighed anew before God and in my interest, so as to leave me in my present state where Providence has placed me.[2]

Blanchet then summed up his reasons for refusing the appointment and called attention to his lack of personal qualifications and his failures as a director of the missions. Finally he suggested a substitute, his brother Augustine, who had always shown considerable interest in the affairs of Oregon:

> I am already old and "hors d'age"; my powers diminish; I am slow at business and it is only by close application that I arrive at a knowledge of anything; I have a treacherous memory; my vigor is gone; I do not know English; I have never had time to study due to the demands of the ministry where I have always been busy. Why then go against nature, wish to draw light from where there is only darkness? What can I say and do further? Even here they see that I am not in my place; they advise me to abandon it since I am not capable of guiding and governing; it is my wish to give my place to another; I ask only a corner on the Columbia.[3] I am

and there was some justification for Blanchet's suggestion of a bishop from the United States. In Blanchet to Signay, November 27, 1841. QAA., he wrote of his hopes of converting the Americans, "We must absolutely have a priest, English or Scotch or Irish. Our protector [McLoughlin] is under the impression and it is my opinion, that with a priest who can speak English, the Methodists will melt away like wax; all the Americans of the Willamette, the English Protestant half-breeds coming from Red River will become Catholics in less than a year. The plan of the company is to have many families to settle the country north of the Columbia to which the Americans pretend to have a claim. Every year a large number of families will arrive at this post. Our Columbia will become a great country." If the plans of the vicar general were any indication of the trend of events, which they were not, there was some reason for the fear so often expressed that Oregon was in danger of coming under "popish domination."

[2] [Blanchet] to Turgeon, April 8, 1844. QAA.

[3] Blanchet refers here to difficulties which were occasioned by Father Langlois who, impulsive and imprudent and evidently more inclined to

blamed at all times; at all times I am taken to task; I am at fault, lacking. So, for the greater glory of God and in the interest of my fellow creatures, would it not be better that I live as I am, rather than to try to rise to become a useless and even a blamable leader. My Lord, intercede for me. I have thought that my brother might replace me if that should be found agreeable. He has greater powers of intellect than I; he has more energy, more talent, greater capacity than I. Storm heaven that I be listened to.[4]

Bishop Signay's estimate of the capabilities of his vicar general did not agree with this and in April he wrote to reassure the bishop-elect:

When this reaches you, you will learn that the Rev. Fr. De Smet has asked the Holy See to erect a vicariate apostolic in the territory of Oregon and all the country which is situated north to the Arctic pole, and to you has been confided the care of this region under the title of a bishop *in partibus*. Although the Fathers of the Council of Baltimore had recommended the Holy See to give this care to Fr. De Smet, he has been so well protected that he has succeeded in evading the burden, which he wished to fall on your shoulders, so that it might rest on the worthy founder of the mission, which has been erected into a vicariate apostolic. If I deserve any blame for having sought to have you made the recipient of a dignity which you are so far from ambitioning the good Father deserves much more, for he has worked harder than myself to have it conferred on you. As he is on the ground, you can show your resentment over it at your convenience.[5]

The bishop urged upon him the duty of submission and suggested

give than to receive orders, was not long in the Columbia territory before he discovered many flaws in the administration of ecclesiastical affairs, which he criticized openly and without ceasing. Demers to Cazeau, November 19, 1843. QAA., characterizes Langlois' conduct as disgraceful and says that the vicar general is such in name only, that he must keep silence and take the place of an inferior to keep peace. The outspoken Demers did not admire either the " conduct of Langlois or the patience of Blanchet."

[4] [Blanchet] to Turgeon, April 8, 1844. QAA.

[5] Signay to Blanchet, April 12, 1844. QAA., tr. in part in Garraghan, *op. cit.*, II, 283; Garraghan, 284, cites a letter of Blanchet to De Smet in which he refers to De Smet's influence in having him appointed vicar apostolic.

that with the help of the Jesuits his position would not be too difficult:

> I have no need, I hope, to exhort you to submit to the choice of the Holy See. You understand, I have no doubt, that divine Providence having directed this choice, you would act against it were you to seek to avoid it. Moreover, the burden which is confided to you ought, it seems to me, to be less painful to you who have been charged with it until now than to another, especially since now that you are assured of the collaboration of the Jesuit fathers, you will have more help to aid you to carry it.[6]

Continuing in the same letter, the Quebec prelate gave suggestions and instructions about the consecration of the bishop-elect:

> There remains now, my dear Lord, to have you consecrated. I would be most happy if it were possible for you to come to receive the holy anointing in your dear Canada but I fear that you will find insurmountable obstacles to this voyage, which would keep you too long a time away from your [. . .]. The shortest for you will be to go and ask this favor from that bishop of California, whom Sir George Simpson saw at Santa Barbara in 1842 and of whom he spoke to you in a letter written from that place.[7] As for going to the Sandwich Islands, it would be necessary for you to be sure that you would meet there the bishop who is often traveling to and from the many islands which are under his jurisdiction. They fear much at Paris that Bishop Rouchoux, who left nearly eighteen months ago to return to the Sandwich Islands, has been lost with all the priests and religious who accompanied him. . . .[8] To return to your consecration, if, after having consulted the Rev. Father De Smet and the other confreres who are nearest to you, you judge it apropos to come here, be sure that you will be received with the greatest pleasure by the clergy and faithful of the diocese who know and appreciate all you have done for the extension of the kingdom of God in that pagan country.[9]

[6] Signay to Blanchet, April 12, 1844. QAA.

[7] Francis Garcia Diego y Moreno, consecrated bishop of San Diego or Monterey, October 4, 1840. Cf. Shea, *op. cit.*, IV, 351 ff.

[8] Kuykendall, *op. cit.*, 342, says that Rouchouze left Honolulu at the beginning of 1841 to visit France and secure additional priests and other workers. In December, 1842 they sailed from St. Malo in the brig, *Marie-Joseph*. They were never heard of again.

[9] Signay to Blanchet, April 12, 1844. QAA.

Bishop Signay evidently judged it necessary to write again to reassure the newly appointed bishop, for under date of September 22 we find this letter:

> Through the kindness of an old servant of the Company, an occasion of sending you a letter has presented itself. I will write a few words in answer to yours of March 24 last which came to me a month ago with your report and those of Fathers Demers and Langlois on the different missions in the country which the Holy See has happily placed under your care. Let me begin with the matter of your repugnance to accept the episcopate. I surely do not blame you for the zeal with which you seek to avoid this burden. I know better perhaps than all others how much it overwhelms, and how much one needs help to carry it. But I know also that it is one of the sacrifices, which you may not rightly or conscientiously refuse.[10]

The Bishop urged then the considerations that guide the Holy See in the selection of prelates, of which, next to personal integrity, a knowledge of the country is one of the most important. He had no doubt that a stranger would for a long time struggle under a disadvantage:

> You are very certain in this case as to the dignity (painful to the truth) which the Holy See wishes to confer on you. It could not be given to a person better fitted than you are of receiving it; the bishop charged with the spiritual care of the territory of the Columbia, should not be newly arrived, but should have lived in the country long enough for him to know its needs exactly, to know the character of the various peoples who live there, the establishments which should be made for the good of religion, etc. As to this, who could be better equipped than you? Also, the Holy See always takes care to choose for the episcopacy in far away missions, priests who have already worked there; it thinks rightly that a bishop who has never set foot on the land would lose much time becoming acquainted with what concerns the good of the mission and would not be ready to begin the work as well as if he had already been there some time. Believe me, a priest who might be sent from Canada, already consecrated, could not know conditions. It would be impossible for him, except after a long time, to know all that he ought to know. You would have to instruct him. Is it not better that you do the things on your own account? As to the

[10] Signay to Blanchet, September 22, 1844. QAA.

> rest, you will see that the bishops of Canada, that Father De Smet to whom you did not refuse light as a missionary, that finally the Holy See judge you to be a man capable of governing as bishop the immense territory of the Columbia. After that it seems to me that you can do nothing but submit; and that is, I have no doubt, the course you will adopt if you have not already done so, on the arrival of your bulls and the letters which accompanied them.[11]

He closed with the encouraging news that Father De Smet was on his way to Oregon and finally offered a word of advice regarding the consecration:

> The Rev. Father De Smet with his helpers should be with you in several weeks if, as I hope, he has a good voyage. With your perspective and the powerful help that you will receive from this holy missionary and his confreres, you ought to find yourself in a less painful position than at present. Another motive to make you receive with resignation the burden which the Sovereign Pontiff imposes on you. . . .
> I am anxious to know where you will go to receive the episcopal anointing. It would seem that Canada will have the preference, if I am to judge by the passage of your letter where you speak of the necessity of sending a priest of the mission in Canada. If you come, may it not be with the intention of putting off onto another the burden of the episcopacy. As to this voyage I do not dare to make myself the judge of its opportuneness. Consult Father De Smet as to that and the other missionaries and act on their advice; they are better prepared than I to counsel you.[12]

In spite of his repugnance Father Blanchet was after all the logical candidate for the position and before long his objections were overcome and he began to make the necessary preparation for his consecration. The time between the arrival of the news of his appointment, early in November, and the end of the month was a busy period. There were consultations to be held, appointments to be made, a statement to be given to the people. On November 22, shortly before embarking on his long voyage, Blanchet issued his first pastoral letter to the clergy and faithful in which he calls their attention to the erection of the vicariate apostolic and the advantages that should follow from such an organization. He

[11] *Ibid.*   [12] *Ibid.*

deprecates his appointment and asks prayers for the success of the important journey he is about to undertake for their well-being and that of the Church in Oregon.[13]

[13] Francis Norbert Blanchet, by the mercy of God and the favor of the Holy Apostolic See, Bishop-elect of Philadelphia and Vicar Apostolic of Oregon.

To the clergy and faithful of our Vicariate Apostolic, greeting and benediction in our Lord.

The numerous benefits which it has pleased God to extend to us, Our Very Dear Brethren, since our entry into this country, even to this day, have increased every year. We have often recalled them to your memory to urge you to give thanks. But that which should cause you greatest joy is the most recent benefit that the Lord has accorded to you through our Holy Father the Pope, Gregory XVI, happily reigning, who has deigned to erect as a Vicariate Apostolic, the mission of Oregon, which formed heretofore, a part of the diocese of Quebec and a part of that of St. Louis. The letters apostolic, which announced to us this happy news, were dated at Rome, the first of December, 1843.

The advantages which ought to follow the erection of the country into a Vicariate Apostolic and the residence of a bishop in the midst of you, are precious and well-designed to cause you to rejoice. We would willingly mingle our joy with yours, if we did not have to regret to see ourself named by the Holy See to fill a post so important. You have every right to think and to hope, seeing our unworthiness and our repugnance, that the burden of the episcopate was not sought by us. We have been mistaken in our expectation. Urged by our ecclesiastical superior and by our worthy co-laborers in this country, fearing to resist the order of Divine Providence and to oppose the Will of God, we have finally accepted. We confide all to the great and infinite goodness and mercy of our God and hope for the powerful help of your prayers. Come then, Our Very Dear Brethren, come to our aid, raise to heaven your supplicating hands for us; obtain for us from the Giver of all perfect gifts, graces, strong and powerful, those gifts of the Holy Spirit, of which we have such great need. It is especially during our absence, when we go to receive the episcopal consecration that we expect the help of your prayers for us. Distance will not diminish the attachment and the love which we hold for you. The cross of Jesus Christ was planted in this country, your faith was reawakened, it was strengthened, you were saved from the tyranny of the demon, your wives and children have been instructed and regenerated in the sacred waters of baptism. You have entered into your rights, your faith and your docility have edified us, your perseverance in good has filled us with happiness.

Courage, then, just souls and fervent Christians, still other days of combat and victory are before you, a crown of glory will be your recom-

All details were at last arranged and on December 5, 1844, the bishop-elect took passage on the bark, *Columbia*, Captain Duncan, en route for Canada, via England. The journey was a long one although the route followed was the ordinary one of the day, since travel overland was out of the question during the winter months. The first break in the journey was at Honolulu, reached after twenty-six days. There a stop of twelve days was made, Blanchet

pense. As for us, Our Very Dear Brethren, who until the present could not abandon you to sin, we shall remember without ceasing, that you have been our well-beloved brothers and our very dear children, that we are your father and your first pastor. Ah! be sure that all our compassion and all our tenderness are yours, that we shall not cease to pray the Father of mercies to save you from the flames of hell. Only have good will, make generous efforts, tear away the veil the demon would place before your eyes, break the chains that attach you to sin, return to our God, " Work out your salvation with fear and trembling," " the charity of our Divine Saviour, Jesus Christ, urges you," could you refuse longer to Him your heart and all the tenderness of your love? Let us, on our return among you, have the consolation to see you entered in the way of justice, of peace, of happiness. We did not at first think to absent ourselves for more than a few months, but we have been inspired to go to Europe in the interest of our Vicariate Apostolic. We hope to go even to the holy city, the city of Rome, to see there the tombs of the apostles, to visit the vicar of Jesus Christ, the common Father of all the faithful. In prostrating ourselves at his feet, in offering him the tribute of our profound homage, we shall not fail to offer him your most sincere wishes also, the sentiments of your great veneration, of your deepest respect. With what interest will not the Holy Father hear of your progress in religion, of your faith, of your fervor. What will be his joy, when he learns by what good examples virtue is propagated, religion flourishes, the kingdom of Jesus Christ is spread in this country! In his deep joy the head of the Church will bless you and will bless your country and all those who live here. Make yourselves worthy of these graces and favors by a renewal of fervor and of zeal in the doing of good and the avoidance of evil.

We have named and we do name to replace us, the Reverend Father Pierre De Vos, S. J., administrator of our Vicariate Apostolic; you will obey him as you would ourself. He is charged to provide for your spiritual needs.

* * * * * * *

The present letter shall be read and published at the Masses in the churches or parochial chapels, the first Sunday or feast after it has been received.

Given at Vancouver, the 22 November, 1844. PAA.

spending the time with the Picpus fathers [14] who had come from France several years before. They had erected a beautiful stone church, had a large congregation and were doing much good, after the days of bitter persecution which had accompanied their first efforts to introduce Christianity among the native population. On January 12, 1845 travel was resumed and for nearly two months the *Columbia* sailed south, doubling Cape Horn on March 5. The stormy Atlantic was still to be braved and it was not until May 22, that the ship put into port at Deal, England. From there Blanchet proceeded to Dover and thence to London, where he remained ten days, the guest of the Abbé Mailly, pastor of the French chapel in London.

Early in June, he was again on his way. Embarking at Liverpool, he crossed the Atlantic, reaching Boston June 19 and Montreal five days later. He went on to Quebec where he found the church draped in mourning on account of the burning of the suburb, St. Roch, a month before, and that of St. John a few days previously. Blanchet had hoped to be consecrated in Quebec by the prelate who had sent him to Oregon but Archbishop Signay was away making the visitation of his diocese and Blanchet, finding it would be impossible to have the ceremony there, returned to Montreal. On July 11 *Le Canadien* announced that bishop-elect Blanchet would be consecrated July 25, along with Charles Prince, bishop-elect coadjutor of Montreal. Accordingly on Saturday, July 25 there took place in St. James Cathedral one of the most impressive ceremonies that had ever been witnessed in the city. The Church was filled with an immense crowd which was thrilled by the inspiring spectacle of the consecration of two bishops. There were present besides the two bishops-elect, five others, the Bishops of Montreal (Ignatius Bourget), of Kingston (Remi Gaulin), of Sidyme (Pierre Turgeon, coadjutor to Bishop Signay), of Toronto (Michael Power), and of Carrah (Patrick Phelan, coadjutor to Kingston), not less than 143 priests and 57 ecclesiastics. The Most Reverend Ignatius Bourget, Bishop of Montreal, was the consecrator. Blanchet was assisted by Bishop Gaulin of Kingston and his coadjutor, Bishop Phelan; Prince by Bishops Turgeon and Power. The three vicars general assisted at the throne of the officiator: F. Demers, as

[14] Congregation of the Sacred Hearts of Jesus and Mary.

assistant priest, Thomas Cooke and Archambault, as deacons of honor; Francis Porlier was deacon and Remi Robert, sub-deacon. Edward Crevier, curé of St. Hyacinthe, preached the sermon, in which he commended the worthiness of those receiving the honor and outlined the duties and burdens of the office of the episcopacy, calling attention to the obligation of the clergy to share that burden.

The gathering of ecclesiastics, seven bishops, several vicars general, numerous clergy, the great crowd of faithful, silent and recollected, the beautiful church decorated for the occasion, the ecclesiastical vessels of great richness, the tones of the organ, the beauty and gravity of the Gregorian, the majesty of the ceremonies, all combined to make this occasion one unforgettable in the annals of Montreal church history.[15]

The newly consecrated bishop remained for a month and a half in Canada, renewing acquaintances and making appeals for his needy vicariate. Early in August he was in Quebec, where he preached in the cathedral to an interested congregation. He made known to them the progress of religion in the mission founded by Canadian priests and supported by alms from the Propagation of the Faith in Quebec; he extended his thanks for their generosity and begged them to continue their assistance. Then he returned to Montreal to make final preparations for his return to Europe. This journey began on August 12 when Blanchet left for Boston to take ship for Liverpool from whence he went on to London and across the Channel to the continent, where he was to spend a year, traveling from one city to another in the interests of his vicariate. He reached Paris September 8 and found hospitality with the Brothers of St. John of God. Here he evidently planned the work of the coming year, "which was to obtain from Rome some assistant bishops, to look for new missionaries and sisters, and collect funds to enable him to buy the requisites for his Vicariate, and pay the freight upon them and also the passage of the missionaries. All this required much time and traveling, and going backward and forward." [16]

[15] An account of Bishop Blanchet's consecration is given in *Le Canadien*, Quebec, July 30, 1845; also in *Mélanges Religieux-Scientifiques, Politiques et Littéraires*, Montreal, July 29, 1845.

[16] Blanchet, *op. cit.*, 59.

Bishop Blanchet first wished to visit Belgium in order to petition the Motherhouse of the Sisters of Notre Dame de Namur for more subjects who would assist the first six who had accompanied De Smet to Oregon.[17] But he had first to get means with which to travel. Having learned in London that the Abbé Mailly had an unforeseen debt against his vicariate, he had been forced to leave with his agent £127 of the £200 he had brought from Quebec. What remained was sufficient to take him to Paris only. A generous Irish priest came to his assistance there, provided for him in Paris and arranged for his trip into Belgium.

Returned to Paris in November, Bishop Blanchet sent an account of his progress and success to Bishop Turgeon. He discussed first the distressing condition of his finances. On his arrival in London the previous September he had made the staggering discovery that he must face immediately a debt of £1397.00. When his agent, Abbé Mailly, had first examined the note he had read it £139, overlooking altogether the figure 7! The bishop could have managed that; he had no means of paying the real sum. He left behind all that he could spare of the money he had brought from Quebec but it was a very small part of the amount required.[18] Hence it was that the Bishop of Drasa [19] arrived in Paris almost penniless. As was noted above an Irish priest gave him assistance there and paid his passage into Belgium. On his return, he applied for aid to the Society for the Propagation of the Faith at Paris and at Lyons and had the satisfaction of seeing things gradually adjust themselves,

[17] Blanchet secured these religious: Sisters Lawrence, Mary Bernard, Renilde, Odelie, Aldegonde, Francesca. There is an amusing account of the bishop's first attempt to visit the motherhouse in *In Harvest Fields*, 102, " One evening after 9:30, a gentleman knocked at the gate of the Mother House of the Sisters of Notre Dame at Namur. The sister portress (doubtless through the grill) without asking his name, courteously informed him that it was too late to admit guests. Since the visitor was in citizen's clothes, she did not suspect his clerical character. He made no demur but slipped her a letter, requesting her to give it to the Mother General, and walked quietly away. What was the consternation of the Mother General to discover the letter was from her Sisters in Oregon! The visitor was Archbishop Blanchet."

[18] Blanchet to Cazeau, September 24, 1845. QAA.

[19] Blanchet's title was changed from that of Bishop of Philadelphia to that of Drasa before his consecration.

although his problems were by no means completely solved. He had found generous religious, willing and eager to devote themselves to the work of his vicariate; but he had no guarantee yet that he could transport them from Europe to Oregon. He explains his predicament to the Canadian bishop:

> . . . my accounts have been arranged little by little, thanks to the help of the prayers which have been offered for my mission and the aid which Divine Providence has sent. . . . I am not free from worry about next year. My petitions and representations to the two councils will indeed reduce the pressing need in which I found myself in the autumn of 1845. I have asked 50,000 francs to pay the note of my vicar general, which will amount to that; and 30,000 francs for the expense of my passage to Oregon with the eight sisters and the six Brothers of the Christian Schools [20] and two priests whom I have at my disposal. I know that I cannot count on any money from Lyons for the expense of my return but I have firm confidence that they will allocate to me the 50,000 francs which I have asked. . . . This is my situation.[21]

His campaign had only begun. It took him from one country of Europe to the other before it was finished. Meanwhile, he made arrangements for notices to be printed regarding Oregon and renewed the consecration of his vicariate to the Blessed Mother:

> But what to do now?—seek—that I shall begin very quickly. They have counselled me to begin in Brittany and I shall go from there to other dioceses. The notice sent from the press of the *Mélanges*, having been corrected and printed in Belgium, has been spread there; I shall also distribute it here in France. Such are my hopes and my methods. On their success will depend the number of persons I shall take with me. My vicariate apostolic of Oregon was consecrated to the Blessed Virgin on September 14 in the Church of our Lady of Victories at Paris; prayers were said there for me, for my mission, its needs in Canada, in Belgium, in Oregon. How could I lose confidence? It is in the midst of distress and destitution that man feels his weakness, his powerlessness and the need which he has of having recourse to God who has created all things out of nothing. It has occurred to me to think that without

[20] These Brothers of the Christian Schools never reached Oregon.
[21] Blanchet to Turgeon, November 29, 1845. QAA.

these difficulties I should have been too confident and that this apparent evil will turn to good.²²

His spirit of confidence did not prevent a realization of the necessity of prudence and he had sent a warning to Demers that expansion in Oregon would have to be checked:

> ... I have written to my vicar general by the Company ship which will return the month after the closing of the accounts, March, 1846 to stop, not to undertake anything more; I have told him of my difficulties of this year and next; that for lack of means I cannot leave next spring or next autumn. As to whether I shall leave alone or accompanied, either in the spring or in the autumn, I shall decide that after having consulted all the papers of the vicar general, of the sisters and of the [...]. I should dislike much to leave behind the helpers Divine Providence has given. Who will send me these brothers and these sisters after my departure? Who will hasten to furnish them the means to pay their expenses? My arrival six months later in Oregon will not make any great difference, although my departure from here six months earlier might be an irreparable mistake; the purpose for which I made the voyage would be lost.²³

Bishop Blanchet had not been too busy or too occupied with his own affairs to notice conditions in the countries through which he traveled. In this same letter to Bishop Turgeon, he comments on and commends the faith of the people of Belgium and France:

> I should have beautiful things to say of Belgium and France if time permitted! What fervor! what piety! what devotion among those who are good! Since 1830 it is admirable, inconceivable to see the number of religious establishments in Belgium. Religion has made progress there; it is the same at Paris and elsewhere. One can travel in soutane without running the risk of being insulted. The devotion to the most holy and immaculate Heart of Mary has made progress and wrought wonders at Paris. The church of our Lady of Victories is always crowded, everyone sings; everyone prays; they prostrate at the singing of the *refugium peccatorum*.²⁴

Paris was left behind on December 17, and the missionary traveled to Marseilles to spend the festival of Christmas. He went

---
²² *Ibid*.   ²³ *Ibid*.   ²⁴ *Ibid*.

on to Rome early in January, 1846 and was granted an audience with Pope Gregory XVI. The first weeks were devoted to visiting the great basilicas, the churches, the monuments of the city. Blanchet descended into the catacombs several times and obtained the relics of Sts. Jovian, Severin, Flavia and Victoria. But the great achievement of these months was the completion and presentation of his *Memorial* on Oregon to the Sacred Congregation of Propaganda. Blanchet described it briefly in a letter to his friend, Bishop Turgeon:

> A word about my *Memorial*: it asks the establishment of an ecclesiastical province with the division of Oregon into eight dioceses and two more for the English part which is to the north. The metropolitan will be at Oregon City, a second bishop at Walla Walla and a third on Vancouver Island. We shall be content with three bishops for the present but the others will be asked and placed at need. It is thus that the Sacred Congregation has acted with regard to Australia. It was said that I should consult those interested, doubtless the archbishops of Quebec and Baltimore. Others thought that should not be necessary. If there should be a consultation, I hope that his Lordship, the Archbishop of Quebec, will sustain and perfect the work which he has so well begun. The archbishopric of Quebec enjoys a great reputation at Rome. Without regulars, the diocese has done what others have not been able to accomplish. As soon as my *Memorial* is printed, I shall send it to your Lordship. I think it will please you.[25]

The *Memorial on the Importance and the Necessity of the Establishment of an Ecclesiastical Province in Oregon* [26] is a remarkable document which Blanchet addressed to the cardinals of the Sacred Congregation de Propaganda Fide. Blanchet tells them that he has come to Rome to place at the feet of the Vicar of Jesus Christ the homage of the Catholics of Oregon and to present a plan which will assure the future of the Church in the Northwest. It is divided into two sections: I—The State of the Country and the Good done to the present; II—What Remains to be done. The first contains a geo-

[25] Blanchet to Turgeon, March 18, 1846. QAA.

[26] A copy of this *Memorial* from the Baltimore Cathedral Archives, henceforth BCA, and a photostat copy from Propaganda Archives in Rome are in the Guilday Transcripts.

graphical description of the Oregon country and an estimate of its importance, which Blanchet rated high, an account of the discoveries and explorations by Europeans and Americans with the beginnings of English and American colonization. There follows the story of the introduction of Christianity on the Pacific coast by the establishment of the Russian Church with bishop and clergy in Alaska. Then is summarized the history of the evangelization of the two Californias, the success and failures of the Jesuits and Franciscans, due, according to Blanchet, to their neglect to secure a hierarchical set-up and a native clergy.[27] The coming of the representatives of the Protestant sects—Methodists, Presbyterians and Anglicans—are next described and finally, the arrival of the Catholic priests. In a paragraph or two is given the state of religion in 1838 with an account of the progress that has been made since that time.

In the second part Blanchet discusses the future of religion in the northwest and offers his plan to secure its success. In his eyes it was necessary to have established there an ecclesiastical province, a metropolitan with several suffragan sees, in order to offset the influence of Russian orthodoxy and Protestantism, especially Anglicanism, both of which have a great reverence for the episcopacy. And secondly, it was essential in order that a native clergy be formed and schools established to instruct the faithful and fortify them in the practice of Christian virtue. Blanchet emphasizes the close bond that should exist between prelate and priest and for that reason he believes that the bishop should be closely connected with the training of the clergy. Both in the *Memorial* and elsewhere, Blanchet insists on the restriction of the privileges of religious communities in Oregon. The problem of the rights and jurisdiction of bishops over regulars in their dioceses was a matter which gave him much concern and of which he heard " incessant talk " in Rome. Perhaps this accounts for a change in his attitude toward the Jesuits to whom he had given a whole-hearted welcome a short time before.[28]

[27] Garraghan, *op. cit.*, II, 287, says it was rather a matter of destruction by hostile governments.

[28] It undoubtedly influenced him to draw up an addition to his *Memorial*, presented to Brunelli, May 6, in which he asked further powers:

1. Independently of the ordinary powers of authority, those granted besides to the metropolitans of Quebec and Baltimore.

Blanchet emphasizes the extent of the Oregon territory and the number of Indians to be converted.[29] He calls attention to the constantly increasing number of emigrants from the eastern United States, people whose dispositions are for the most part favorable to the Church and who, with the aid of a zealous priest, might be converted to the faith.

Finally, he outlines, as an ideal to be realized in the future, what to him was the logical organization of the Oregon territory, a metropolitan, Oregon City, with nine suffragan sees, Nisqually, Walla Walla, Fort Hall, Colville, Vancouver Island, Princess Charlotte Island, New Caledonia, with two in the country extending to the Arctic Ocean, Mt. St. Elias being a possible dividing point.[30] At the present he will be content with three, the archdiocese of Oregon City with jurisdiction over Nisqually, the diocese of Walla, Walla, including Fort Hall and Colville, that of Vancouver Island, including Princess Charlotte Island and New Caledonia with all the English and Russian possessions to the Arctic Ocean.

Early in May he recommenced his travels. On his way to Paris, he visited Leghorn, Genoa, Marseilles, Lyons and Chalons. He spent some days at Avignon, where seven seminarists offered themselves for the Oregon missions, and a week at Lyons, where he was the guest of the grand seminary. He addressed the 300 students, of whom three asked to accompany the missionary bishop to his diocese. These, B. Delorme, J. F. Jayol and F. Veyret, were to be among the group that sailed with Bishop Blanchet the following year. From

2. In all that concerns the exercise of the external ministry all authority without distinction over the missionaries, secular and regular, as to the administration of temporal goods in the diocese confided to my care. Of such sort that to carry out the orders of the Holy See, the regulars may not have recourse to an authority foreign to the mission.

3. The power to suspend the formation of the religious novitiate until the time when there will be formed the nucleus of a native secular clergy, sufficient to support and sustain the action of the bishop.

4. That these last two powers (Nos. 2 and 3) will be equally accorded to the bishops or vicars apostolic of the province.

[29] Blanchet estimates the number of Indians as 200,000 which is far too many.

[30] It is worthy of note that this plan, "amazing and startling" as it was, has with the development of the country been carried out rather closely in the present organization of the province of Portland-in-Oregon.

Lyons, Blanchet went on to Paris, which he left June 17 to visit again the cities of Belgium, where he had been so well-received before. At Liege, he assisted at the great Corpus Christi procession at which were present seventeen bishops, a large number of priests and an immense religious crowd. During the next two months he was traveling continuously—through the country of the Rhine, stopping at the principal cities; down the Danube to Vienna, where he remained three weeks, the guest of the Redemptorist fathers. On returning, he visited Augsburg and Strasburg, where he remained a week with its illustrious bishop. It was on his return to Paris that he learned that his vicariate had been erected by briefs, dated July 24, 1846, into an ecclesiastical province with the three sees of Oregon City, Walla Walla and Vancouver Island. The vicar apostolic was called to the metropolis of Oregon City, Reverend A. M. A. Blanchet, canon of the Montreal cathedral, to that of Walla Walla, and Vicar General Demers to that of Vancouver Island.

From Paris on August 31 Blanchet wrote to Bishop Turgeon to announce the good news:

> I have the honor to announce to your Lordship that the Holy See has put the last seal of approval to the acts of the Sacred Congregation. I say it, humbling myself before God at the sight of my weakness; I have been charged with a new burden; Oregon is an ecclesiastical province since last July 24. Mgr. A. M. Blanchet and Mgr. M. Demers have their bulls according to the request of my *Memorial*. I rejoice for the people and am grieved on my own account. May we walk always in the steps of the most illustrious bishops who rule and govern the diocese of Quebec with so much wisdom.[31]

And shortly after, Archbishop Blanchet communicated the news to the Archbishop of Baltimore. Evidently there had been no consultation regarding the new province with the archbishops of Baltimore and Quebec. At least in August the metropolitan of Baltimore knew nothing of it except what he had learned from an indirect report from Rome. In that month he wrote to Bishop Kenrick of Philadelphia seeking confirmation of the announcement of the proposed establishment which he seems to have found disturbing:

> I have lately received indirect information from Rome that an application had been made to erect an archiepiscopal See with

[31] Blanchet to Turgeon, August 31, 1846. QAA.

ten suffragans in Oregon. It is said also that the application was received with much favor. Should you know anything about the affair, and be at liberty to communicate it, you will much oblige me by letting me know whether there is any foundation for the report. The measure bears on its face a character of extravagance; but the source through which I have heard it is one of high respectability.[32]

His query was answered the following month by the new Archbishop of Oregon City who informed him concerning the ecclesiastical province just erected and gave him the names of the prelates who were to administer its affairs. Blanchet expresses his willingness to have submitted the plan to Baltimore but that would have necessitated a journey to America and would have meant the loss of precious time. He is, however, happy that his province will be a part of the Church in the United States:

> ... I would have been most willing that this important measure should have been proposed to the venerable prelates of the Council of Baltimore; I should also have wished much to have assisted at the last council of that city but if I had returned so soon to America, I should have been obliged to come again to Europe. This would have delayed my return to Oregon for a year and the important measures taken by the Holy See would thus have been put off. However, it was important that my sojourn in Europe should not be longer prolonged so that my suffragans might take possession of their sees as soon as possible and that work might be begun without delay simultaneously in several places for the conversion of the Protestants and the savages. The distance of Oregon from the province of Baltimore, the difficulties of the roads, the expenses of the voyage, the inconvenience of a long absence place great obstacles in the way of a reunion with the province of Baltimore. The difficulties of these reunions have contributed not a little to bringing a successful issue to this measure ... we congratulate ourselves on being a part of the Catholic Church in the United States. We shall be attached in mind and in heart to the rules of the Councils of Baltimore. Already we have procured the statutes of the first Councils, we desire, also, to have those of the Council held last spring. Will you be kind enough, my Lord, to send me several copies?[33]

A few days later, Blanchet wrote to the Cardinal Prefect of

---

[32] Eccleston to Kenrick, August 18, 1846. BCA.
[33] Blanchet to Eccleston, September 16, 1846. PAA.

Propaganda to express his deep appreciation for the interest he had taken in the Oregon missions and for the favorable action of the cardinals with regard to his *Memorial*:

> I thank your Eminence for having deigned to announce to me yourself this important news. It has been most agreeable to learn that a measure so grave has been so happily and so promptly terminated. It is sweet to think that it has in such a high degree drawn not only the attention and care of your Eminence and their Eminences, the Cardinals of the Sacred Congregation, but even the attention and the wishes of two illustrious sovereign pontiffs.
>
> I profit by this occasion to ask your Eminence to place at the feet of His Holiness the homage of my profound veneration, the ardent wishes that we have for the prosperity of his reign, while we implore His Holiness to bless the bishops of Oregon, the missionaries and all the people confided to their care.[34]

He had written some months before (May 29, 1845) to the Jesuit General asking that twelve Jesuits be sent to join those already working in Oregon, to take charge of Indian missions in New Caledonia and around Puget Sound, which Blanchet felt were in danger of falling into the hands of the Protestant missionaries.[35] It was impossible for Father Roothaan, the General, to send this number, not because he was unwilling to assist but because the men were not available. He did appoint two and Blanchet writes to thank him. The letter gives a glimpse into conditions at home where dissensions and disputes threatened the unity of the small band of workers. Evidently the difficulty had to do with the ownership or use of land which had been given to the Jesuits by Archbishop Blanchet:[36]

---

[34] Blanchet to Cardinal Prefect of Propaganda, October 6, 1846. PAA.

[35] This letter is given in Garraghan, *op. cit.*, II, 285-286. Garraghan, 289, quotes a letter of Roothaan, in which he gives his estimate of Blanchet: "For the rest I don't conceal my fears that difficulties may arise with his Grace. He is indeed a very pious man, but one very much under the sway of imagination, who indulges a good deal in theory and weighs less the practical side of things. Hence, he is unsteady and changeful and often hesitates considerably. Of such character does this excellent man appear to be not only in my own opinion but in that of other persons here and these of the highest standing. . . ."

[36] Cf. Garraghan, *op. cit.*, II, 297 ff.

> I recently received your letter brought me by the Italian fathers destined for Oregon; I am happy to be accompanied by them. I thank you for having informed me that Father Demers has been invested with the powers with which I had charged him as Vicar General and administrator of the Vicariate Apostolic. The good and Reverend Father De Vos, having seemed to me to act conscientiously in refusing the jurisdiction,[37] it is not that which has caused me pain, but rather that he has never consulted my Vicar General in this circumstance and in that of the boundary of the piece of land granted. It has been painful to me to receive lines which demanded that a man in whom I had put my confidence should keep at a respectful distance from the establishment of the fathers. Imprudences on the part of another member before the public have not helped to maintain that harmony so necessary to do good. I hope that my presence may remedy this evil.[38]

One last letter of this period remains, written shortly before the final departure from Europe. It tells the story of the last weeks; the false starts and disappointments that attended every move. Obstacles seemed to appear at every step and it was not until February, 1847 that the *Oceanic Maritime Society*[39] was able to secure and have ready to sail *l'Etoile du Matin,* the ship which carried Archbishop Blanchet and his group of twenty-one missionaries to Oregon. He had brought the sisters of Notre Dame from Belgium to Paris in December expecting to leave during that month but it was found to be impossible. The late sailing increased the dangers of the voyage and Blanchet was apprehensive.

> Although adoring the designs of Divine Providence in the multiplied contradictions and the long delays which I have experienced; and in all submitting willingly to the bitterness which heaven may reserve to us at Cape Horn, which we shall double in the month of May, the winter season in the tropical regions, I cannot be under any illusion about the dangers which we shall have to run by leaving two months too late. *L'Etoile*

---

[37] De Vos was appointed vicar general before Blanchet's departure for Europe. Garraghan, *op. cit.*, II, 366, says that he on the advice of De Smet withdrew from the post. Roothaan expressed his disapproval of the appointment.

[38] Blanchet to the General of the Jesuits, October 7, 1846. PAA.

[39] This society was founded in France to facilitate the passage of priests who were anxious to devote themselves to the work of the missions in parts of the world with which communication was difficult.

du Matin will carry the hope of Oregon; it is already a great disappointment not to be able to arrive until autumn, when we should have arrived in the spring in time to begin the work of the mission; by autumn we should be seeking winter quarters. . . .⁴⁰

However, he has put his trust in Mary, "our good Mother," and he consoles himself with the thought of her powerful protection. Besides, Captain Menes, a good Breton Christian, has had much experience—"his twenty-six years on the sea make him dear and precious to us; he has doubled Cape Horn four times, even in the months of June and September." The personnel of the missionary party consisted of "seven sisters of Notre Dame de Namur, five priests, two subdeacons and one ecclesiastic who has received the tonsure. That makes fifteen, I am the sixteenth. For this number I paid 1600 frances per person. The three Jesuit fathers and the three coadjutor brothers of their order paid for themselves."

On February 22, 1847 this little band put out to sea to begin their six months of ocean travel. Prayer, reading and study were the daily occupations of the missionaries, "the beauties of the vast sea and of the spangled vault, especially of the southern bright starry firmament at night, were subjects of profound meditation on the powerful creating hand of God." It was not until August that the "land of promise" appeared in sight but finally the bark safely crossed the bar of the Columbia and late in the afternoon of August 13, 1847, cast anchor in Gray's Bay. Then it was that the missionaries in "their exceeding great joy, chanted a *Te Deum*, which the echoes of Cape Disappointment and the neighboring hills repeated with emulation." On August 17, the ship went aground at the mouth of the Willamette and two days later the priests and sisters left her to travel to St. Paul, which they reached on Saturday, August 26, late at night. The Archbishop went first to Oregon City where he celebrated Mass in the Cathedral and then on to Champoeg, where accompanied by a large crowd of Catholics and Protestants, he entered the church at St. Paul vested in his episcopal robes, mozette, miter and crosier. After the *Te Deum* and benediction of the Blessed Sacrament and appropriate words from the Archbishop, all retired happy.⁴¹

⁴⁰ Blanchet to [———], January 28, 1847, QAA.
⁴¹ Blanchet, *op. cit.*, 61.

CHAPTER VIII

THE FIRST PROVINCIAL COUNCIL

By 1844 the days of pioneer missionary work in the country west of the Cascades were drawing to a close. Fathers Blanchet and Demers realized the coming change and prepared themselves to meet it. The steady stream of settlers who came from the eastern United States in 1842, 1843 and 1844 decided beyond doubt the question of predominance;[1] by 1844 American influence was an accepted fact and the provisional government that had been established was, in spite of Hudson's Bay Company cooperation, largely American in its ideas and practices. Even before Blanchet's departure for Europe, Oregon City had begun to replace Fort Vancouver as a center of activity and the newcomers, with customary American enterprise, had made plans for other towns. The missionary was an interested spectator of this development. " The Columbia," he wrote to Bishop Turgeon, " is no longer without interest; she becomes and will become, more and more interesting. The Americans who have arrived here by hundreds, bring with them their industry and well-known activity. They talk of towns to be built; there are four under construction . . ."[2] Each one of these tiny outposts of civilization needed its church or chapel and so the demands of the white settlers, for the time at least, crowded the Indian from the plans of the missionaries. Blanchet regretted this but felt that there was nothing he could do about it. As he said in a letter, " You will see with sorrow that we have done nothing for the savages. Not having received priests last autumn, it has been necessary to concentrate our efforts. . . ."

[1] In 1841 the first pioneer settlers came over the trail, a band of thirty persons; in 1842 more than a hundred; in 1843 the " great emigration " of 1000; in 1844 the numbers are uncertain, estimates varying from 475 to 700.

[2] Blanchet to Turgeon, April 6, 1844. QAA. The four towns were Fort George, Linntown, Champoeg and Oregon City.

Early in March, 1844 Blanchet and Demers visited Oregon City, in order to make the necessary arrangements for the opening of a church of which Demers was to be first pastor. In a letter to Father Cazeau, he gives a few details of his experiences and of the conditions under which this foundation was made:

> Here I am the first pastor of Oregon City among the *Poston telehom*, the Americans, and never could I have come under more favorable circumstances to make my entry in their midst. You have heard me speak, I suppose, of a certain Waller, self-reverend, mad Methodist who cut down a cross among the Clackamas; he has succeeded in making himself detested by his own co-religionists who accuse him of subterfuge and proved lies with regard to a plot of land of which he has despoiled Dr. McLoughlin. . . .[3]
>
> Imagine his rage when he saw me; without doubt he will do, as do those in the Islands, pray publicly against the usurpation of papism, especially since he saw that last Sunday I had a numerous congregation . . . I do not expect to change them overnight, but little by little, prejudices will disappear, when they see for themselves the absurd tales spread against our religion.[4]

Somewhat perhaps to his astonishment Demers discovered that the American settlers were often likable, tolerant and inclined to give him a fair chance to explain to them the mysteries of the faith. He seems to have shared with Father De Vos[5] the work at Oregon City and often during these years the priests had a little band under instruction and more than one of these was received into the Church. One of the best known was Peter H. Burnett, first chief justice of Oregon, and later first governor of California, who, becoming convinced of the truth of Catholicism, asked admission into the Church. He was baptized by Father De Vos in June, 1846.[6] Another was Dr. J. E. Long, secretary of the Provisional

---

[3] Alvin Waller arrived in Oregon on the Lausanne in 1840. He later played an unhappy part in helping to defraud McLoughlin of his land claim at Oregon City.

[4] Demers to Cazeau, March 8, 1844. QAA.

[5] Garraghan, *op. cit.*, II, 367, says that De Vos was placed in charge of the parish in Oregon City early in 1845.

[6] Burnett gives the story of his conversion in *The Path which Led a Protestant Lawyer to the Catholic Church* (St. Louis, 1909).

Government, who with his wife became a Catholic in July, 1845.[7] The action of both men was undoubtedly a factor in the early success of the missionaries among the Americans. In October Demers reported to Cazeau:

> I do not know whether I had occasion to tell you of the conversion of a man sometime after Easter; he was a deist more than anything else.[8]
>
> His example has been followed by another, Dr. Long, who has become a Catholic with his wife; they are both truly edifying. Having been instructed and well-grounded, as one said, no one that I know, dares to ask him the reason for his return to the religion of his ancestors. Several others read, listen and examine in silence the truths of papism, determined to become papists, once convinced that the truth is there and not elsewhere. The Americans begin to familiarize themselves with our dogmas, and so little by little the absurd prejudices which the spirit of error has invented against our holy religion are disposed of. Let us hope that it may continue so and that more than one of the scattered sheep may return to the fold.[9]

This progress was not the only kind that might have been noted during the absence of Bishop Blanchet. In November, 1844 before his departure for Europe, Blanchet had appointed Demers his vicar general and administrator, evidently with instructions to begin an extensive building program. Accordingly Demers planned churches, chapels, convents, schools and pushed on their construction without much thought of the cost. In an enthusiastic letter to Cazeau written in February, 1845 he gives an account of this activity:

> Besides a chapel for the sisters which is being built, we will soon begin a church and an episcopal residence which ought to be finished by the return of Bishop Blanchet. Don't you think that even the word—episcopal—already begins to give tone and relief to our growing Oregon? Still another chapel—the habitants who live on the great prairie are busy constructing it under the direction of Father Vercruysse;[10] it is necessary

---

[7] Cf. Garraghan, *op. cit.*, II, 367, for a letter of De Vos regarding this conversion.

[8] This may have been George Le Breton.

[9] Demers to Cazeau, October 10, 1845. QAA.

[10] Garraghan, *op. cit.*, II, 369, gives a sketch of the work of Father Louis Vercruysse. This chapel was built, not with contributions from the Association of the Faith, but with money contributed by the settlers themselves.

because during the winter season these men cannot, except with difficulty, come to the old church on account of the poor roads and the waters which obstruct the passage in more than one place. . . .

I still want to build a house and a chapel at the Fort on the land which has been allotted us. We fear much that things will change at this important post after the departure of Dr. McLoughlin and we have good reason for thinking thus. Mr. Douglas, well as he knows our dogmas, still remains attached to his Presbyterian church. . . . It is expected that he will have a minister who will remain at the Fort and that we shall be politely shown to the door. Hence it is, that it is prudent for us to have a house of our own, so that we may help our Canadians who are always there in large numbers.[11]

Construction costs were high and these unpretentious buildings loaded the Oregon vicariate with a debt that mounted before long to frightening heights. Although Bishop Blanchet had encouraged such a program, Demers began to think that he might have gone too far and to wonder whence the funds necessary to finance such operations were to come. Toward the end of 1845 he shared his anxiety with Cazeau:

. . . I ask you at once if you have seen Bishop Blanchet; I think you will answer no; according to his last letter he seemed resolved to make the sacrifice and not to go to Canada so that he might be able to return next spring by the Company vessel. If this is the case he will have but little time in Europe to look for and prepare the things which are necessary, of which I gave him a long list. May God guard and bring him back to us but not with empty hands; for he has need of a large purse to pay the expenses which we have incurred this year in building churches, convent, houses and all the rest. My church at the Falls (Oregon City) will be finished, as far as the exterior is concerned next month; they say it will be an ornament to our little city. It is sixty feet long by thirty wide, built on a foundation six feet high, with side chapels, gothic cornices and windows. But for all that it takes *ayo talla*, many piasters. The workers are not ashamed to ask two and three a day; but everything is so dear here that even with that they could never make a large fortune.[12]

[11] Demers to Cazeau, February 21, 1845. QAA.
[12] Demers to Cazeau, October 10, 1845. QAA.

His anxiety over the debt led the priest to appeal to the Society for the Propagation of the Faith at Lyons, of which he asked a large allocation to cover the calculated expense of 80,000 francs. However, in spite of the worry over money matters he seems to have been particularly happy in this struggling frontier town and to have found conditions there much to his liking. In February, 1846 St. John's Church was blessed and Demers sent an account of the event to Quebec:

> My church at Oregon City was blessed February 8, Septuagesima Sunday; there was a large crowd; all the pews were filled with the curious who seem to have been urged, however, not by a spirit of criticism but by a praiseworthy curiosity. They have seen the ceremonies and listened to the explanations which were given. Since that time the congregation has continued to be numerous; they listen with pleasure and interest to the explanation of Catholic dogmas, and little by little prejudices disappear; they end by having a taste for a religion they had despised, which they hated only because they did not know it.[13]

Demers felt keenly the need of a priest to whom the English language was a native tongue. He and Father De Vos made some progress and the citizens of Oregon City do not seem to have found their lack of facility with English too great a handicap. Both men were well-liked and found many things about this settlement which had an appeal. Father Demers was especially enthusiastic: "The good God has willed that I succeed with them; and I have gained their esteem and even their affection—*ad majorem Dei gloriam*. . . . The first favor which I shall ask of his Grace on his return, if he has not brought another, will be that he place me at St. John's; this place is mine; this church is mine by all sorts of titles." [14]

Still the Americans continued to come, "the emigrants arrive in great numbers; some by the Columbia from Walla Walla; others by land with their animals, horses, cows, and wagons making a road through the woods and forests; nothing stops them; there is not, anywhere under the sun, a people like them, I think." With their coming the "Oregon question" was often a matter for discussion.

[13] Demers to Cazeau, March 5, 1846. QAA.
[41] *Ibid.*

These newcomers could tell of the agitation in the eastern United States for American control and of the extensive claims that President Polk had advanced. Difficulties were constantly arising and the demand for some sort of settlement became urgent. The appearance on the coast of British and American ships-of-war did not tend to ease the situation. There was constant speculation about the possible action of the British parliament and the American congress; it could be no more than speculation for news traveled slowly in 1845. But the feeling of unrest grew and men were anxious about the outcome. The missionary, keenly alive to the dangers, sent some observations to Quebec:

> I have received a letter from Father Mailly . . . who says they are menaced by war without giving any further details. . . . Here we know nothing regarding the boundary which we suppose to be the cause of this war. It is to be hoped that this affair may soon be ended for the peace and tranquillity of Oregon. A large emigration has come to augment our American population. The emigrants, coming chiefly from the northern states, represent every kind of people, good and bad. There are two parties, that which favors the Hudson's Bay Company and that which would drive it from the country, although without it they would die of hunger on arriving here. . . . I tell you and the bishops that we fear trouble in the country and in a short while perhaps. Even for religion I fear there will be some sort of a struggle; the Methodist party seems terrified at the advance of papism; it is said that the Catholics will become powerful and make conversions; this last, I rejoice to tell you, is true; for there is an extraordinary desire to be instructed in the truths of Catholicism and the change in ideas is proportional.[15]

In November, 1845 Demers wrote that the British frigate, *La Modeste*, had come to spend the winter off the coast of Oregon and was at the disposition of the officers of the Hudson's Bay Company. One of the officers of the ship, Dr. Gibson, had reported that the American war ship, *Salamander*, had been met at the Sandwich Islands and was bound for the Oregon coast. The fear of war oppressed all, " We think here that there will be a war which will cost much more than the possession of the country will be worth. Already several Americans are established at Cowlitz and still

---

[15] Demers to Cazeau, March 11, 1845. QAA.

farther, well persuaded that that country will belong to them; it is known that they would not like to become British subjects."[16] And in December, Demers, knowing the tension between British and American, felt that he should order the prayer for peace to be said in all the churches. "The situation in the country," he wrote to Cazeau," is suddenly delicate. The fire is near the powder; should an American receive an injury which might wound national sentiment a little, the fort might be attacked and would very likely be burned; we should be in the midst of the horrors of a disastrous war."[17] The position of the priests was difficult, "if we should meddle there, especially if we should try to influence our men toward England, it would go against us and our missions; but do not fear, not at all, we shall remain perfectly neutral. . . ."

Not all of the time of the missionaries was devoted to a consideration of the uncertainties of Oregon sovereignty. Work continued and progress was made in spite of new obstacles to success which constantly appeared. The French Canadians who had welcomed the missionaries with so much enthusiasm in 1838 were not the most satisfactory of parishioners. Early accounts of these settlers picture them as industrious and well-behaved. Jason Lee's first impression of them was a favorable one, "We found at least a dozen families, mostly French Canadians, . . . They seemed prosperous and happy and gave us a very polite and generous welcome to the best they could set before us."[18] But through the 1840's the French Canadians showed little progress and made slight contribution to the development of culture and industry. Rather were they characterized by shiftlessness and dissipation.[19]

Under McLoughlin's rule the sale of liquor had been fairly well controlled. After his retirement it seems to have been manufactured and sold freely and to have wrought havoc among the settlers of French Prairie. Demers thus described conditions:

> I wrote you last autumn but I do not know if my letter ever reached you. I spoke to you of the disgust that I have taken

[16] Demers to Cazeau, November 14, 1845. QAA.
[17] Demers, to Cazeau, December 20, 1845. QAA.
[18] Tobie, *op. cit.*, 152, quotes Lee's diary.
[19] Clark, *Willamette Valley*, I, 236.

toward the country as likewise Father Bolduc since they have
begun to make whiskey which has made sad ravages among our
men. . . . I told them publicly that if they continued to drink
I would not remain in the country nor would Father Bolduc;
that it was too hard for me after having taken so much pains
to put them on the right road, etc., etc., to see them lose in so
short a time the fruit of our toil and labor; that I would
rather live on roots and moss with the savages than in the
midst of drunkards.[20]

There was no permanent improvement in the character and conduct of these Oregon pioneers; indeed, a gradual deterioration is to be noted and Demers' judgment that "the conduct of the Canadians on the Columbia is far from edifying and contributes not a little to retard the conversion of the Indians to whom they should be models" was confirmed in later years until in 1852 Blanchet was forced to conclude with Father Cenas, who had been stationed at St. Paul, that "there are few among the Canadians of Oregon who give consolation to the missionaries . . . they have little firmness of character, no solid faith, nothing but routine in their religious practices. Their wives and children are little better. I have done what I could but I am discouraged."[21]

In the meantime, Demers discovered another enemy to the progress of Catholicism, ". . . our religion is established on the ruins of Methodism but another enemy, a hydra with hideous visage has begun to show its infernal head. It has lately been discovered in existence in the country, that is free masonry. You will see in the *Spectator* a notice on this subject; they have already held an assembly."[22]

Such were the problems that Demers and his fellow workers had to face during the two years of Blanchet's absence. The Oregon to which the Archbishop returned in August, 1847 was not the Oregon, that he had left in December, 1844. These years had seen many changes—political, social, religious. The "Oregon question"

[20] Demers to Cazeau, March 5, 1846. QAA.
[21] Blanchet to Archbishop of Quebec, January 5, 1852. QAA.
[22] Demers to Cazeau, March 5, 1846. QAA. Bancroft, *Oregon*, II, 30, notes that the first issue of the *Spectator* contained a notice for a meeting of masons to be held February 21, 1846. The grand lodge of Missouri issued a charter on October 19, 1846 to Multnomah lodge in Oregon City.

had been settled, once and for all, and the United States had extended her sovereignty over the western territory, north to the forty-ninth parallel. The power of the Hudson's Bay Company had disappeared. McLoughlin had severed his connections with it, declared his intention to become a citizen of the United States, and had settled at Oregon City. The population was entirely changed. The ever-increasing immigration from the eastern United States had for several years overshadowed the French Canadian as the dominant element in the new American territory. The center of interest was no longer Fort Vancouver on the Columbia but Oregon City, the growing town on the Willamette. The Methodist group was still a power, but now its interest had definitely shifted from missionary work and seemed to be concerned with an attempt to control the political situation in Oregon.

But in spite of these changes no one could have foreseen that the Church in this western land was close to disaster, nor that it was to undergo trials in the next ten years, which would threaten its very existence. The prospect seemed fair in 1847 as the prelates looked over the province. It is true that there were troublesome problems to be solved but there was no indication of the catastrophe which would so soon plunge the people of Oregon into panic and destroy in a day the work of nine years of painful effort.

When in August, 1847 Archbishop Blanchet arrived from Europe to take possession of his recently-erected province, none of this was apparent; a spirit of joy and general rejoicing made happy his return, and if we may judge from his own account, he received a cordial welcome from clergy and people. To quote him, "from the arrival of the archbishop to the sad event which put the Catholic missions of Oregon upon the brink of their ruin, there were but festivities and rejoicings in the archdiocese, especially at St. Paul." [23] On Sunday, September 12 the archbishop administered the sacrament of confirmation there, and on the following Sunday, he "made an ordination," raising Mr. Jayol to the priesthood. On September 26 he was at Vancouver to give confirmation and the next three Sundays he spent with the people of Cowlitz, where he confirmed fifty persons. He returned to St. Paul toward the end of October

[23] Blanchet, *op. cit.*, 61.

and ordained deacon Delorme. But the culminating point of all the rejoicing came on November 30, when Father Demers received episcopal consecration at the hands of the archbishop, in the presence of a numerous clergy and a large crowd of interested spectators. It was a happy occasion for all except the recipient of the honor who was far from content at the prospect before him, " I do not know in what terms to express my misery! . . . What should I do? I do not wish to accept but at the same time I have not the courage to carry out the plans I spoke of in my last letter. I am loath to abandon his Lordship in the critical circumstances in which he is placed." [24]

The thought of the great expanse of territory confided to his care was overwhelming and the bishop was far from enthusiastic about undertaking his new duties for conditions at the time were not such as to warrant too great hopefulness. Some of the country he had seen; some of the Indians he had met and he knew all too well the obstacles that lay in the way of making the diocese of Vancouver Island and the districts of Princess Charlotte Island and New Caledonia strongholds of the faith. He wrote to Cazeau, " I have been charged with more than 30,000 savages, plunged for the most part in the darkness of infidelity and I have for co-laborers, only two priests [25] who have begun a small establishment in New Caledonia at the head of Lake Okanogan from where they began their exploration of this vast territory. . . . Vancouver Island . . . is to be my place of residence . . . The population is composed of savages, all pagans, except some hundreds of children who were baptized in 1843 by Father Bolduc, the only missionary who has yet visited this country. This is the vast field which Providence has confided to my care." [26] There was some justification for the bishop's feeling that the only means which Providence had placed at his disposal for building in this solitary and savage country were " poverty, destitution and without doubt divine Providence."

Meanwhile, Bishop A. M. A. Blanchet had arrived at Walla Walla. Consecrated by Bishop Ignatius Bourget of Montreal, September

[24] Demers to Cazeau, September 22, 1847. QAA.
[25] Fathers John Nobili and Anthony Ravailli. For their work in New Caledonia cf. Garraghan, *op. cit.*, II, 325-334.
[26] Demers to Cazeau, in *Rapport* (1849), 96-97.

27, 1846 he had spent some months in Canada, making final arrangements for the journey to the west. Knowing the scarcity of priests in the Oregon country, he had appealed to the bishops of eastern Canada and to the superior general of the Oblates at Marseilles for volunteers for his far-away diocese. And to an extent which he had not expected, he had been successful in gaining recruits. Thus he writes to one of the bishops:

> Yesterday's post brought me such consolation that I am almost overcome. The bishop of Marseilles announced to me that the Oblates had embarked February 1 from Havre for New York and would there await my orders. The bishop of Montreal who wrote me January 14 was most favorable toward Oregon. The administration has today given to Father Brouillet, curé of Acadie, permission to follow me and has promised him letters of excorporation. . . . So I have what I wanted for this year. There remains for me to pay my debt of gratitude to God. Help me to satisfy this demand. I asked at least one secular priest—prudent, virtuous, of some experience. I asked at least two Oblates. I asked 1000 or 1200 louis. I shall have all that and perhaps more! *Misericordias Domini in aeternum cantabo. Omnes gentes plaudite manibus.*[27]

The bishop of Walla Walla made the long journey across the United States from Westport, Missouri. Leaving Montreal in March he went to St. Louis where he busied himself with the numerous details attendant on travel to the west in 1847 and where he "experienced worries and perplexities, which followed me for the rest of the journey." Shortly after his arrival at Walla Walla in September he sent an account of his adventures to Bishop Turgeon and included some useful advice for those who might have to travel the same road:

> If there is any priest who wishes to come here by the same route, there are several things he should have in order not to find himself in my embarrassing situation. If he is alone and without baggage, the best plan would be for him to procure at Westport or elsewhere a good guide, accustomed to these trips, to purchase a pack-horse (they call them prairie horses), and then to join a caravan because of the danger there would be in traveling alone or in small numbers, especially in passing through the lands of the Pawnees and the Sioux. If he has

[27] A. M. Blanchet to [————], February 24, 1847. QAA.

baggage, it will be necessary to purchase a wagon at St. Louis and to buy some oxen, five or six years old, not too fat; if the load does not weigh more than 1200 to 1500 pounds, three pair will be sufficient for the wagon but it is necessary to have one or two extra pair in case of accidents, which are likely to happen. The provisions are sea biscuits and flour; one pound a day ought to be sufficient for each person. It is essential to have plenty of meat, bacon and salted or chipped beef, three fourths pound of bacon each day is enough for each; also, tea, coffee, sugar, rice, etc., etc. A milk cow is of great service. My best oxen cost me $40 and $50 the pair; my wagons $80 each, my horses from $25 to $30. Although I had purchased twelve pair of oxen, I had trouble in making the trip; many are dead or have been abandoned, unable to walk farther. The cause of the death of such a great number of animals this year has been lack of food. The number of wagons to come and go will be over a thousand. The early emigrants had pasturage for their stock but the later arrivals found nothing or almost nothing for theirs to feed on. Father Brouillet tells me that from Fort Hall to Walla Walla there were no less than a hundred wagons abandoned on the road because there were no more beasts to pull them. My wagons are still usable but the oxen are so worn with fatigue, hunger and thirst that it was necessary to leave along the way some of the supplies carried from St. Louis, such as the plow, etc. . . . My expenses for the trip exceeded my estimate. I had planned that they would be about £500 at the most; and they almost doubled this amount. Farewell then, to the hope of beginning the episcopal establishment with the money subscribed by Quebec and Montreal; one must live while awaiting such help as may come to us from France.[28]

This frontier bishop found many obstacles to even the beginnings of his work but he made some plans which he hoped eventually to put into effect:

The Oblates wish to establish a mission on the Yakima River, twenty-two miles north of Walla Walla. As for me, I must remain at the fort with my priests until God makes known to us His will regarding the beginning of a mission. It will doubtless be amongst the Cayuse but the chiefs are away and will perhaps not return soon and I am unable to do anything before their arrival. One of them, Tawato, called by the French, "Young Chief," has begged for priests for several years and is ready to give us some land, but there are two other chiefs, Tilocate and Gros Ventre, whom I would like to

[28] A. M. Blanchet to Turgeon, 1847. QAA.

> unite, so as not to have to establish more than one mission for the whole nation. If I am successful Dr. Whitman, Presbyterian, laborer, merchant, having the office of minister may say that his days are numbered. Already the Indians dislike him and wish him far from them. It seems certain that his establishment will fall into our hands. They say it is a beautiful place for a mission. . . . The Methodist mission at the Dalles is finished. The savages say that they will no longer endure the ministers and wish to have some missionaries. Those who know tell us we shall find there several sites well-placed for a mission. I would not be averse to establishing my episcopal residence there. It is accessible from the sea by boat and can be reached from the Willamette in three or four days. Salmon is plentiful, the earth rich and it will be an important place in the future. It is true that it is in the extreme western part of my diocese but communication should become more and more easy.[29]

The Indians were not always friendly but there were a sufficient number of chiefs who were willing and anxious to give their assistance:

> The great chief of the Walla Wallas, Piopiomoxmox (he is sixty years old) which signifies Yellow Bird but which the French translate as Yellow Snake, did not appear well-disposed at first but at present I think he is more friendly. . . . Some of the men were baptized before my arrival; others who have not been, call themselves Catholics and make the Sign of the Cross. There is one named Patatis, baptized Pierre, who acts as missionary on all occasions whether in preaching or in leading the prayers although he does not half know them. He is going to be a great chief and will have a great influence with a large number of young natives for he is beloved of all, whereas Piopiomoxmox is feared. . . . Cannassissi, the chief of the Dalles Indians, says that his people would not be as bad as they are if they had priests to instruct them. The Nez Percés are too distant to be attached to the Presbyterian minister who resides among them. I am going to send them a missionary very quickly. As you see, the harvest is indeed ready but the laborers are few. The number of houses in my diocese, properly speaking, is five; there is neither church nor chapel, as you know.[30]

---

[29] *Ibid.*

[30] *Ibid.*; another account of this journey compiled and edited by Raphael N. Hamilton, S. J., is published in *Illinois Catholic Historical Review*, IX (1926), 208-222.

As for the archdiocese of Oregon City, Blanchet seemed to have found conditions satisfactory although Demers, in a letter written before the archbishop's return, points out difficulties awaiting him. He fears that the new priests are scarcely suited for the work and he finds the debt that has been incurred staggering:

> First I will speak to you of Father De Smet. Do not be astonished if I tell you that the good Father has made his voyage in Europe like a man who had never been in this country or who had no idea of its needs. He has failed to bring the most necessary things; of those which cannot be bought here except for a high price, he has brought nothing. As for books, which Father Langlois asked, I doubt if he has brought a single one, it is the same with many other articles. Besides the Jesuits are dissatisfied, they did not come here to establish schools but to found missions for the Indians. Following advice given to the Father General by Father De Smet he has ordered that they form an establishment in the Willamette Valley, which will be a mother mission, a central place which can furnish the needs of the missions of the mountains. But the Willamette is not any more central for the mountains than Kingston is for Rimouski. You know already what distances there are and how many of the voyages are not only difficult but dangerous. The Fathers here feel keenly the mistake in calculation and the inconvenience of being stationed at Willamette but they can do nothing. . . .[31]
>
> I hope that his Lordship will not follow Father De Smet's example. He took a list made out by me but I am afraid that he has not had the necessary time; I fear above all that he will not bring money. . . . I have told you that his Lordship ordered us to build without economy—churches, houses, convents without too much calculating the cost; we have not done all that he said but our accounts are none the less, enormous, frightening—150,000 francs or almost.[32]

To sum up: " By the arrival from France and Canada, the ecclesiastical Province of Oregon City possessed in the fall of 1847, 3 bishops, 14 Jesuit Fathers, 4 Oblate Fathers of M. I., 13 secular priests, including a deacon ordained in 1849, and a cleric, T. Mesplié, ordained in May 1850; 13 sisters and 2 houses of education." [33] With this band of zealous workers the prospects were

---

[31] Cf. Garraghan, *op. cit.*, II, 295-303.
[32] Demers to Cazeau, March 5, 1846. QAA.
[33] Blanchet, *op. cit.*, 62.

fair. There can be little doubt that Archbishop Blanchet had ambitious plans for the extension of the influence of the Church in Oregon. The Holy See had approved the general outline of his ideal. He had secured helpers—priests and nuns—for the missions and schools. His brother, Augustine, Bishop of Walla Walla, was already established in his diocese; Bishop Demers, the third of the Oregon prelates, was soon to leave for Europe to ask aid for his diocese. The plans were made; the execution of all of them was destined to be postponed; some of them were never to be realized.

Scarcely had the joyous strains of the festivities at St. Paul died away, when there came the report of the murder of the missionary party at Waiilatpu. It opened a decade of years of trial and difficulty for the Catholic clergy and for the time at least, put an end to the hope of progress that might reasonably have been expected. The story of the Whitman tragedy has been told many times; there is no need to review it here except in so far as it affected the activities of the Church in Oregon. The motives that prompted it, the uncertain reasoning on the part of the Indians, the rancor and bitterness against a man, who, according to his own notions, had worked for their welfare can be understood now. So too can the outrageous charges made against the Hudson's Bay Company and the Catholic clergy. The intense excitement and fear that characterized the period are explanation enough. Every writer of the time and almost every one since, who has had any interest in Oregon history, has discussed the question, whether or not the Hudson's Bay Company and the Catholic missionaries were responsible for the massacre. They have been cleared of all complicity; whether or not the presence of Bishop Blanchet and his priests in the Walla Walla country complicated the situation is another matter. It was unfortunate, without doubt that they settled where they did, but that they had any part in the plans and activities of the Indians is unbelievable.

But catastrophe had come and for at least another decade its effects were felt by all who had anything to do with the Church in the province of Oregon City. Hopes and ambitions that had seemed so surely to be fulfilled, were laid aside and efforts were confined to the struggle for existence. There was now no question of expansion.

Bishop Blanchet, who had come to Oregon City shortly after the massacre, made an attempt to return to his deserted missions. But he was halted at the Dalles, where he was informed that it was desirable that no more missions be established until the presence of United States troops in the country should render such efforts safe and judicious. The bishop remained at the Dalles during the winter, opened the mission of St. Peter's and attended the Indians, as they wandered about the country. Father Rousseau stayed on cultivating a land claim but refrained from teaching the natives, as he had been ordered. The Oblates who had accompanied Bishop Blanchet to the west and who had established missions in the Yakima Valley, returned to their posts as soon as actual fighting ceased. Their work was carried on under great handicaps and never attained any real success.

The report that Archbishop Blanchet sent to Quebec in March, 1848 was not encouraging:

> It was on the 13th of August of last year, that the ship, *l'Etoile du Matin*, crossed the bar with the aid of a pilot after a journey of five months and a half from Brest to Cape Disappointment, bringing with me, religious, Jesuit Fathers and secular priests, to the number of twenty one persons.
>
> This was not without need; the mission is in a state of suffering in spite of the efforts of my worthy administrator, aided by the Fathers and the secular priests. Now that all are placed, there remains a frightful gap between the Indians and well-disposed Americans; how will it be filled! Emigration increases more and more; one finds American establishments at all points of Oregon, even at Puget Sound. How our poor savages are exposed! How the demon tries to repare his losses or to retard the good. He has made the most of all the evils. He has succeeded in causing a war between the savages and the Americans. I leave to others to give you the details of the massacre which was the occasion of this sad war in which our people have been engaged. It has been feared that if the united nations gain the advantage, our dwellings will be in grave danger.
>
> Such is the terrible trial which we had to bear after our arrival, for I speak here of three bishops; it was in the midst of this terrible scourge (the war) which reddens the earth with the blood of those whom the Church has confided to our care, that we made our entry into the country; that we assembled and held the first provincial council in order to give form to our

Church, to give it a living soul, an ecclesiastical discipline fitting and necessary.[34]

The Archbishop sends a warning that fantastic tales, regarding the participation of the clergy in the massacre, are likely to appear in the papers:

> Your Lordship should not be surprised to see some calumnies appear against us in the American papers. They have suspected the Bishop of Walla Walla of being capable of having counselled the massacre of Dr. Whitman and the others. After the murder they accused him or at least Vicar General Brouillet of having baptized nineteen of the murderers the day after the massacre and of building on their land. In their blind fury the soldiers, all filled with the deepest prejudice, would have put to death, hung or shot, the bishop and his clergy if they had been found.
>
> The good Bishop of Walla Walla did what he could to stop the evil and the murders among the savages. He succeeded certainly; and it was Father Brouillet who saved the life of the Rev. Mr. Spalding at the risk of exposing his own. It is for lack of knowledge and understanding that several of our fellow citizens remain in error. But the truth will be known sooner or later. All intelligent men know it and we have known it for a long time.[35]

The foregoing was written immediately after the adjournment of the first provincial council of Oregon. The three bishops, finding themselves together, determined to study the needs of their respective dioceses and to plan, as far as they were able, to meet the new difficulties that had been forced upon them. Thus on February 28, March 1 and 2 the meetings were held at St. Paul. On March 4 Blanchet wrote to Cardinal Fransoni:

> It is with a deep feeling of gratitude toward God that I inform your Eminence that I happily returned to my post on August 28, 1847, after five months and a half of sailing; that the Bishop of Walla Walla arrived at his on the 5th of the following month; that the Bishop of Vancouver Island was consecrated on the 30th of the following November; that I received the pallium in the month of February, 1848, that Divine

[34] Blanchet to Turgeon, March 3, 1848. QAA.
[35] Ibid.

Providence having reunited us, we have held our first provincial council.

I have the honor of sending the decrees of the council to your Eminence, together with the petitions which have been reported, begging you please to lay them at the feet of His Holiness, as likewise the homage of our gratitude, of our love, and the assurance of our attachment to the Holy See and of our veneration for the successor of St. Peter.[36]

In July Archbishop Blanchet discussed some of the acts of the provincial council in a letter to the clergy, but it was not until December, 1848 that he issued a general circular in which he promulgated the decrees of the council. At that time after setting forth the rulings decided upon, he exhorted his people to maintain that high standard of Christian conduct, which would edify all and lead them to friendship for and unity within the Church of Christ.

This decade of beginnings (1838-1848) was but a small part of Archbishop Blanchet's service in the Northwest, where he continued to guide the Church in the Province of Oregon City until 1881, when he resigned and retired from active life.

Bitter trials had followed upon the Whitman massacre. Indian wars put an end to missionary work among the natives; anti-Catholic bias forbade intimacy with many of the whites who clung to the belief that the Catholic priests had been responsible for the tragedy of November, 1847. In 1848 with the discovery of gold in California, fully half of the French Canadians abandoned the prosaic fields of Oregon to join the constantly growing number of fortune hunters who thronged into the southern territory. Finding themselves deserted by those to whom they had ministered, priests and nuns gave up their northern establishments and sought other fields of labor. By 1855 the number of priests had been reduced to seven and there were no religious in the province of Oregon City.

But slowly conditions improved: new settlers made their homes in the west; priests arrived to work among them and sisters came to open schools and hospitals; even the missions to the Indians, seemingly ended forever by the wars between white and red, were begun again, though never on the scale that Archbishop Blanchet

[36] Blanchet to Fransoni, March 4, 1848. PAA.

had planned. In 1862 Blanchet moved his residence to Portland, then replacing Oregon City as the center of activity. In 1866 he attended the second Plenary Council of Baltimore and three years later went to Rome to participate in the Vatican Council. The last years of his active administration witnessed a real growth and in 1879 the Archbishop asked for and received an assistant, Bishop Charles John Seghers, who was appointed coadjutor. Two years later, he announced that Pope Leo XIII had accepted his resignation "after sixty-two years of the priesthood; after forty-three years of toilsome labors on this coast; after an episcopate of thirty-six years; after thirty-five years spent at the head of this Ecclesiastical Province," in which he had seen the transformation from "nothing but darkness and the shadow of death," to "flourishing dioceses and vicariates, prosperous missions, a zealous clergy, fervent communities and a Catholic people of whom we may expect great works and noble deeds."

ESSAY ON THE SOURCES

It has not seemed necessary or particularly useful to append a list of all the works consulted in the preparation of this dissertation. Rather an attempt will be made to give a critical analysis of the literature of the field and to select that which has proven most helpful.

I. BIBLIOGRAPHICAL AIDS

In addition to the standard volumes of bibliography for American history — Henry P. Beers, *Bibliography in American History* (New York, 1938), and Channing, Hart and Turner, *Guide to the Study and Reading of American History* (New York, 1912), those dealing exclusively with the Pacific coast were found useful. Although Hubert H. Bancroft's conclusions must be followed with a certain caution, his thirty-four volume *History of the Pacific States* (San Francisco, 1882-1890), holds a wealth of information and his first volume of the *History of Oregon*, with its list of books, pamphlets, newspapers and manuscripts is especially valuable. Footnote references enhance the worth of this bibliography to the student of Oregon mission history. Robert E. Cowan, *A Bibliography of California and the Pacific Coast, 1510-1906* (California, 1914), Eleanor R. Rockwood, *Books on the Pacific Northwest for Small Libraries* (New York, 1923) and F. W. Howay, "Early Literature of the Northwest Coast," in the Royal Society of Canada, *Proceedings*, XVIII (May, 1924) have useful lists while George W. Fuller, *A History of the Pacific Northwest* (New York, 1931), Harvey W. Scott, *History of the Oregon Country* (Cambridge, 1924), the Most Rev. Edwin V. O'Hara, *Pioneer Catholic History of Oregon* (Paterson, N. J., 1939) and Rev. Gilbert J. Garraghan, *The Jesuits of the Middle United States* (New York, 1938), III, all have helpful suggestions. Charles W. Smith of the University of Washington has compiled two collections that are indispensable: *Pacific Northwest Americana, a Check List of Books and Pamphlets Relating to the History of the Pacific Northwest* (New York, 1921) and *A Union List of Manuscripts in Libraries of the Pacific Northwest* (Seattle, 1931). The bibliographical section of each issue of the *Canadian Historical Review* (1920—) contains many titles of value.

There are a number of short bibliographies that refer to Archbishop Blanchet. Following his article on Blanchet in the *Dictionary of American Biography*, Richard J. Purcell gives a brief account of the literature; L. W. Reilly does likewise in the *Catholic Encyclopedia*;

as does Peter Guilday in "Guide to the Biographical Sources of the American Hierarchy," *Catholic Historical Review*, V (1919-1920), 126.

II. GENERAL WORKS

The most extensive account of the Pacific Northwest is that of Bancroft whose four volumes, *The History of the Northwest Coast*, I—1548-1800 and II—1800-1846 (San Francisco, 1886) and *History of Oregon*, I—1834-1848 and II—1848-1888 (San Francisco, 1886) contain an abundance of material. Robert Greenhow, *The History of Oregon and California and the Other Territories on the North-West Coast of North America* (Boston, 1845) is still of value. The first short general account of recent years is that of Joseph Schafer, *A History of the Pacific Northwest* (New York, 1905), which does not discuss the work of the Catholic missionaries. This was followed some years later by Fuller's *A History of the Pacific Northwest*, which is the best general history that we have, and by John W. Caughey's *History of the Pacific Coast* (Los Angeles, 1933), which, however, concentrates on the California story to the neglect of that of the north Pacific coast. Samuel F. Bemis, *A Diplomatic History of the United States* (New York, 1936) and Thomas A. Bailey, *Diplomatic History of the American People* (New York, 1940) give the political background of the period. Of the histories of Oregon, that of William H. Gray, *History of Oregon, 1792-1849* (Portland, 1870) is useful in spite of its anti-English, anti-Episcopalian and anti-Catholic bias; the four volumes of Horace S. Lyman, *History of Oregon* (New York, 1903) are a fair treatment; Harvey W. Scott's six volumes, *History of the Oregon Country* (Cambridge, 1924), compiled by Leslie M. Scott, are specially interesting for their quotations from the files of the *Oregonian*. The third contains an account of the arrival of the Catholic missionaries. Charles H. Carey, *History of Oregon* (Chicago, 1922; new edition, 1935) has written the best general account of the state and his volume is without doubt the finest reference work for Northwest history. Clinton A. Snowden, *History of Washington* (New York, 1909) gives the pioneer history in the first two of his four volumes. Edmond S. Meany, *History of the State of Washington* (New York, 1910) contributed a short history. Adrien G. Morice, O. M. I., *The History of the Northern Interior of British Columbia* (London, 1906), is an interesting account of that section and offers a discussion of the work of early missionaries. Toward an understanding of men and events in the country where Blanchet and Demers began their work, the three volumes of Robert C. Clark, *History of the Willamette Valley* (Chicago, 1927) are indispensable.

III. CHURCH HISTORY

John Gilmary Shea has an account of the foundation of the Oregon missions and of the establishment of the hierarchy in the Pacific northwest in the fourth volume of his *History of the Catholic Church in the United States, 1844-1866* (New York, 1892). If we may judge from footnote citations this is largely based on Blanchet's *Sketches*, on the mission reports from Quebec and on De Smet's account of western missions. Blanchet's *Historical Sketches of the Catholic Church in Oregon during the past Forty Years* (Portland, 1878; Ferndale, Washington, 1910), is an important source of information. A new edition of it, along with various other documents of interest to historical students, was recently published by Clarence B. Bagley under the title, *Early Catholic Missions in Old Oregon* (Seattle, 1932). The first volume contains the *Sketches*, which Mr. Bagley thought a most important document for early Oregon history. We may deprecate the missionary's lack of appreciation of the efforts of non-Catholic workers but at the same time gather many items of interest from the *Sketches*, which were compiled from diaries and journals in which the pioneer priest kept an account of each day's happenings. O'Hara's *Pioneer Catholic History* is one of the few volumes which deal exclusively with the Church in Oregon. Garraghan's *Jesuits of the Middle United States* discusses the Oregon missions but, interested primarily in the work of the Jesuits in the northwest, he has skimmed the contribution of the Canadian priests, although he treats fully the establishment of the hierarchy and the ministry of the Jesuits in the Columbia region. No account of the literature would be complete without at least a mention of Father De Smet's numerous writings. His letters form a considerable body of first-hand and generally accurate information on conditions in the western country in the 1840's. They were written primarily to attract interest to the missions, as a means of securing material aid for them. Hiram M. Chittenden and Alfred T. Richardson have collected and edited them in their *Life, Letters and Travels of Father Pierre-Jean De Smet, S. J., 1801-1873* (New York, 1905).

IV. SPECIAL WORKS

The archival material of the Hudson's Bay Company was only recently placed at the disposal of students and steps were taken toward the publication of sources important in Oregon history. That work has been postponed indefinitely on account of the war. Until access can be freely granted the final story of this period cannot be written for the connection between the Honourable Company and the missionaries, Protestant and Catholic, was very close. None of the general accounts of the Company adequately describes that organization on the Pacific coast. George C. Bryce, *The Remarkable History of the Hudson's Bay Company* (London, 1902), continues to be of use. Robert E. Pinkerton, *The Hudson's Bay Company* (New York, 1931) has written an interesting account but probably Douglas MacKay, *The Honourable Company* (New York, 1936), the work of an employee of the Company, has given the most complete and accurate history which has yet appeared. A number of biographies of John McLoughlin have been written, none of them altogether satisfactory. That of Frederick V. Holman, *Dr. John McLoughlin* (Cleveland, 1907), has been followed by two others, Robert C. Johnson, *John McLoughlin* (Portland, 1935) and Richard G. Montgomery, *The White Headed Eagle* (New York, 1934). Carey, *History of Oregon*, gives guidance to the literature on McLoughlin in his chapter, "The Reign of Dr. McLoughlin." The other Hudson's Bay Company officers, especially James Douglas and Peter Skene Ogden, have received some attention. Walter N. Sage, *Sir James Douglas and British Columbia* (Toronto, 1930), relates the story of the former chief factor in Oregon. T. C. Elliott, "Peter Skene Ogden, Fur Trader," *Oregon Historical Quarterly*, XI (1910), 229-278, has written the best account of Ogden.

Of immense value toward the understanding of the period and the circumstances under which the missionaries worked is the constantly increasing number of monographs dealing with the Protestant missions and missionaries. John M. Canse, *Pilgrim and Pioneer: Dawn in the North West* (New York, 1930), presents a picture of the missionary labors of Jason Lee and his fellow-Methodists as does Cornelius J. Brosnan, *Jason Lee, Prophet of New Oregon* (New York, 1932). Two older volumes, that of Daniel Lee and Joseph H. Frost, *Ten Years in Oregon* (New York, 1844) and that compiled by Miss A. J. Allen, *Ten Years in Oregon. Travels and Adventures of Doctor E. White and Lady* (Ithaca, N. Y., 1850) give accounts by members of the mission. Perhaps the fairest treatment is that of W. P. Strickland, *History of the Missions of the Methodist Episcopal Church* (Cincinnati, 1850).

V. PERIODICALS AND NEWSPAPERS

Of the historical periodicals, by far the most useful was the *Oregon Historical Quarterly* (1900—), the volumes of which are rich in material. The *Washington Historical Quarterly* (1906-1908; 1912-1935) and its successor, the *Pacific Northwest Quarterly* (1936—), the *Pacific Historical Review* (1932—), are likewise of value. Two Canadian publications, the *Canadian Historical Review* (1920—) and the *British Columbia Historical Quarterly* (1932—) are helpful.

The Catholic periodicals are primarily of assistance by the occasional source material, mentioned in another section of this essay. The centenary celebration of the establishment of the Oregon missions (1938) was the inspiration for the appearance of a number of articles, dealing both with John McLoughlin and the first missionaries.

The Portland *Oregonian* (1850—) is an important source for Oregon history from the date of its foundation and has as well more than an occasional reference to earlier events. The *Catholic Sentinel*, established in accordance with the wishes of Archbishop Blanchet in 1870,

Essay on the Sources 193

has much useful material. The *Christian Advocate and Journal* of New York (1826—) is an important source for the Methodist missionary work, as is *Zion's Herald* of Boston (1823—).

VI. PRINTED SOURCES

Donald C. Shearer, *Pontificia Americana: A Documentary History of the Catholic Church in the United States, 1784-1884* (Washington, D. C., 1933) has included the principal documents of the Sacred Congregation de Propaganda Fide which deal with Oregon; he gives as his sources, R. De Martinis, *Iuris Pontificii de Propaganda Fide*, Pars Prima (Rome, 1888-1897) and F. J. Hernaez, *Colección de Bulas, Breves y otros Documentos relativos a la iglesia de America, y Filipinas* (Brussels, 1879). Of the greatest importance for the history of early church activity in Oregon are the reports of the Society for the Propagation of the Faith at Quebec, published each year under the title, *Rapport sur les Missions du Diocese de Quebec qui sont secourues par l'Association de la Propagation de la Foi*, which give extracts of letters, journals and diaries sent by the missionaries twice a year with the Hudson's Bay Company's express. Written with the idea of spreading information about missionary work and of gaining material help for that work, they supply interesting notes, especially with regard to the Indian missions, which are found nowhere else. The struggles of the first years are vividly told and the personal reactions, the ambitions and ideals, the prejudices and fears of the two French Canadian missionaries may be closely followed. Gifted with a keen appreciation for beauty in nature both Blanchet and Demers saw and described the splendors in mountain, river and valley as they traveled over the country, at the same time noting the manners and customs of the Indian tribes that they met. *Les Annales de l'Association de la Propagation de la Foi* (Lyons, 1822—), have some few notices but due to the fact that most of the missionaries' accounts had been published in Quebec, they were not reprinted by the Lyons society. The *Berichte der Leopoldinen-Stiftung im Kaiserthume Oesterreich* (Vienna, 1831—) contain letters of the bishops of the Oregon province.

A number of the Catholic historical magazines have published documents concerned with the Church in Oregon. The *Records of the American Catholic Historical Society* (Philadelphia, 1884—) give translations of the correspondence between St. Louis and Quebec, which relates to the establishment of the vicariate apostolic in 1843. The *Illinois Catholic Historical Review* (Chicago, 1918—) published Bishop A. M. A. Blanchet's journal of his journey from Westport, Missouri, to Walla Walla in 1847. The *United States Catholic Magazine* (Baltimore, 1843—) contains a long account of Demers' work among the Indian tribes of British Columbia, which he sent to Father De Smet. The decrees of the first Provincial Council are published in the *United*

States Catholic Historical Magazine (New York, 1887-1893); these may also be found in *Acta et Decreta Sacrorum Conciliorum Recentiorum.* Collectio Lacensis (Freiburg im Breisgau, 1870-1890).

Not dealing directly with missions and missionaries but often contributing toward an understanding of conditions under which they worked, often too giving shrewd estimates of their methods and worth, are the journals and accounts of travel of the period. One of the most important of these is the journal of the "imperious, aggressive, self-assured, severe in his judgments, painfully eager for success" George Simpson, edited by Frederick Merk under the title, *Fur Trade and Empire; George Simpson's Journal, 1824-1825* (Cambridge, 1931). The journal covers a period prior to the arrival of the missionaries but there is no more revealing account of the country to which they were to come and of the methods and outlook of the men among whom they were to work and by whom they were often to be influenced. Of lesser significance is Simpson's *Narrative of a Journal Round the World during the Years 1841 and 1842* (London, 1847). Several of the thirty-two volumes of Thwaites' *Early Western Travels* (Cleveland, 1904-1906), as De Smet's *Letters and Sketches* (XXVII) and Alexander Ross' *Adventures of the First Settlers on the Oregon or Columbia River* (VII), are interesting and informative to the student of the period. Not less so are the accounts of some of the Hudson's Bay Company employees, among them that of Daniel W. Harmon, *A Journal of Voyages and Travels into the Interior of North America* (1922). Likewise of value are the documents of non-Catholic mission history which have often appeared in the historical publications of the northwest, as "A Document of Missionary History, 1833-1843," from the archives of the Methodist Board of Missions in New York, edited by Robert M. Gatke in the *Oregon Historical Quarterly*, XXVI (1935), 71-94, 163-181.

VII. MANUSCRIPT SOURCES

Quebec

Due to the fact that the Oregon country was (1838-1843) presumably under the jurisdiction of the Diocese of Quebec and that the first missionaries were sent to the western territory by Bishop Signay, the archiepiscopal archives of that city are rich in documentary material for this part of the history of the Church. The voluminous reports which Blanchet sent twice a year to the Bishop of Quebec, often supplemented by additional accounts to his coadjutor, Bishop Turgeon, and to his secretary, Father Cazeau, are of the greatest importance in revealing the fortunes of the pioneer priests. Their activities from day-to-day and from month-to-month are carefully recorded along with their judgments of men and of events. Copies of many of these are in the Guilday Transcripts.

Portland, Oregon

Some of the material in the Portland archiepiscopal archives is duplicated in Quebec but there is much there that is new. The correspondence of Blanchet with Bishops Signay and Turgeon of Quebec and with Bishop Provencher of Red River, with his brother, Augustine, and with various Canadian friends, all adds information regarding missionary life of the time and tells a part of the development of the Oregon frontier that is usually overlooked. The letters of Demers, Bolduc and Langlois to their superior, Blanchet, supply details regarding their methods, their difficulties and occasional successes. The journals, geographical and historical sketches, records of the mission stations, account books, are invaluable source material.

Baltimore

Baltimore became interested in Oregon only when the matter of establishing the vicariate apostolic was brought to its notice. Consequently its archives contain little for the period, 1838-1848.

INDEX

Aberdeen, Lord, xx.
Acadians, 3.
Acton, C. Cardinal, 146.
Adams, John Quincy, xix.
Alexandria, Fort, 125, 128.
American Fur Company, xiv.
Anderson, A. C., 125.
Ashburton, Lord, xviii.
Assiniboine, Fort, 13.
Astor, John Jacob, xiv.
Atnas, 101, 127.

Bailey, William J., 78.
Bannocks, 102.
Beaver, Herbert, 21, 38, 54.
Belcourt, George, 9.
Beleque, Peter, 19, 26.
Belgium, visit of Blanchet to, 159, 161.
Big Bend, 14.
Black, Samuel, 39.
Blanchet, Augustine Magloire, 2, 59, 150; named Bishop of Walla Walla, 165; arrival at Walla Walla, 179; journey from Westport, Mo., 180-182; at the Dalles, 185.
Blanchet, Francis Norbert, xx, 2; mission in New Brunswick, 3; chosen for the Columbia mission, 5; journey to Oregon, 8-17; arrival at Vancouver, 19; first missions, 20-26, 28-33, 35-37, 39-44; plans for development, 34, 99; efforts to secure helpers, 45, 46, 51, 53, 59; meeting with De Smet, 62; Shepard's funeral, 76-78; incident of Dr. White, 79-85; a difficult land claim, 85-87; controversy with Lee, 87-94; an attempt to form a government, 94-96; difficulty of converting Indians, 100; work of 1840, 104, 105, 110-114; of 1841, 114, 115, 106-110; failure of plans, 120; efforts to secure a bishop in Oregon, 135, 136, 138, 139, 140; named vicar apostolic, 146; unwillingness to accept, 149, 150; first pastoral letter, 155; journey to Canada, 157; consecration, 157; travels in Europe, 159-161, 164, 165; *Memorial on Oregon*, 162-164; return to Oregon, 169, 178; report on first provincial council, 185-187.
Blanchet, Pierre, 2.
Blanchet, Rosalie, 2.
Bolduc, John Baptist Zachary, arrival in Oregon, 59; 60, 65; plans for missions, 119, 120, 177.
Brigades, 37-39, 105, 124.
Brunelli, Cardinal, 163.
Buchanan, James, xx.
Burnett, Peter H., 171.

Calhoun, John, xix.
Calipooias, 33.
Canadians, 21, 26, 42, 54, 74, 78, 85, 87, 91, 176, 177.
Canning, George, xix.
Carriers, 101, 125, 126.
Castlereagh, Lord, xix.
Catholic Ladder, 35, 40, 98, 105, 109.
Cayuse Indians, 17, 181.
Cazeau, Charles, 31, 138, 171, 172, 174.
The Cedars, 2, 4, 5, 6.
Chaudières, 15.
Chinook jargon, 22, 31, 98.
Chinooks, 32, 104.
Cinpoils, 15.
Clackamas, 106, 109.
Colville, Fort, 15, 39, 40, 42, 62, 99.
Congregation of the Sacred Hearts, 133, 157.
Cook, James, xiii.
Cook, Thomas, 4.
Cowichans, 115.
Cowlitz Indians, 32, 97, 98.
Cowlitz, 25, 35, 40, 41, 44, 45, 54, 68, 74, 99, 110, 175, 178.

Dalles of the Dead, 14, 18.
Demers, Modeste, xx, 7, 9; appointment for the Columbia, 10; work with Indians 16, 22, 23, 31-33, 37, 39, 40, 98-101, 105, 110, 114-120, 123-128; meeting with De Smet, 68, 139; named Bishop of Vancouver Island, 165; vicar general, 170-177; consecration, 179.
Douglas, James, at Fort Vancouver, 19, 20, 21; allows mission at

197

198 *Index*

Willamette, 41; advice to Blanchet, 76, 80; expedition to Vancouver Island, 119.
Drasa, Bishop of, 159.
De Vos, Peter, S. J., 171, 174.
De Bourg, William, 130.
Dumoulin, Severus Joseph, 9, 129.

Edmonton, Fort, 12.
Ermatinger, Francis, 62.
Etoile du Matin, L', 168.
Evangelical Ladder, 107.

Farnham, Thomas J., 69, 70, 78, 79.
Flatheads, 61, 62, 72, 110.
Floyd, John, xvii.
Forts: Alexandria, 125, 128; Assiniboine, 13; Colville, 15, 39, 40, 42, 62, 99; Edmonton, 12; George, 42, 67, 99, 104; Hall, 62; Langley, 116; Nez Percé, 99; Nisqually, 36, 40, 42, 44, 99, 110, 115; Okanogan, 16, 40, 99; Vancouver, xv, xvi, 17, 18, 21, 22, 23, 25, 30, 69, 70; Walla Walla, 16, 17, 39, 40, 42, 99, 123.
Franchère, Gabriel, 6.
Fraser, Simon, xiv.
French Prairie, 20.

George, Fort, 42, 67, 99, 104.
Gervais, Joseph, 19, 26, 27, 77, 87, 88.
Gray, Robert, xiii.
Great Britain, xi, xii, xiii, xvii.
Gregory xvi, 146, 162.

Hall, Fort, 62.
House of the Lakes, 14, 15, 19.
Hudson's Bay Company, xiv, xv, xvi, 1, 2, 6, 7, 38, 40, 42, 45, 46, 48, 55, 56, 69, 75, 78, 88, 89, 90, 91, 94, 119, 124, 184.

Indians, Calipooias, 33; Carriers, 101, 125, 126; Cayuses, 17, 181; Chaudières, 15; Chinooks, 32, 104; Cinpoils, 15; Clackamas, 106, 109; Cowichans, 115; Cowlitz, 32, 97, 98; Flatheads, 61, 62, 72, 110; Micmacs, 4; Molallas, 108; Okanogans, 15; Piskoous, 16; Puget Sound tribes, 112, 113, 115, 116, 117, 118; Sauteux, 9; Spokans, 15; Teits, 118; Walla Wallas, 17; of Willamette Valley, 33; Wholerneils, 116; Yougletas, 115, 119.

Jesuits, 64, 130, 131, 145, 146, 147, 152, 163, 167.
Juliopolis, Bishop of, 9, 10, 135.

Keith, James, 2, 7.
Kelley, Hall J., xviii, 69.
Kendrick, Robert, xiii.
Kenrick, Peter Richard, 141-143, 147.
Kitson, William, 36, 40, 110, 114.

Lachine, 2, 7.
Langley, Fort, 116.
Langlois Anthony, arrival in Oregon, 59-61, 65; criticism of Blanchet, 151.
Lavignon, Joseph, 4.
Lee, Daniel, 35, 39, 72, 77.
Lee, Jason, arrival in Oregon, 72; mission plans, 73; carries memorial to Washington, 78, controversy with White, 82-84; correspondence with Blanchet, 87-92; note on French Canadians, 176.
Leslie, David, 16, 93, 94, 95, 99.
Lewis and Clark Expedition, xiv.
Linn, Lewis L., 78.
Long, J. E. 171.
Lucier, Stephen, 19, 26.

MacDonald, Archibald, 15, 40.
Mackenzie, Alexander, xiv.
McLoughlin, John, charge of Columbia, xv, xvi; meeting with Blanchet, 10; relations with French Canadians, 27; interest in missions, 47, 52, 59, 60, 65; at Vancouver, 71; attitude toward Farnham's memorial, 78, 79; attitude toward provisional government, 95, 96; retirement, 178.
McLoughlin, Madame, 144.
Mailly, Abbé, 157, 159, 175.
Mayrand, Joseph, 7.
Memorial on Oregon, 162-165.
Mengarini, Gregory, S. J., 62.
Methodists, 21, 42, 43, 56, 73, 74, 76, 82, 88, 91, 96, 105, 175.
Micmacs, 4.
Molallas, 108.
Monk, Maria, 43, 82.
Moreno, Francis Garcia Diego y, 152.

New Brunswick, 3.
New Caledonia, brigades to, 37, 60. 122, 139.
Nez Percé, Fort, 99.
Nisqually, Fort, 36, 40, 42, 44, 99, 110, 115.

Index

Nootka Sound Convention, xi, xiii.
North West Company, xiv, xv.
Norway House, 10, 11, 12.
Notre Dame de Namur, Sisters of, 66, 159.

Oceanic Maritime Society, 168.
Ogden, Peter Skene, 39, 123.
Okanogan, Fort, 16, 40, 99.
Okanogan Indians, 15.
Oregon City, 171, 173, 174, 178.
Oregon City, Province of, xx, 149, 164, 183.
Oregon country, xi, xvii, 8. 61, 68, 98, 101.
Oregon question, xvi, xviii, xix, 2, 175, 176.
Oregon, Vicariate apostolic of, xx, 143, 144, 145.

Pakenham, Richard, xix, xx.
Pambrun, Peter, 16.
Panet, Bernard, 3, 129.
Pembina, 9.
Philadelphia, Bishop of, 146, 148.
Piskoous, 16.
Plamondon, Simon, 26.
Plessis, Joseph, 129.
Pohpoh, Chief, 106, 108.
Point, Nicholas, 62, 143.
Polk, Franklin K., xix.
Presbyterians, 21, 73, 123.
Provencher, Joseph Norbert, 1, 2, 5, 9, 10, 11, 23, 26, 129, 132, 135, 136.
Provincial council of Oregon, 186, 187.
Puget Sound, 35, 110, 111.
Puget Sound Indians, 112, 113, 115, 116, 117, 118.

Quebec, Diocese of, 129, 131.

Red River, 1, 9, 10, 11, 129, 132.
Richibucto, 4.
Rosati, Joseph, 62, 132, 140, 142, 144.
Rouchouse, Bishop, 53, 133, 137, 138.
Rowand, John, 12.
Russia, xi, xii.
Russian American Fur Company, xii.

St. Joseph de Soulanges, 4.
St. Louis, 59, 123, 130, 131, 139, 141.
St. Paul, 97, 139, 178.
Sandwich Islands, xvi, 59, 132, 133, 137, 138.
Saulte Ste. Marie, 8, 9.

Sauteux Indians, 9.
Shahaptians, 102.
Shepard, Cyrus, 72, 76, 77, 81.
Shoshones, 102.
Signay, Joseph, 1, selects Blanchet for Oregon, 2, 4, 5; pastoral to habitants, 28; efforts to secure recruits for missions, 46-53; sends Langlois and Bolduc, 59; jurisdiction of, 129, 131; approval of establishment of Oregon diocese, 140-147; interest in Blanchet's consecration, 151-154.
Simpson, George, governor-in-chief of Hudson's Bay Company, xv; attitude toward the missions, 46, 48-52, 58.
Smet, Peter John, S. J., De, arrival in Oregon, 51, meeting with Blanchet and Demers, 61-64; return from Europe, 66; approves plans for vicariate apostolic, 139, 140; selected by Baltimore council as candidate, 143.
Spain, xi, xii, xiii, xiv.
Spokans, 15.

Tamakoun, Chief, 109.
Teits, 118.
Temperance Society, 79.
Thompson, David, xiv.
Tsla-lakum, Chief, 35, 41, 98, 110-112, 115.
Turgeon, Pierre, 43, correspondence of Blanchet with, 45, 51, 97, 105, 135, 145, 150, 151, 165, 170, 180.

United States, xi, xii, xiii, xiv, xvi, xvii, 2.

Vancouver, Fort, Company headquarters, xv, xvi; arrival of missionaries at, 17, 18; conditions at, 21; missionary work at, 22, 23, 25, 30; description of, 69, 70.
Vancouver, George, xiii, xiv.
Vancouver Island, Diocese of, 179.
Vercruysse, Louis, S. J., 172.
Verhaegen, Peter, S. J., 62, 64.

Walla Walla, Diocese of, 180-182.
Walla Walla, Fort, 16, 17, 39, 40, 42, 99, 123.
Walla Walla Indians, 17,

Waller, Alvin, 106, 107, 108.
Walsh, Robert A., 136.
Webster, Daniel, xviii, xix.
Whidby Island, 35, 98, 111.
Whitcomb, James L., 87, 88, 82.
White, Elijah, 78, 81 83, 84.
Whitman massacre, 184.

Wholerneils, 116.
Wilkes, Charles, xix, 95, 96.
Willamette, 44, 45, 54, 68, 99.
Willamette Valley, Indians of, 33.

Yougletas, 115, 119.
Young, Ewing, 93, 94.

www.ingramcontent.com/pod-product-compliance
Lightning Source LLC
Chambersburg PA
CBHW071438150426
43191CB00008B/1174